A Beautiful

Year with Jesus

The 365 Day Bible Devotional

ALABASTER

How to Use This Book

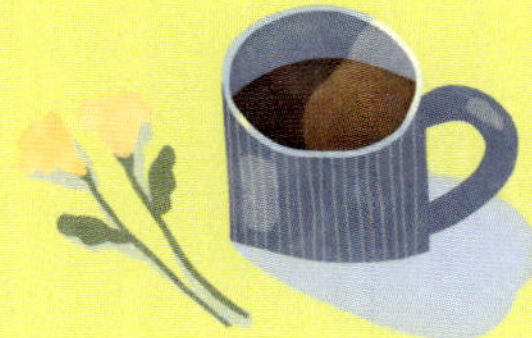

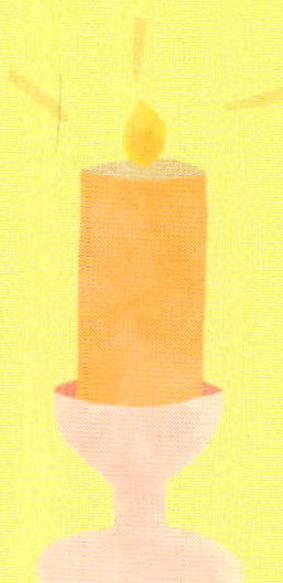

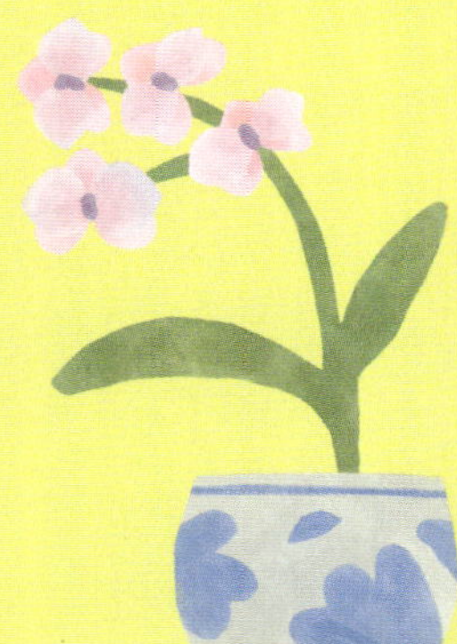

We live in an increasingly distracting world, continuously bombarded with notifications, advertisements, and messages. It can be hard to decipher which voices we should heed and which we ought to ignore. With so much to accomplish and experience, slowing down—pausing even for a moment—can seem impossible.

In such circumstances, finding time for our faith feels daunting. How do we make time for Jesus, for the wisdom and assurances of scripture? Our schedules seem too jam-packed.

Church history has long recognized the value of regular reflection in God's Word. As the psalmist declares, *"Your word is a lamp to guide my feet and a light for my path"* (Psalm 119:105, NLT). When we root ourselves in the wisdom of the Bible, the way forward becomes clearer. We grow more attuned to the movement of the Holy Spirit.

This book aims to help us carve out space every day, amidst our busyness, for moments with Jesus. Featuring 365 brief, thought-provoking, and biblically-rooted devotionals, we hope to provide a resource to fit even the most active calendars. Centered around a grounding verse from scripture, each devotional entry is designed to take no more than five minutes.

As we create new habits and lean closer to Jesus each day, may he become the guiding voice in our lives. May these devotionals illuminate our days, drawing us closer to the One from whom all blessings flow. Amen.

Table of Contents

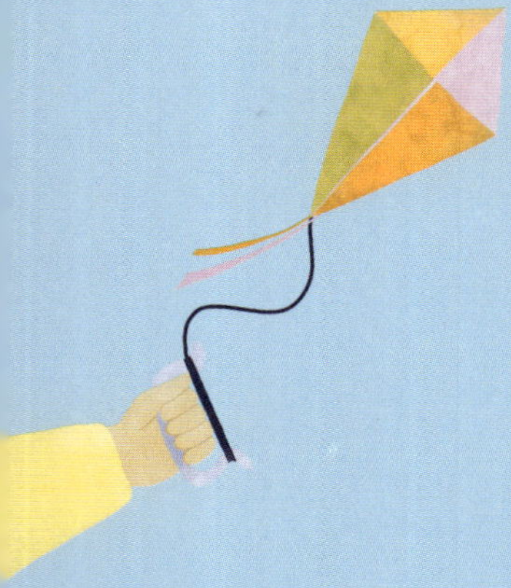

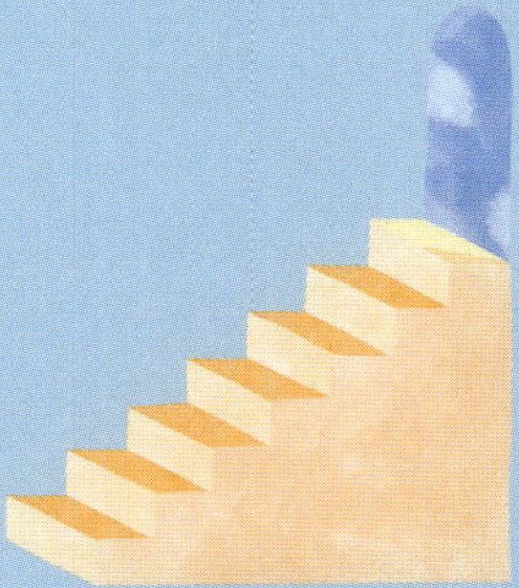

Psalm 5:3

DAY
01

"In the morning, Lord, you hear my voice;
in the morning I lay my requests before you
and wait expectantly." (NIV)

Each morning, it's easy for us to slip into feeling hassled. Mornings can be far from peaceful: rushing to get the kids ready for school, feeding the dog, showering, and getting dressed for work. This often means starting our days from a reactionary place, springing to action without intention.

Our knee-jerk responses are not always in step with our values or true priorities. Ideally, we should begin each day by focusing on what matters most: our relationship with Jesus. Taking a few minutes to sit and feel grounded in the Spirit, reminding ourselves of our highest purpose, enables us to enter the rest of our day with peace and levelheadedness.

Mindfulness—being aware of what we're doing and why—can be a challenging skill to develop. The good news is that when our mornings include prayer, scripture, or a quiet moment with Jesus, it's easier to enter the rest of our day mindfully.

Lord, bringer of each sunrise, calm our anxious thoughts, attune our hearts, and realign our priorities to bring you glory. Amen.

DAY

02 Hebrews 13:8

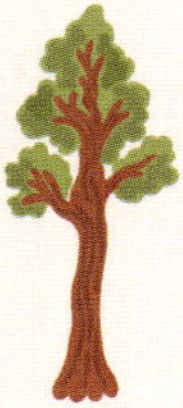

"Jesus Christ is the same yesterday and today and forever." (ESV)

Everything around us changes. Time moves forward, seasons shift, and we, as people, grow and adapt. Our circumstances evolve, our emotions rise and fall, and even our understanding of the world deepens over time. But in the midst of all this change, Christ remains the same. His character is steady, his promises hold firm, and his love never fades.

This truth is not just comforting—it is *foundational.* When life feels uncertain, we do not have to wonder if God's mind about us will change. The same Jesus who walked with his disciples, healed the broken, and calmed the storm is the Jesus who walks with us today. In him, we find security, not because life is predictable, but because he is *faithful.*

Dear Jesus, you are the same yesterday, today, and forever. Help us to trust in your steady presence, knowing that you remain faithful in every season. Amen.

DAY
03

Genesis 50:20

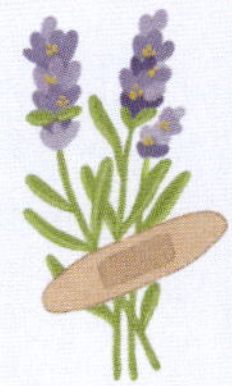

"You intended to harm me, but God intended it all for good. He brought me to this position so I could save the lives of many people." (NLT)

Suffering and pain contain profound mystery. The things we fear will break us God can transform to build us. In Joseph's case, the betrayal of his brothers, long years of imprisonment, and seeming silence of Heaven could have been the script of despair. Yet, woven into the fabric of his suffering was a higher purpose, a divine redemption.

We, too, bear wounds from the past—words spoken in anger, lost relationships, dreams unrealized. Our hearts remember, even when we would like to forget. But healing is not found in denial, nor in the bitter grasp of resentment. It is found in surrender, in yielding our wounds to the One whose hands flung the stars into space and formed us with love and intention.

Joseph recognized that even the most brutal betrayals could be reached by divine purpose. This is the invitation before us: to believe that our pain is not wasted, that God is at work for our healing, and can bring love and goodness even out of situations that cause great pain.

Lord Jesus, help us place our past into your hands. Give us the assurance that your healing brings love and hope into our places of hurt. May we rest in that promise today. Amen.

DAY

04 Colossians 1:16–17

"For through him God created everything in the heavenly realms and on earth. He made the things we can see and the things we can't see—such as thrones, kingdoms, rulers, and authorities in the unseen world. Everything was created through him and for him. He existed before anything else, and he holds all creation together." (NLT)

We are greeted with more stimuli than we can process in any given day. From the freckles framing a friend's smile to the shapes formed in billowing clouds, our eyes absorb, but our brains only highlight a few joyful details.

Yet, God created it all and holds it in perfect, detailed harmony. Even at the microscopic and cosmic levels, we know beauty exists but cannot fully grasp it. Still, God intimately knows every aspect of creation!

There is freedom found in this mystery. God is present in every detail, knowing every moment in the timeline of history. There is no need for us to be in control. We are simply asked to notice the details the Creator has left for us, like little treasure hunts throughout our day. Each detail moves us to awe and wonder over the beauty all around us. And if we are willing, we are invited to create alongside our Creator.

God, as we go about our day, cause the details of your creation to shimmer before us. Open our eyes to the beauty of how you hold the whole world all together. Amen.

Matthew 14:19–20

DAY
05

"... Taking the five loaves and the two fish and looking up to heaven, he gave thanks and broke the loaves. Then he gave them to the disciples, and the disciples gave them to the people. They all ate and were satisfied, and the disciples picked up twelve basketfuls of broken pieces that were left over." (NIV)

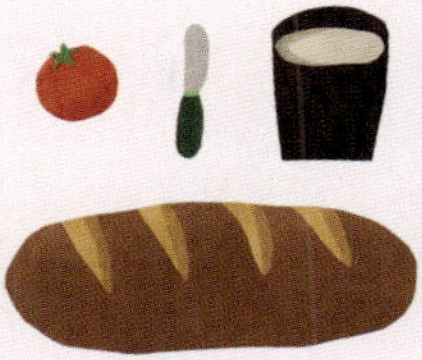

The natural world brims over with abundance. Water falls from the sky; the sun rises every morning; rich soil provides the nutrients plants need to grow. Yet, so many people do not have the basic ingredients needed to survive, let alone thrive. When a few humans hoard their resources, many experience scarcity, not abundance. War, greed, environmental harm, and other forms of violence create conditions in which we feel we have to compete rather than share with one another.

When Jesus takes a meager five loaves of bread and two fish and uses them to feed a whole crowd of several thousand people, he speaks a decisive "no" to competition, hoarding, or scarcity. He tells us there is enough for everyone. Let's give thanks. Let's share. Jesus also invites us to walk in this way of generosity, so that we might live in communities where all eat and are filled, where everyone has what they need.

God, help us see abundance all around us in the natural world and in our communities. Help us receive this abundance with thankful hearts and share it generously. Amen.

DAY
06 Psalm 126:2

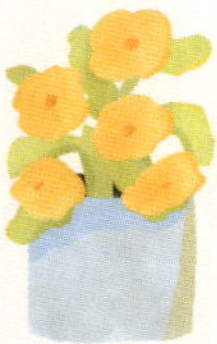

"We were filled with laughter, and we sang for joy. And the other nations said, 'What amazing things the Lord has done for them.'" (NLT)

Too often, we act as if solemnity were the only proper language of faith, treating joy and laughter as trivial. Yet laughter is woven into creation—the delight of a baby playing peek-a-boo, friends giggling freely, a quiet chuckle at life's ironies.

Joy doesn't deny suffering or ignore our world's brokenness. Instead, it reminds us that sorrow is not the only reality. Amid hardship, laughter assures us that we are not abandoned; Jesus' light still shines.

When we become consumed by the difficulties of life, we pray and work toward the establishment of God's love, justice, and healing. This is important work. But even in fierce storms, tunnels provide respite from the rain and allow us to take a breath. Moments of laughter can be like these tunnels—God's invitation to pause, breathe, and recognize the good and joyful around us.

Our laughter can be a declaration that we know God is good. It's an act of faith, affirming that we see God's presence and gifts right here, right now—and so our hearts rejoice.

God, let us smile at the small wonders, and receive your gifts of joy and laughter without hesitation. Amen.

Ephesians 4:2

DAY
07

"Always be humble and gentle. Be patient with each other, making allowance for each other's faults because of your love." (NLT)

We all want a little more patience, even as we resist extending it to others. Sometimes, we even struggle to have patience with ourselves. The biblical command to be patient, however, finds its root not in our capacity for tolerance but in God's forbearance toward us all.

Despite all the times we falter and fall short of God's glory, God's love toward us remains steadfast. Forgiveness is given without limit. Jesus doesn't abandon us in our shortcomings but is present and at work in and through our weaknesses, guiding us toward growth.

Recognizing the boundless mercy of God transforms how we view ourselves and treat others. Our shared flaws and shortcomings become less an irritation and more a reflection of the human condition—that we are all works in progress. When we truly grasp this, we cannot help but be humbled and better equipped to extend grace to ourselves and those around us. True growth takes both the allowance of time and space. Patience isn't just a virtue we strive for; it's a natural outflow of experiencing God's unwavering graciousness in our own lives.

God, grant us the grace to extend ourselves and others the same boundless patience and love that you so freely give us. Amen.

DAY

08 Daniel 3:17–18

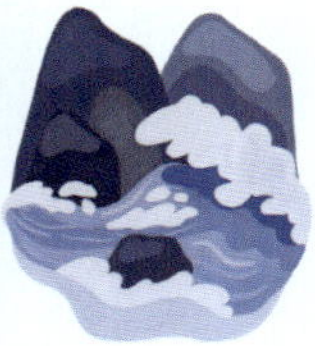

"If we are thrown into the blazing furnace, the God whom we serve is able to save us. He will rescue us from your power, Your Majesty. But even if he doesn't ... we will never serve your gods or worship the gold statue you have set up." (NLT)

In Daniel 3, three faithful servants of the Lord refuse to worship King Nebuchadnezzar's created gods, even in the face of dire consequences. The fire that blazed before them may have looked like certain death to everyone else, but not even death could stop these men from proclaiming faith in the one true God.

What does daring faith do to us? It makes us fearless. It spurs us on with a holy boldness, underwritten by the power of God Almighty. We stand resolute in our pursuit to stand firm in Christ.

But do we always feel like this? Oftentimes, we feel afraid in moments when our faith is pressed. Sometimes, we fear our faith isn't strong enough to stand firm amid such daunting opposition.

Shadrach, Meshach, and Abednego did not enter the furnace confident in their strength or faithfulness, but in God's. To be daring, then, is to fully trust in God even in the face of forces that claim to be more powerful. We are intimately protected by Jesus, who is ready to save.

God, give us daring faith to always proclaim your name to anyone who challenges it! Amen.

2 Corinthians 12:9–10

DAY
09

"Each time he said, 'My grace is all you need. My power works best in weakness.' So now I am glad to boast about my weaknesses, so that the power of Christ can work through me. ... For when I am weak, then I am strong." (NLT)

Better. Faster. Stronger. Prevalent aspirations in a world in which weakness is seen as something to overcome or hide. Yet scripture invites us to view weakness not as a liability, but as a doorway. When we come to the end of ourselves, we have a unique opportunity to step into God's grace and power.

Our wisdom and strength have clear limitations. Plans fall apart, and good intentions falter. Our natural instinct may be to double down on our own capabilities, hoping greater effort will ensure future success. But disappointment also offers a different path: shifting our trust away from our own abilities and toward the sufficiency of God. Weakness becomes strength as we lean on the One who spoke light into darkness, who restores the broken to new life through Jesus.

Weakness is not the end of us; it's the beginning of God's might within us. It teaches dependence, deepens our trust, and reminds us that life is sustained not by our efforts, but by the unfailing strength of God.

Mighty God, may we rest in the truth that our weakness opens the door to your strength, which is always enough. Amen.

DAY

10 Psalm 42:11

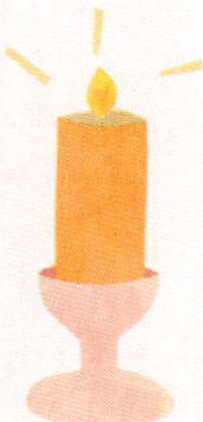

"Why am I discouraged? Why is my heart so sad? I will put my hope in God! I will praise him again—my Savior and my God!" (NLT)

In life's darkest moments, it's easy to respond in distress. With crises at the center of our attention, we often forget the light still in our midst. Perhaps we've experienced mountaintop moments that felt like they were never going to end, until we enter an unexpected storm, leaving us with a sense of defeat and uncomfortable questions.

Psalm 42 confronts the "why" behind these feelings of despondency. The Bible often shows the necessity of checking our hearts when they are not refreshed in Jesus. But instead of condemning ourselves for negative feelings, we can act as curious scientists who get to the root of the problem we face.

Hope is a word that acts as a long-lasting flashlight in the deepest of pits. As one acrostic describes it, the phrase reads: **H**old **O**n, **P**ain **E**nds. We can place our hope fully in God without hesitation. We can praise our Creator in the most doubtful of times. For we know God is a resilient force that will always see us through.

Jesus, you are our Living Hope. Help us to hold onto you as you forever hold onto us. Amen.

1 Peter 2:1, 3

DAY
11

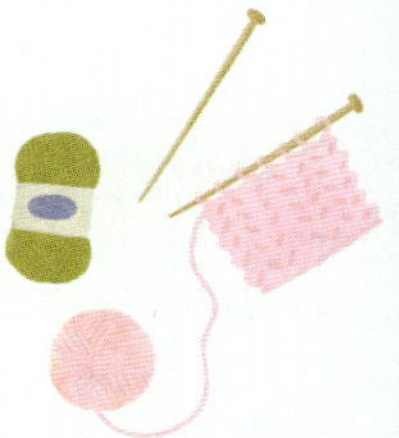

"So get rid of all evil behavior. Be done with all deceit, hypocrisy, jealousy, and all unkind speech. … now that you have had a taste of the Lord's kindness." (NLT)

Many negative postures hinder our growth, but none is as stunting as that of envy. That restless impulse of constant comparison and gnawing discontent at another's blessings steals our joy. It distances us from authentically celebrating with others.

The scriptural antidote for this spiritual malady is not some half-hearted measure of adopting a positive attitude. Masking envy only causes it to morph into other debilitating and destructive behaviors—deceit, jealousy, and unkind speech. Getting rid of such bitter poison in our lives requires nothing less than letting it go—spitting it out, and refusing to go back to that well in our thirst for contentment. Instead, we must seek our nourishment in the goodness of God.

Cherishing every moment we are given, every blessing we receive, we find satisfaction in the abundant grace of Christ. By gratefully abiding in the peace of a life well-lived and well-loved rather than focusing on the fleeting possessions and achievements of others, envy has no room to grow, and joy abounds.

God, help us release the grip of envy and instead hunger for the pure nourishment of your grace, finding our contentment in you alone. Amen.

DAY

12 Exodus 35:10, 29

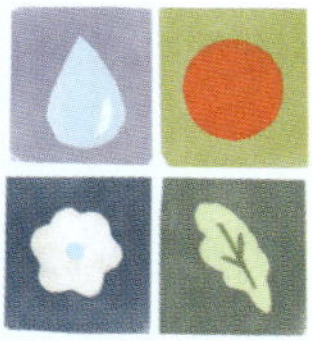

"Come, all of you who are gifted craftsmen. Construct everything that the LORD has commanded. … So the people of Israel—every man and woman who was eager to help in the work the LORD hadw given them through Moses—brought their gifts and gave them freely to the LORD." (NLT)

We all have a natural eagerness to create. Creativity stimulates our spirits and calms our souls. Once complete, we want to display our art, even if it's a finger-painted drawing hung on the refrigerator.

When Moses called the Israelites to create the Tabernacle according to God's instructions, he was calling them into creative worship. As the people collected the highest quality materials, the Creator began working. First, God called the artists to worship: to offer their skills as a testament to God's glory. God stirred in their hearts, giving them the skills and knowledge to raise to the level of craftsmanship worthy of God's dwelling place among the people.

We see the work of artists and think our efforts are subpar. But Jesus is still working. Just like the building of the Tabernacle, God equips us when we offer up our skills for worship. If one soul draws nearer to their Creator, God is capable of dwelling even in the refrigerator artwork.

Holy Creator God, we offer up our meager talents and finest materials as worship so that you may dwell amongst them and bestow beauty. Amen.

DAY
13

Matthew 5:9

"God blesses those who work for peace, for they will be called the children of God." (NLT)

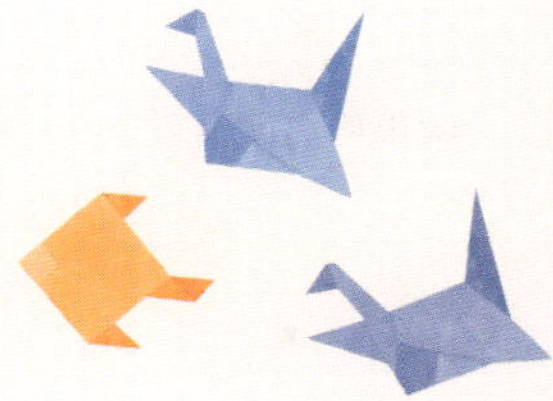

It's an unfortunate fact that conflict is inevitable. It happens in small moments—a misunderstanding between friends or acquaintances. Deeper than that, our closest relationships can experience more difficult conflicts, stemming from broken trust or vulnerable feelings left uncared for. Whether we're directly involved or feel caught in the middle, Jesus calls us to work towards peace.

Peace doesn't look like ignoring a problem or difficult emotions. It comes from offering care and mutual empowerment, paying attention to problems, and addressing them. To be a peacemaker means pursuing restoration; it moves us from a mindset of "live and let live" to "love and be loved." Jesus models this kind of peacemaking throughout his life and ministry, and we are called to follow his example.

God, teach us how to be peacemakers. Please grant us the strength to keep working towards peace, no matter how big the conflict in front of us feels. Amen.

DAY

14 1 Peter 5:6–7

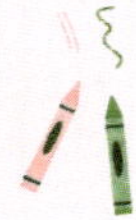

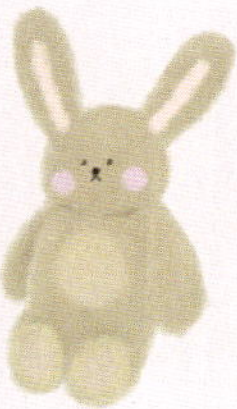

"So humble yourselves under the mighty power of God, and at the right time he will lift you up in honor. Give all your worries and cares to God, for he cares about you." (NLT)

Life often feels like a tug-of-war, with worries pulling us in every direction. Our initial impulse is to grasp for control, believing our strength lies in our grip. Yet, another gentler path exists: surrender. Imagine releasing the rope and letting go of the burdens we were never meant to carry alone.

Scripturally, this is not a call to passive resignation but an active dependence upon our Creator who alone carries and controls what we cannot. Such a posture of self-surrender is not an expression of weakness. It is the means to a greater strength—a strength born, not of the limitations of our own efforts, but of the God who can do more than we could ever hope for.

True power lies in relinquishing our attempted stranglehold on the concerns of each day. There is a profound release, an abiding peace that comes when we trade the exhausting struggle of trying to be masters of our destiny for the quiet assurance of being held by God. The God who has proven time and again to be able to bring good out of evil and life from death.

Caring Jesus, grant us the grace to surrender our burdens and find strength in your loving embrace. Amen.

Colossians 3:13

DAY
15

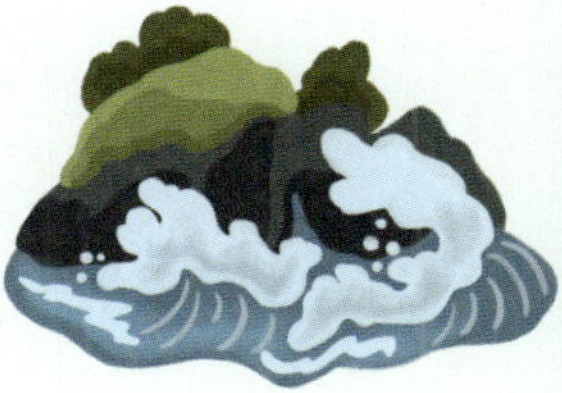

"Make allowance for each other's faults, and forgive anyone who offends you. Remember, the Lord forgave you, so you must forgive others." (NLT)

Let's face it, forgiveness is hard! It's so much easier to resent a mistake someone made or fixate on the harm we've experienced than to do the work of forgiveness. Nevertheless, the clear call from scripture is to forgive. So, how do we do that?

It's helpful to think of forgiveness as a journey, rather than a destination. Forgiveness is a process that includes observing our emotions, showing ourselves the compassion we need to heal, and figuring out what we need from the other person to repair the relationship.

At the same time, we must accept that we can't control others. Those who wrong us, or wronged by us, may or may not want to repair—a reality that makes forgiveness so vulnerable. When our repair work goes unreciprocated, we must begin a process of releasing resentment so we can move forward. At the end of the day, all we can do is follow the example of Jesus and walk down the road of forgiveness as far as it depends on us.

Jesus, show us the path you're calling us to walk that brings us closer to forgiveness. Help us to forgive just like you forgave us. Amen.

DAY 16 Psalm 34:17–18

"The Lord hears his people when they call to him for help. He rescues them from all their troubles. The Lord is close to the brokenhearted; he rescues those whose spirits are crushed." (NLT)

Grief can feel overwhelming. Anyone who has experienced the all-consuming heartache knows it can show up in the most surprising ways and unexpected places. There's no cure for grief—the only way out is through it. Over time, it fades and becomes less present in our lives. But how do we make it through until then?

Psalm 34 reminds us that when we call for help, when our hearts are broken, and when we feel crushed, God hears us and moves close to us. Grief isn't something we have to experience alone. When it feels like no one around us can understand the depth of pain we're enduring, we can rely on Jesus. His presence brings peace and comfort in the moments when it feels simply impossible.

God of healing, please be near to all of the brokenhearted. Grant us comfort as we process and move through our grief. Amen.

Psalm 73:28

DAY
17

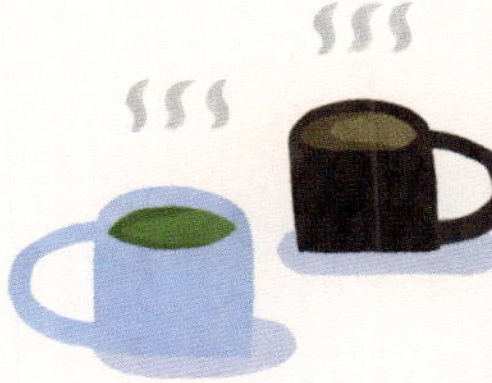

"But for me it is good to be near God; I have made the Lord God my refuge, that I may tell of all your works." (ESV)

To be near God is not simply to acknowledge God's presence but to dwell with it—to seek a divine refuge, a source of strength, and a place of belonging. Intimacy is more than knowledge. It is a relationship. It's returning to God in moments of joy and ache, speaking honestly in prayer, receiving love without striving, and allowing that love to shape how we show up in the world today. Intimacy invites both stillness and surrender. It draws us into a life of communion, not performance.

It is the quiet confidence that, no matter what life brings, we are held in God's care. Throughout scripture, we see that nearness to God transforms. Moses, having spent time in God's presence, descended the mountain with his face radiant. David, in seasons of triumph and trial, returned again and again to the refuge of the Lord. This closeness is not reserved for a select few but offered to all who draw near. In Jesus, we find security, love, and the deepest fulfillment of our souls.

Lord, draw us closer to you, that we may know you not just from a distance, but as our refuge and home. Amen.

DAY

18 Psalm 30:11–12

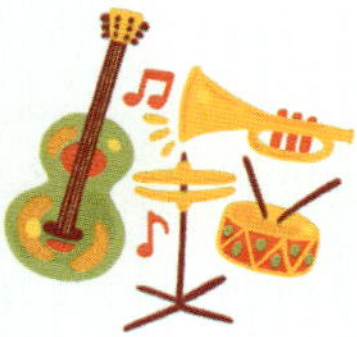

"You have turned my mourning into joyful dancing. You have taken away my clothes of mourning and clothed me with joy, that I might sing praises to you and not be silent. O Lord my God, I will give you thanks forever!" (NLT)

A person clothed in joy is unmistakable. Like a couple on their wedding day or a child receiving a puppy, there is no stopping the delight radiating from their eyes or the singsong tone in their voice. Whether or not anyone asks, they are happy to proclaim the source of their joy.

In Psalm 30, David describes a joy that is even more radiant: the joy of worship. Written for the dedication of the Temple, the psalm extols God for goodness in every situation. God's dwelling place becomes a tangible symbol for divine presence in our daily lives. Surrounded by God, we can't help but shout for joy!

As we reflect on God's provision through our worship and adoration, we don radiant robes of joy. Our hearts grow lighter as we cast off mourning and enter into the presence of God. And in our exuberance, the reason for our joy becomes a testimony brightly etched into our faces.

We give thanks to you forever, Jesus! May we remember today that our worship to you is the beacon of our joy. Amen.

Colossians 3:1–2

DAY 19

"Since you have been raised to new life with Christ, set your sights on the realities of heaven, where Christ sits in the place of honor at God's right hand. Think about the things of heaven, not the things of earth." (NLT)

In writing to the Colossians, Paul paints a picture of a life wrapped up in Christ. He writes about "putting on" compassion, kindness, humility, patience, and love as if they're clothes we wear. This goes against many of the cultural scripts that speak of these qualities as innate or natural rather than something we "put on." While they may come more naturally to some, Paul's call to all followers of Christ is to "wear" these qualities.

It's a reminder that God's ways can often feel far away from who we are. But if we pay attention to the life of Jesus and the testimony of scripture, we get a glimpse into the realities of the Kingdom of God. When we meditate on these realities and set our eyes on the things of Heaven, it can teach us to adopt these qualities, reflecting God's ways here on earth. Over time, we'll develop a habit of practicing them, and they might start to feel more natural. This is God partnering with us to bear the fruit of the Spirit within us.

God, show us how to put on compassion, kindness, humility, and love. Attune us to your ways. Amen.

DAY

20 Hebrews 12:1–2

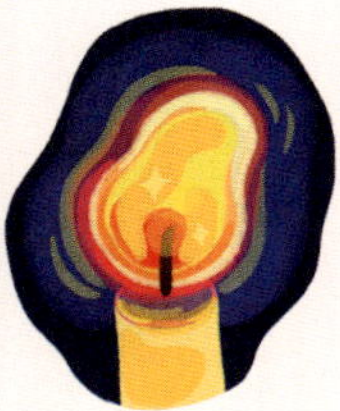

"Therefore, since we are surrounded by so great a cloud of witnesses, let us also lay aside every weight, and sin which clings so closely, and let us run with endurance the race that is set before us, looking to Jesus, the founder and perfector of our faith." (ESV)

In the ebb and flow of our lives, we are pulled in many directions. Each expectation and distraction demands our attention. But amid these competing interests exists an invitation to focus, to anchor our hearts and minds on a singular, steadfast person: Jesus.

The call to "fix our eyes on Jesus" is more than a simple directive; it is a profound act of redirection in a constantly shifting and moving world. We as humans are inclined to wander toward the urgent, the loud, and the temporary. But in moving our gaze toward Jesus, we choose to look beyond these fleeting distractions. We can look to the One who is both the beginning and end.

As we look to Jesus, we are reminded of our true purpose: to run the race with endurance. A race not defined by the world's expectations, but one shaped by the grace and strength God provides. Our humanity is not a liability to the Kingdom, but by focusing on Jesus, we lay aside every burden, every distraction, and run not in our own strength but in his.

May our eyes remain fixed on Jesus, the founder and perfecter of our faith, that we may live and move forward in grace and strength. Amen.

Matthew 17:20

DAY
21

"'You don't have enough faith,' Jesus told them. 'I tell you the truth, if you had faith even as small as a mustard seed, you could say to this mountain, "Move from here to there," and it would move. Nothing would be impossible.'" (NLT)

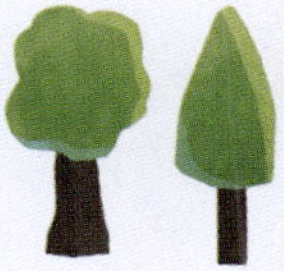

Every day, challenges stand before us—from the stress of difficult relationships to weariness in caring for a loved one. These are mountains that we struggle to scale, let alone perceive any possibility of moving. Before these seemingly insurmountable towers of life, Jesus assures us that even a sliver of belief in God can shift our perspectives and empower us.

Often, we perceive faith as something we must manifest. But scripture reorients this, declaring faith a gift. It is not something we conjure on our own, but grace extended to us by God. Faith, however small it feels, is rooted in God's unwavering belief in who we can become in Jesus. When we live out of the love of Christ, we are reminded that, through him, all things are possible.

Let's plant our seed of faith in the small things—choosing kindness over anger, offering forgiveness despite hurt, persevering through difficulty. We are empowered by a God who believes in us more than we can imagine.

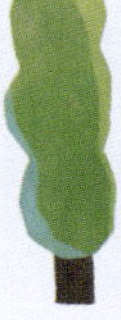

God, grant us the grace to nurture even the smallest seed of faith you place within us, trusting in its power to move the mountains in our daily lives. Amen.

DAY

22 Proverbs 19:21

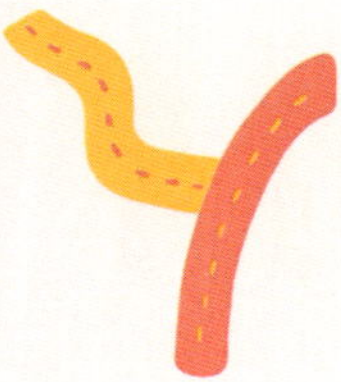

"You can make many plans, but the Lord's purpose will prevail." (NLT)

Humans are naturally driven creatures. Whether building life plans or vision boards, we long to see the future mapped out according to our dreams and desires. But Proverbs 19 shows that no matter how methodical our planmaking is, God's purpose will prevail beyond what we could ever imagine.

"Purpose" is used interchangeably with words such as "counsel" and "decree" in several Bible translations, revealing the intentional order and direction God provides in our lives. Scripture reminds us to walk wisely by following the guidance of the One who embodies all wisdom.

Rather than straining to arrange our next steps, we should rely on the knowledge that God has already laid out our future exactly as it is meant to be. Instead of thinking we are solely responsible for our lives, what does it look like to surrender control and embrace the plans God has designed specifically for us? When we trust in God's blueprint, our hearts rest knowing the plan is for our deepest good.

Almighty Lord Jesus, you know what is best for us! Help us to surrender to your will, and lead us in the direction you desire. Amen.

Jeremiah 31:13

DAY
23

"The young women will dance for joy, and the men—old and young—will join in the celebration. I will turn their mourning into joy. I will comfort them and exchange their sorrow for rejoicing." (NLT)

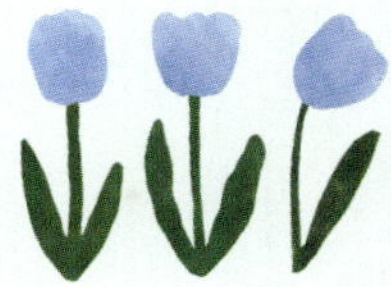

In a society obsessed with markers of wealth and status, it's easy to become so focused on making a living that we neglect the things that make life *worth* living.

What brings deep joy to our souls? Maybe it's a spontaneous dance party or a home-cooked meal with loved ones; perhaps it's painting with watercolors or strumming on the guitar. Maybe it's taking a walk outdoors and listening to the birds, or maybe it's playing with kids or watching a toddler discover the world.

Our world does not always value dancing, merriment, or play. But God treasures these things. God knows our souls need them. In Jeremiah 31:13, God affirms the value of gladness, promising to restore joy to those who mourn. In difficult times, God invites us to look ahead with hope toward a day when dancing will return—and even to find sustaining moments of joy in the midst of the hardship.

Jesus, help us make room in our busy lives for dance breaks, time with loved ones, and all the things that make our hearts glad. May these things be available to everyone. We dance in your grace. Amen.

DAY

24 Joel 2:12–13

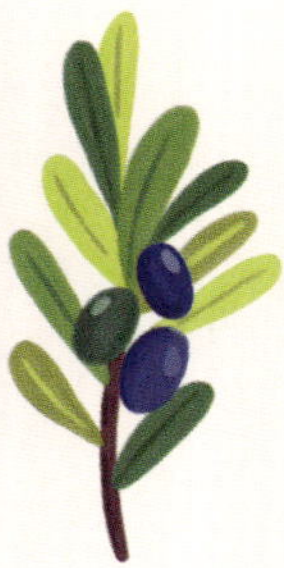

"That is why the Lord says, 'Turn to me now, while there is time. Give me your hearts. Come with fasting, weeping, and mourning. Don't tear your clothing in your grief, but tear your hearts instead.' Return to the Lord your God, for he is merciful and compassionate, slow to get angry and filled with unfailing love. He is eager to relent and not punish." (NLT)

It is never comfortable to admit we're wrong. It is much easier to find reasons to keep to harmful but familiar rhythms. But when we bring our mistakes to God with an honest heart, the process of returning to the One who extends mercy begins.

In simple terms, repentance means turning back toward the Lord—forsaking the ways that trespass, and asking God to forgive us. Joel 2 takes it one step further. Repentance is a matter of completely giving over our hearts to the restorative cleansing of Jesus. Instead of tearing our clothing according to the biblical display of grief, God asks us to spiritually tear apart our hearts so all sin might be fully exposed. Bearing a heart in step with the fruit of repentance allows us to commune with Jesus without trespasses getting in the way. Only in this low place of admitting our sins are we freed from the burden of carrying them.

Merciful God, thank you for giving us the gift of repentance so that we can be made right. May we turn back to you and experience your compassion. Forgive us our trespasses and renew our hearts. Amen.

Matthew 11:29–30

DAY 25

“Take my yoke upon you. Let me teach you, because I am humble and gentle at heart, and you will find rest for your souls. For my yoke is easy to bear, and the burden I give you is light.” (NLT)

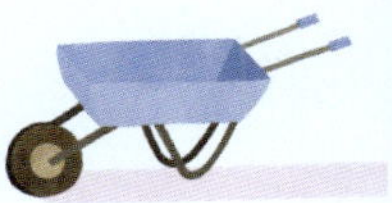

A Swedish proverb tells us, “shared joy is a double joy; shared sorrow is half a sorrow.”

When we share our burdens with trusted loved ones and receive an empathetic, caring response, we feel some of the weight leave our shoulders. Imagine how much more relieved we can be in Jesus, who invited his disciples to take his yoke upon them, assuring them that, once they did so, their burdens would be light.

Jesus embodies gentleness and compassion. He reminds us that with God in our lives, we are never alone in our griefs, sorrows, worries, or fears. We don’t carry our burdens by ourselves.

Jesus’ invitation into humility and rest is a healing balm for souls so often held captive by striving, arrogance, and the need to prove ourselves through shows of strength. Shedding these false needs releases a heavy burden indeed.

God, may the weariest places in our souls find rest. You do not burden us, but instead, you meet us in our sorrows. Thank you for releasing us from the unnecessary burdens we pick up from the world around us. We are lighter and freer with you. Amen.

DAY 26 Psalm 27:1

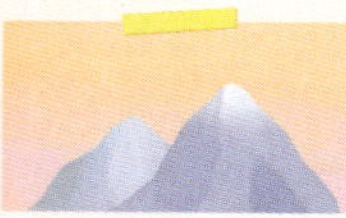

"The Lord is my light and my salvation—so why should I be afraid? The Lord is my fortress, protecting me from danger, so why should I tremble?" (NLT)

We're all too familiar with fear. From the eerie feeling of unease to heart-pounding fright, when we're frightened, we feel vulnerable. Yet, in leaning into God, we discover resolute light that guides us through the darkest alleys of apprehension. Fear, formidable as it may seem, finds its match in the unwavering strength of faith—a beacon that illuminates the path to liberation and transcendence.

Faith is not the absence of fear but the triumph over it. It's the audacious belief that God stands steadfast, working always for the good of creation. Moments of worry and pain will come, but through faith, we remain assured that God's goodness, peace, and mercy will have the final say.

Fear frequently disguises itself as rationality, obscuring our sight with apprehension and cynicism. However, faith allows us to surpass the confines of our earthly perspective—to catch a glimpse of the divine vision God intends. The Spirit bestowed upon us isn't one of fear but power, love, and self-control. Faith becomes the catalyst for tapping into this holy wisdom, empowering us to navigate the tumultuous seas of fear with unwavering courage.

Faithful God, remind us that, in Jesus, fear is but a fleeting shadow in the eternal radiance of your providence. Amen.

Psalm 143:10

DAY
27

"Teach me to do your will, for you are my God. May your gracious Spirit lead me forward on a firm footing." (NLT)

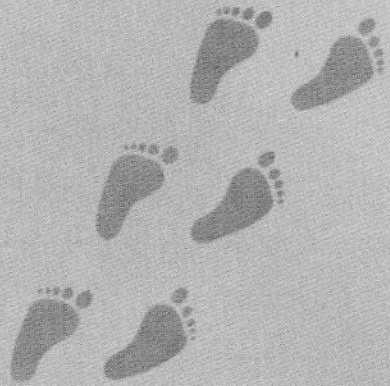

When Jesus spoke to the disciples at the Last Supper, he promised to send an Advocate to guide the world into all truth. At Pentecost, the Spirit of God descended on the apostles like a mighty windstorm and tongues of fire, granting the followers of Jesus extraordinary gifts. Later, Paul wrote about the Holy Spirit producing fruit in us and transforming us. This same Spirit was hovering over the water in Genesis before creation.

The Holy Spirit is the imprint of God here on earth. The Spirit marks out a path for us and guides us from within. We must choose to walk in step with or ignore the Holy Spirit. To follow this God-sent Advocate, we need only to be still and listen long enough to hear what the Spirit is whispering to us. In choosing the path of the Holy Spirit, we stand firmly in the legacy of our spiritual ancestors and their history of faith. We can move through life on firm, faith-filled footing.

Jesus, open our ears to the voice of the Spirit, and help us to see the way marked out for us. Amen.

DAY
28 Proverbs 3:5–6

"Trust in the Lord with all your heart; do not depend on your own understanding. Seek his will in all you do, and he will show you which path to take." (NLT)

Faith requires intentional surrender, loosening our grip on the steering wheel of our lives. We map out our futures with careful precision, take comfort in preparations, and trust in what we can see. But life has a way of unraveling even the best-laid plans, leaving us at the crossroads of fear and faith. In these moments, God whispers: "Trust me." This trust empowers us to let go of the need to control, of the illusion that certainty is security, of the fear that if we release our grasp, everything will fall apart.

The truth is, we were never meant to carry the weight of our destiny. The Creator who formed the heavens and traced the rivers into the earth is the same One who guides our steps. Jesus journeys with us through these paths, not leaving us to trek alone. God calls us not to hold tight to specific outcomes, but to trust. Not to chart our own course, but to listen for the Spirit's guidance.

To let go is not to lose, but to rest in the hands of the One who knows the way and holds us fast. In that release, there is peace.

Lord, teach us to trust you enough to let go. Amen.

Psalm 66:1–2, 4

DAY 29

"Shout joyful praises to God, all the earth! Sing about the glory of his name! Tell the world how glorious he is … Everything on earth will worship you; they will sing your praises, shouting your name in glorious songs." (NLT)

The call to worship is familiar. Praise is a central spiritual practice, allotted dedicated time during church services, and its own genre of music. But aside from tradition or convention, why do we give praise to God? What moves us to lift our voices in song?

Contrary to what we may believe, worship is not something we offer for God's sake. It's not a divine ego boost or a means of heavenly placation. Rather, giving praise serves *our* good. There's an old adage that when our feelings become too big for words, we sing. Music gives shape and expression to our deepest thoughts, allowing us an outlet when we feel overcome.

Giving glory to God invites us to think on all we have to give thanks for. The culture around us constantly reminds us of things that are broken, corrupt, and upsetting. To sing praise amid such a bleak cacophony reminds us that gloom is neither inevitable nor all-encompassing. The wonders and blessings of God are all around us.

Merciful Savior, as we praise you, declaring your goodness, use our song to renew our hope and strengthen our faith. When we behold your wonders, we cannot help but sing. Amen.

DAY

30 James 3:13

"If you are wise and understand God's ways, prove it by living an honorable life, doing good works with the humility that comes from wisdom." (NLT)

We may have heard the phrase, "Don't just talk the talk, but walk the walk," by which we mean words mean nothing without noticeable action. As believers, we have the beautiful privilege to show what we know about God. How far can words carry a humble life if behavior never reflects it? James 3:13 speaks to this idea and insists that knowing God's ways requires wisdom, challenging us to show the fruit of this wisdom in *how* we carry out our lives.

A humble heart does not coast on down-to-earth words to reveal meekness of character, but exhibits a sincere effort to show the servant-hearted character of Jesus. It requires us to put aside our preferences and comfort and step into community to genuinely serve.

We are called to willingly extend help to those in need, knowing that true honor comes in putting others first. Humility is the visible fruit of embodied wisdom.

Jesus, create in us a humble heart to serve others around us, ultimately serving you in the process. Amen.

Ephesians 5:1–2

DAY
31

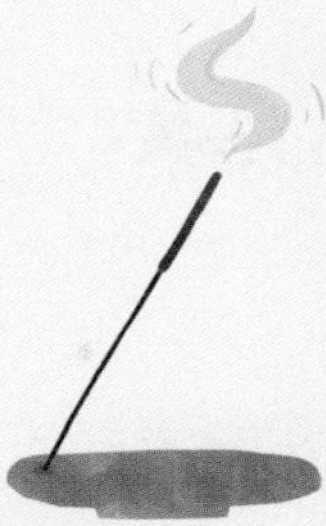

"Imitate God, therefore, in everything you do, because you are his dear children. Live a life filled with love, following the example of Christ. He loved us and offered himself as a sacrifice for us, a pleasing aroma to God." (NLT)

Too often, we focus on coming out on top. In a fast-paced world that celebrates success above all else, it's easy to default to a mindset that says we must be the best. However, when we look at the stories of Jesus, we see a life lived according to a different set of priorities and expectations.

Jesus set an example of standing up to influential religious leaders, empowering the powerless, and challenging the status quo. It didn't always lead to immediate structural change. He wasn't always seen as "successful" by our metrics. He lived simply, shirked personal glory, and was bound and beaten by governing powers. Regardless of the initial responses, Jesus continued to operate in love, sacrificing himself for the sake of others.

These sacrifices echo throughout history, and we have the opportunity to imitate Jesus today, regardless of how "successful" it feels. We are invited to redefine success to align with the biblical definition—offering a sacrificial love to others that will have ripple effects far beyond our imagination.

God, teach us to value the ways of Jesus over worldly successes. Amen.

DAY

32 Proverbs 16:32–33

"Better to be patient than powerful; better to have self-control than to conquer a city. We may throw the dice, but the Lord determines how they fall." (NLT)

Most of us don't relish waiting. Sitting still feels counterintuitive in a world so constantly in motion. We have grand plans and strive to achieve our goals as quickly as possible. And yet, all of us have found ourselves, at one time or another, stuck in the uncomfortable position of having to be patient.

It may seem like a nuisance or a hurdle, but in actuality, patience is a gift. Our waiting spaces offer opportunities to lean on God, to rely upon the Spirit, and to trust that Jesus is working in our lives.

As we anxiously await the future, desperate to leave our present pains behind, or excitedly anticipating all that God has in store, let us not overlook the spaces of stillness and peace. God's timing is perfect, leading us down good and righteous paths. We can follow the lead of the Good Shepherd. There is no need to rush ahead or forge our own way.

Seasons of patient waiting enable us to develop discernment. As we open ourselves to what God intends, we experience lessons and opportunities we might otherwise miss.

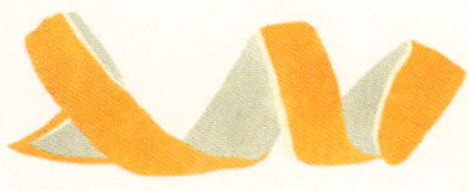

Creator God, grant us patience and faithfulness this day and every day of our lives. Amen.

DAY

Romans 5:4–5

33

"And endurance develops strength of character, and character strengthens our confident hope of salvation ... For we know how dearly God loves us, because he has given us the Holy Spirit to fill our hearts with his love." (NLT)

Sometimes, hope seems like nothing more than wishful thinking—a crossing of one's fingers for a particular outcome without any active participation or a solid basis for believing it will happen. The hope to which scripture points, however, is more than a fragile wish; it is a resilient force rooted in God's unwavering love for us. This divine unconditional love, borne of sacrifice and victorious even over death, is the foundation upon which our hope stands firm.

Even in suffering, what at first seems like defeat can become instead a crucible, where endurance takes root and character blossoms. The development of such character not only challenges but also deepens this hope we have been given. Remembering God's faithfulness and trusting in God's love, our hope is not passive, but a confident expectation, a defiant stance, an active resistance against the fear and darkness before us.

Loving Savior, strengthen us with the resilient hope born of your love, enabling us to stand firm against despair. Amen.

DAY

34 Colossians 3:17

"And whatever you do, in word or deed, do everything in the name of the Lord Jesus, giving thanks to God the Father through him." (ESV)

We usually equate thankfulness with politeness, saying "thank you" when someone does something nice. But biblical thankfulness goes deeper than that. It's not just about good manners or certain situations—it's a spiritual posture.

The Greek word for "thanks" is *eucharistia*, derived from *eucharisteo* and meaning "to give thanks." This word is closely linked with *charis*, meaning "grace." Thanksgiving is not merely a polite expression but a recognition of the grace of God in our lives. It is a response to the grace we have received in Jesus, shaping how we live and speak. In Colossians, Paul calls us to do everything, whether in action or speech, in the name of Jesus and with a heart of gratitude. This means acknowledging God's goodness in every circumstance, from mundane to extraordinary. True thankfulness transforms our perspective, reminding us that every moment is an opportunity to reflect God's grace.

Intentionally seeking gratitude, we align ourselves with God's will, recognizing the ongoing work being done in and through us. May our lives be marked by the constant expressions of thank yous to our heavenly Father.

Lord, may our hearts overflow with gratitude as we intentionally look to recognize your grace in all things. Amen.

Ecclesiastes 3:12–13

DAY 35

"So I concluded there is nothing better than to be happy and enjoy ourselves as long as we can. And people should eat and drink and enjoy the fruits of their labor, for these are gifts from God." (NLT)

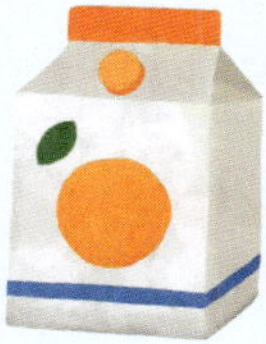

Everyone loves a bit of excitement. Our best-loved stories chronicle grand adventures. Social media urges us to seek out the unique and exhilarating to display to the world. In comparison to such high-stakes happenings, our daily lives can feel small or uninteresting. We may feel we have nothing much to recount or share.

Scripture challenges this notion, declaring the ordinary little moments of our lives to be divine gifts. Each morning is a blessing; every meal is a bounty of divine provision. The joys of a simple life are as valuable and beautiful as the extraordinary. They are reminders of God's fingerprints covering each and every one of us. And, in enjoying the delights of what we have here and now, we experience a contentment far better for us than striving after the ever-moving target of "more" and "better".

Let us not merely notice and acknowledge life's ordinary delights, but celebrate them.

Jesus, all that we have comes from you. Help us to see the beauty all around us and approach each day you bless us with in a spirit of grateful festivity. Amen.

DAY

36 Psalm 23:4

"Even when I walk through the darkest valley, I will not be afraid, for you are close beside me. Your rod and your staff protect and comfort me." (NLT)

As we walk through life, there will be dark days. Scripture is filled with examples of God's people navigating upheaval and confusion. When he wrote Psalm 23, David knew that darkness can envelop us like cold, rigid stones. For a season, the valleys where the dead were buried and superstitions reigned were more of a refuge to David than friends' homes. Even in those seasons, David found comfort in the Lord.

Knowing that God walks with us brings hopeful light into our darkest valleys. Our shepherding God provides for and protects us through all things. Walking alongside our Divine Protector, we are cared for in ways that bring peace close.

When we feel engulfed in darkness, it's hard to see our hand in front of our face. But God is near with protection and comfort. Our fears are not ignored as God walks every step with us. God is shining a light amidst our darkness; we need not be afraid.

Jesus, our Good Shepherd, thank you for being our lantern of comfort and provision in the darkest walks of life. Amen.

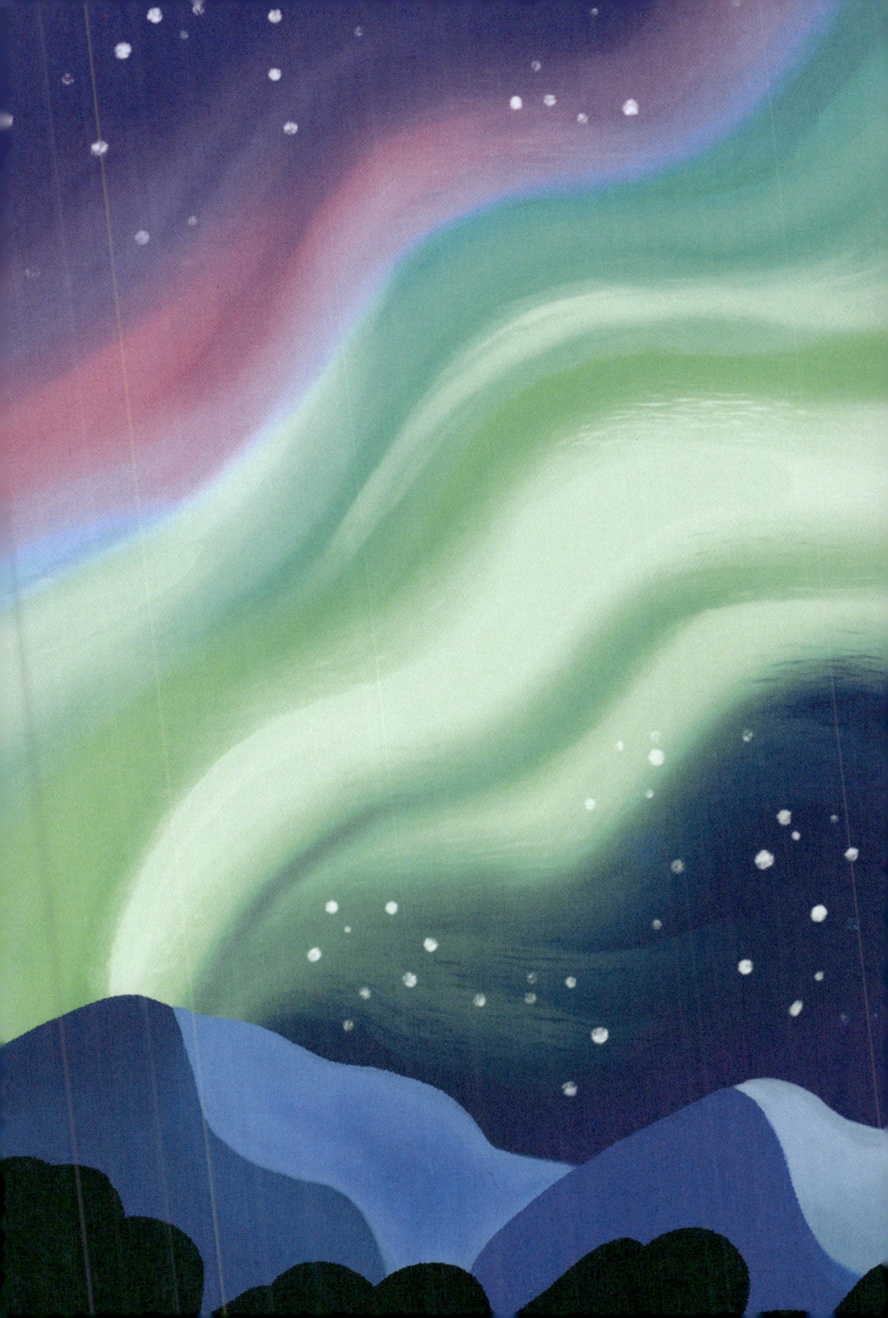

DAY
37 John 14:27

"I am leaving you with a gift—peace of mind and heart. And the peace I give is a gift the world cannot give. So don't be troubled or afraid." (NLT)

What images come to mind when we hear the word "peace"? Maybe it's a world free from war. Perhaps a memory of time spent with close friends or family. Or maybe it's the image of sitting by a trickling spring in a calm forest. However, we imagine peace, its presence in our life takes many forms.

Jesus speaks about peace as a gift he leaves for us. In other words, God's peace is not just the absence of something, but rather the presence of something else. God's peace can show up when we least expect it—in grief, conflict, stillness, or in joy. The substance of God's peace surpasses understanding. It is a gift originating from God's very being, a glimpse of the harmony and clarity we were created for. When we experience hardship, conflict, anxiety—anything that leaves us uneasy or stressed—we are invited to take a moment to still ourselves and embrace God's gift of peace.

God, we thank you for the presence of your peace in our lives. Amen.

John 14:1–3

DAY
38

“Don’t let your hearts be troubled. Trust in God, and trust also in me. There is more than enough room in my Father’s home. If this were not so, would I have told you that I am going to prepare a place for you? When everything is ready, I will come and get you, so that you will always be with me where I am.” (ESV)

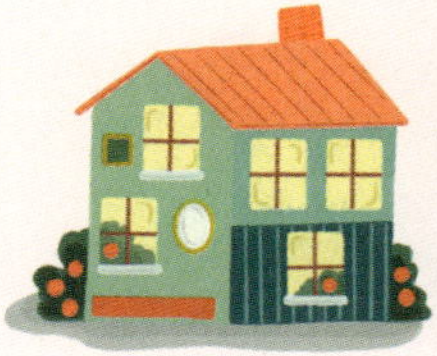

Every life contains seasons of difficulty—relationships break, our health flags, or the future seems unclear. In such times, Jesus offers a steadying hand: “Let not your hearts be troubled.” These words are not merely a call to inner peace, but an invitation to trust in something greater than the present moment.

Jesus does not promise an absence of hardship, nor that faith will erase all sorrow. Instead, he points to a deeper reality: “I go to prepare a place for you.” This is not only a future promise of Heaven but a declaration of his constant, active care in the here and now. Like a devoted gardener lovingly waters and prunes the garden, God tends to the details of our lives, shaping even our struggles into something purposeful.

Encouragement from Jesus is not shallow optimism—it is rooted in the certainty of his presence. And just as he promised to return for his disciples, so too will he bring us, in his perfect time, to a place where sorrow has no hold.

Welcoming Jesus, when our hearts are troubled, help us to trust in your goodness and faithfulness. Amen.

DAY 39 Matthew 28:20

"Teach these new disciples to obey all the commands I have given you. And be sure of this: I am with you always, even to the end of the age." (NLT)

Just before his ascension, Jesus tells his followers to go out and baptize, teach, and make more disciples. A life of wandering from town to town, building relationships, and moving on to the next town leaves a lot of space for loneliness. But Jesus doesn't just send us on a mission, he promises to be with us, always.

Sometimes it feels lonely doing the work we're trying to do. When we have a sense of a mission or a calling from God, we often feel out of step with our friends, family, or the world around us. Our communities may even push us in a direction that feels misaligned with our purpose. When we decide to go against the grain, loneliness and insecurity can begin to emerge within us.

In these moments, God invites us to be still and listen. Jesus didn't just call us to go forth; Jesus promised to be with us. In our moments of loneliness, we can take solace in the assurance of scripture that we are never truly alone. Our savior is with us.

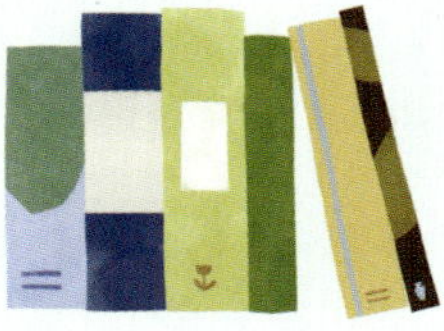

Jesus, thank you for your presence in our lives and in our loneliness. Please help us to remember your promises when we feel discouraged. Amen.

Matthew 5:13–14, 16

DAY 40

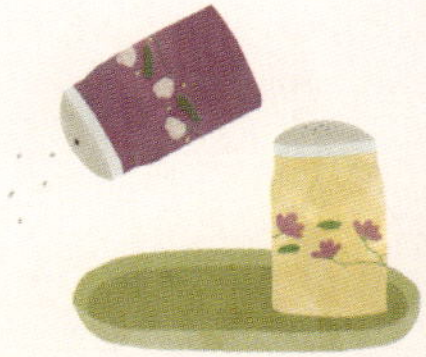

"You are the salt of the earth. But what good is salt if it has lost its flavor? ... It will be thrown out and trampled underfoot as worthless. You are the light of the world—like a city on a hilltop that cannot be hidden ... In the same way, let your good deeds shine out for all to see, so that everyone will praise your heavenly Father." (NLT)

A single flame in the darkness commands attention; a pinch of salt transforms the flavor of an entire meal. Likewise, Jesus calls his followers to be unmistakably his in a world that often drifts toward shadows and dullness. "You are the salt of the earth. ... You are the light of the world." These are not merely suggestions; they are declarations of identity.

Salt prevents decay and awakens the senses. In the same way, our lives, as followers of Jesus, are more satisfying, flavorful, and nourishing for those around us. Light, by its nature, is impossible to ignore. Even the smallest glow shatters darkness, revealing what was hidden and helping people find their way. To live as salt and light is to embody the character of Jesus—preserving what is good, illuminating what is true, and reflecting his compassion in every interaction. We stop striving to be noticed, but remain faithful where we are placed, allowing God's presence to shine through us. A candle does not strain to illuminate; it simply burns. So too, when we remain connected to Jesus, our lives naturally give light.

God, let our lives reflect your light and preserve what is good. Amen.

DAY

41 2 Peter 1:5–7

"... Make every effort to respond to God's promises. Supplement your faith with a generous provision of moral excellence, and moral excellence with knowledge, and knowledge with self-control, and self-control with patient endurance, and patient endurance with godliness, and godliness with brotherly affection, and brotherly affection with love for everyone." (NLT)

The call to excellence can be intimidating. Hyperaware as we are of our growth edges and shortcomings, it can feel like we are incapable of the exemplary or exceptional. This insecurity is often the result of conflating excellence and perfection. Perfection is an unattainable goal, but excellence is a posture we adopt.

Pursuing excellence is a continual process, one that comes from giving our best in all areas of life. It is born out in responding to the lessons and teachings of God on a daily basis and striving to live according to Jesus' example.

In 2 Peter, we see this pursuit outlined for us tangibly. God's provision and promises move us to try our best. In our attempts to live out Jesus' teachings, we gain more experience and knowledge. That knowledge helps us to do better as we go forward, avoiding the pitfalls of our past. And out of this growth, we become more disciplined, more patient, more loving—more like Jesus. The truth is, the pursuit of excellence is synonymous with living faithfully.

Jesus, in your mercy, you do not demand perfection. Help us to continue the lifelong process of growth as we strive to be more like you. Amen.

DAY

Ezekiel 36:26–27 42

“And I will give you a new heart, and I will put a new spirit in you. I will take out your stony, stubborn heart and give you a tender, responsive heart. And I will put my Spirit in you so that you will follow my decrees and be careful to obey my regulations.” (NLT)

Everyone needs a spiritual heart transplant. Because the heart was built to be a home for the indwelling God to renew us from within, we must address the rocky terrain of unresponsiveness and pride. Selfish interest and guardedness must be washed away. Ezekiel 36 shows us that God longs to renovate our hardheartedness into a soft, tender spirit that responds to the divine voice.

Our generous Creator promises to smooth out our stubborn nature and make our inner worlds completely new. God is not one who ever leaves us the same, but rather catalyzes lasting change; the Master of transformation, the One who loves us too much to let our hearts remain as they are.

This sacred makeover results in a desire to follow the Spirit’s direction over our lives. If God’s love language is obedience, then a heart that yields to holy decrees is what Jesus creates in us, because he always has our best interest at heart.

God of transformation, thank you for giving us your Spirit to make our hearts new. May we heed the Spirit’s leading. Amen.

DAY 43 Philippians 4:6–7

"Don't worry about anything; instead, pray about everything. Tell God what you need, and thank him for all he has done. Then you will experience God's peace, which exceeds anything we can understand. His peace will guard your hearts and minds as you live in Christ Jesus." (NLT)

Sometimes, it all becomes too much. Despite our best efforts, anxiety swirls around us, moving from the babbling brook of worry to the deafening roar of panic. In this space of sensory overload, God meets us and sits with us. Where the oceans once raged, God provides still waters. Where once there was a cacophony of thoughts and fears, the Holy Spirit brings quiet.

Into this pregnant pause, the soothing and encouraging words of scripture remind us that no matter what we face, we are held tenderly in the palm of our Creator's hand. When we feel shaken, we can trust in the comforting and steadying presence of God.

Our God desires our good. More than that, through the moving of the Holy Spirit, God actively works for it. Although we may feel alone, Jesus is right beside us. We may feel fragile and vulnerable, but our God strengthens and preserves us.

Nurturing God, help us rest in this knowledge. Fill us with a sense of hope and trust, and let our anxious thoughts begin to dissipate. Amen.

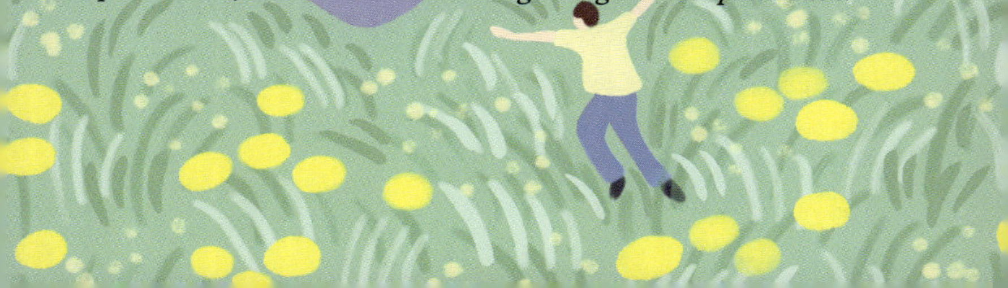

1 Peter 3:8–9

DAY
44

"... Sympathize with each other. Love each other as brothers and sisters. Be tenderhearted, and keep a humble attitude. Don't repay evil for evil. Don't retaliate with insults when people insult you. Instead, pay them back with a blessing. That is what God has called you to do, and he will grant you his blessing." (NLT)

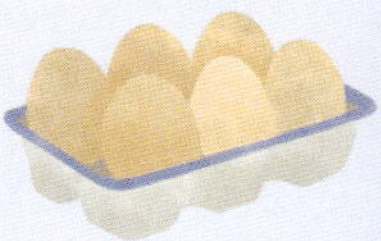

Some people are easy for us to love. Others get under our skin and test the limits of our patience. In either case, scripture calls us to be tenderhearted, to bless even when wounded, to extend kindness where none is deserved. This is not a passive call to endure but an active invitation to reflect the mercy we have received.

The truth is, we, too, have been difficult. We have spoken in haste, failed to listen, and burdened others with our words and actions. And yet, God's love has never wavered. God has been the sculptor, shaping our rough edges with gentleness, sanding away our self-righteousness, and teaching us grace. To love as God loves, we must interact with others with the same patient hand.

To be tenderhearted is to choose understanding over resentment, to remember that beneath every difficult exterior is a soul longing for kindness. Like water smoothing the sharpest stone, love from God has the power to transform even the hardest of hearts, including our own.

Jesus, shape our hearts to love as patiently as you have loved us. Amen.

DAY 45 Psalm 119:15–16

"I will study your commandments and reflect on your ways. I will delight in your decrees and not forget your word." (NLT)

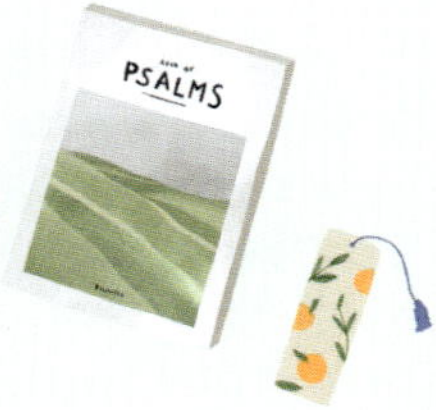

Throughout scripture, the greatest commandment given is to love God wholeheartedly and love our neighbors as ourselves. Psalm 119's assertion to meditate on God's decrees can be understood to mean meditating on love. As we do so, we might reflect on questions like these: What does love look like in our lives right now? Where are we receiving love? Where are we giving love?

We can make daily and life-altering decisions alike with God's ways of love in mind, asking ourselves: What is the most loving thing to do in this situation? Which is the path of greatest love for other people and ourselves?

The psalmist assures us that when we fix our eyes on God's ways and remember God's words, we will find delight. The road might not be easy or straightforward, but we will be guided by God's Spirit of love at every step—and we will find joy in the journey.

Christ Jesus, help us to fix our eyes on love today. Help us see more than the broad, big-picture idea of it, but the specifics of what love looks like in our lives right now. Amen.

DAY

Zechariah 4:10 46

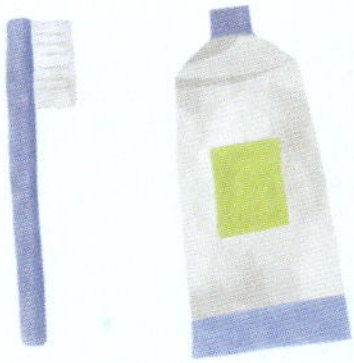

"Do not despise these small beginnings, for the Lord rejoices to see the work begin, to see the plumb line in Zerubbabel's hand." (NLT)

Sometimes we have a vision for our lives that feels so big that we don't know where to start. It can be easy to feel overwhelmed by the number of choices in front of us, all different paths to the same destination. At the same time, those same choices can feel underwhelming, like none of the steps are big enough for us. We can cycle through these overwhelmed and underwhelmed feelings so much that we get stuck and never take a step towards the vision we have.

Zechariah 4:10 reminds us to embrace the small steps—that the act of getting started can delight God. Every small step has the potential to bring us closer to something bigger than we could ever imagine. Beginnings like these are tiny seeds; they may seem small and insignificant, but through the years, they can turn into large trees that produce fruit. If we can see our humble beginnings as God does, we too can delight in the potential within each small step forward.

Jesus, grant us the eyes to see potential in every step we take. May we delight in the process as we watch those steps bring us towards the vision you've given us. Amen.

DAY
47 Psalm 18:6

"But in my distress I cried out to the Lord; yes, I prayed to my God for help. He heard me from his sanctuary; my cry to him reached his ears." (NLT)

In stressful situations, we often say desperate times call for desperate measures; we might do things we would not otherwise do. Perhaps we are tempted to lie, steal, or harm people in our frenzy to meet our own needs. Scripture offers a different way. Rather than solving our problems at another's expense, we are invited to call upon God and ask for help.

There is no shame in crying out for help. Rather, there is great power in identifying the deepest desires of our hearts to the One working for our good. Often, God meets our needs through community. As we seek divine assistance, we can seek support from other people as well. And we find energy and joy in working with others toward shared goals.

Asking for help requires courage, confidence, and strength. When we do so, we are assured that God hears.

Lord Jesus, give us faith to ask for help. Help us know that you hear us, even if you do not always respond in the ways or the timeframes we prefer. Provide abundantly for our needs and the needs of our communities. Amen.

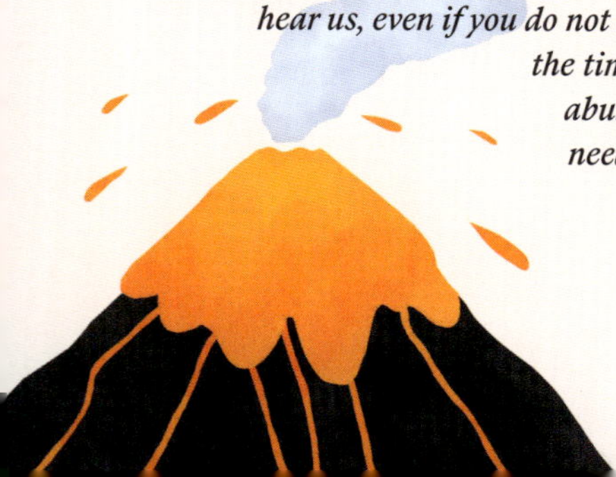

Psalm 1:2–3

DAY **48**

"But they delight in the law of the Lord, meditating on it day and night. They are like trees planted along the riverbank, bearing fruit each season. Their leaves never wither, and they prosper in all they do." (NLT)

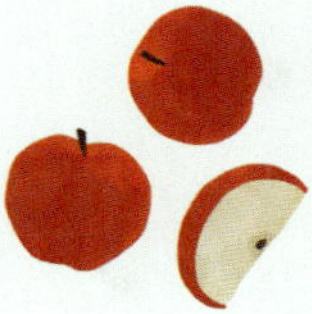

Trees do not yield *edible* fruit year-round. In autumn, a tree's branches may bend with abundance, while in winter, it grows in perseverance against the cold. In spring, it awakens with blossoms, and in summer, roots stretch deeper into the soil, drinking unseen nourishment. No matter the time of year, trees live according to their purpose, drawing from the river.

Maybe this is what it means to bear fruit and prosper in each season. At times, our fruit may be visible—we grow in wisdom and grace, aware of God working through us. There are obvious results. Then there are seasons of quiet growth, when our outward life is unspectacular, yet beneath the surface, God is strengthening us. God deepens our roots through trials, teaching us endurance. Or God prunes us in seasons of waiting, refining our hearts. Even in barren times, Jesus' living water sustains us, unseen but unwavering.

Whether the fruit is visible or happening underground, God is always at work, nourishing and preparing us for what is to come, inviting us to reach toward the river of life, lean into the process, and work of our creative Gardener.

God, help us trust that you are at work in every season of our lives. Amen.

DAY

49 Exodus 14:14

"The Lord himself will fight for you. Just stay calm." (NLT)

Faced with fear, our natural instincts for protection kick into action. While each person may fight their battles differently, peace and calm are rarely our default responses.

The Israelites left Egypt in fear. With the sea on the horizon and their Egyptian enslavers quickly approaching, they were terrified. Commentary must have flown from all directions at Moses. Our moments of crisis can sound the same.

But Moses embraced the holy pause. Standing there filled with peace from God, he reminded the people of the goodness they had seen and the battles God had already conquered. The holy pause that allowed Moses to remember is also available to us.

Moses led out of a peaceful pause, and we can do the same. We may not know what God is doing in each moment. But just as God already had a solution in mind for the Israelites, so too is a plan ready for us. When caught in fear, the peace of the Holy Spirit fills us. God will fight on our behalf.

Victorious God, we thank you for moments of pause that we may rest in your plans. Amen.

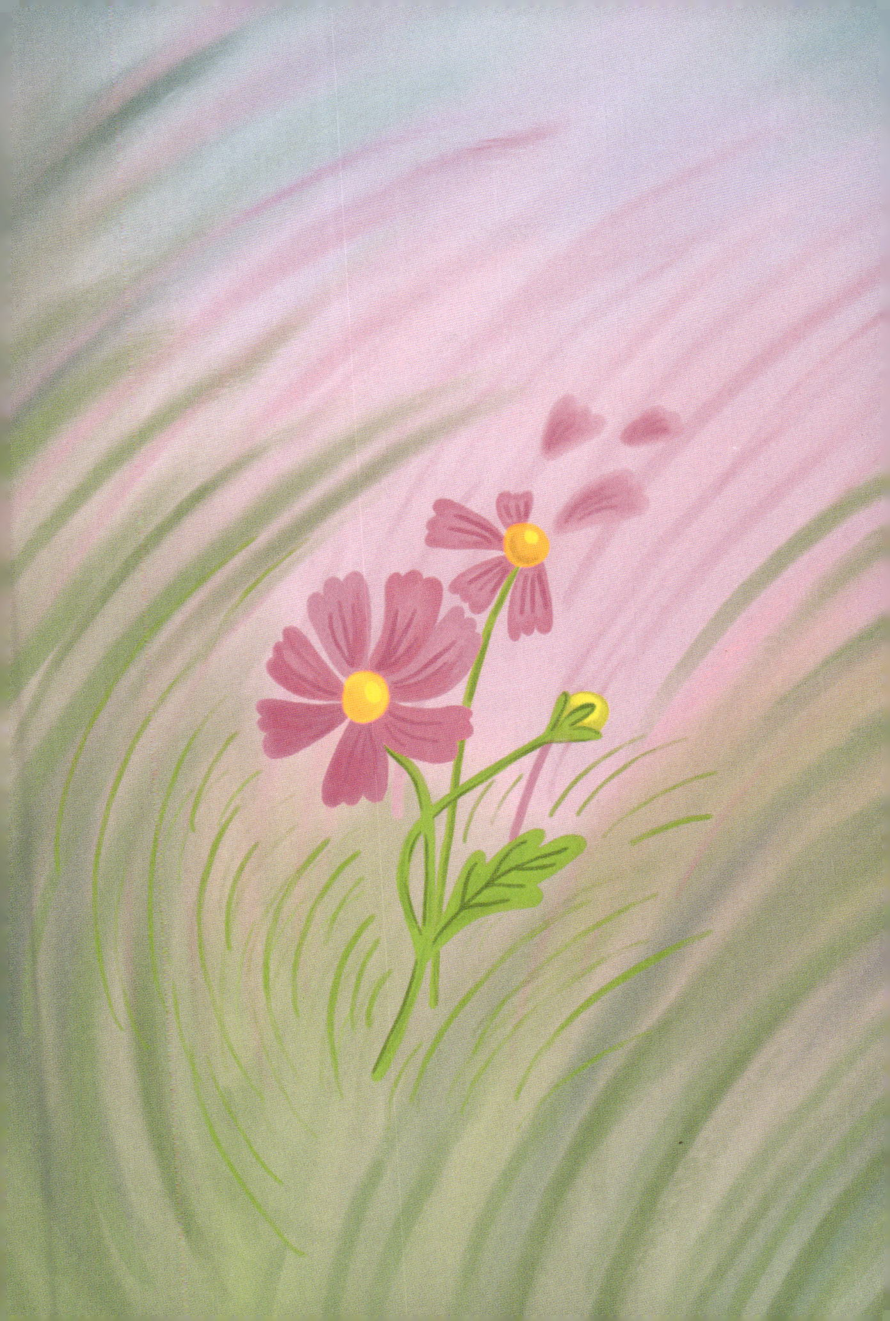

DAY

50 2 Corinthians 4:8–9

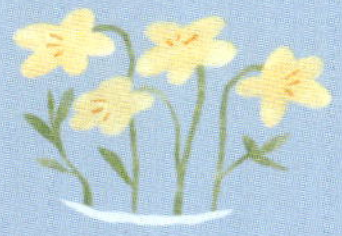

"We are pressed on every side by troubles, but we are not crushed. We are perplexed, but not driven to despair. We are hunted down, but never abandoned by God. We get knocked down, but we are not destroyed." (NLT)

Throughout Paul's missionary journey, he experienced hardship and persecution as he worked to fulfill Jesus' calling for his life. In his letters to the Corinthians, he alludes to these difficulties and shares some of his pain. But Paul's reflections weren't confined to hardships; he also shared the resilience he experienced with God on his side.

Like many of us, Paul frequently found himself in situations in which he was socially or politically powerless. There were many reasons to be afraid, abandon his call, or feel lost in despair. Powerless though he was by the world's standards, Paul had confidence in the power of God's Kingdom. Standing firm in that power made Paul resilient—the hardships became manageable, and he was able to keep moving forward in his work for Jesus.

In the spaces in which we feel powerless, we, too, can tap into the power we have in the Kingdom of God and be resilient in the face of hardship.

God, grant us the resilience of Paul, and remind us that no matter where we are, your power prevails. Amen.

Ephesians 4:29

DAY
51

"Don't use foul or abusive language. Let everything you say be good and helpful, so that your words will be an encouragement to those who hear them." (NLT)

Words are powerful tools. A single word has the capacity to encourage someone or wound them, to build bridges or burn them down. Scripture reminds us to be mindful of the impact of what we say and how we say it. We must think before we speak so that whatever we communicate is constructive rather than destructive.

Taking a moment to consider the many different ways we express ourselves and how our words might be heard ensures that we will not be misunderstood, but also that we will not offend the other person. Sometimes the difference between a message being received as a blessing rather than a curse is a matter of listening first and speaking second.

Talk need not be cheap if we practice discernment both in what others need to hear and what we say. A kind and gentle word can make a world of difference in the noisy and negative conversation space surrounding us. It can be the first step toward introducing a little bit of grace and transforming an otherwise contentious environment.

Teacher, grant us the wisdom and love to speak words that build up and bless those who hear them. Amen.

DAY

52 Lamentations 3:22–23

"The faithful love of the Lord never ends! His mercies never cease. Great is his faithfulness; his mercies begin afresh each morning." (NLT)

In the intricate tapestry of our lives, mercy is a golden thread, delicately woven by the hands of a compassionate Creator. At times, we may find it challenging to embrace the truth that we are cherished. The weight of shame and guilt casts a shadow on the idea that we are genuinely loved.

As we wrestle with our vulnerability, scripture reminds us that our God is one of second chances, of restoration and renewal. As beloved children of God, we are enveloped in a love that is not negated or diminished by our flaws and failings. God's love is steadfast, unchanging, and all-encompassing. When we stumble, God is there to lift us back up.

God extends mercy through Jesus, a gift freely given and not earned. And in return, we are moved to share that gift with others, extending grace and understanding to those around us when they misstep. In this way, we imitate God's unconditional love and grace, and we show others that no matter what, they are valued and accepted. We become a beacon of hope in a broken world.

God of mercy, envelop us in your grace and lead us forward into the brighter tomorrow you've prepared. Amen.

Matthew 22:37–38

DAY
53

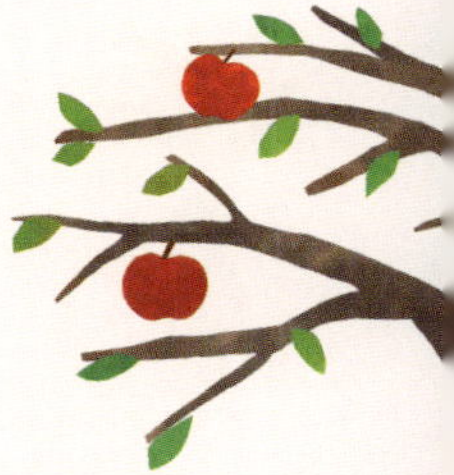

"Jesus replied, 'You must love the Lord your God with all your heart, all your soul, and all your mind.' This is the first and greatest commandment." (NLT)

God's highest desire for us has always been love. When we consider the first commandment, we can hear the heartbeat of the Lord crystal clear. God longs to be the steadfast lover of our souls. There is no greater love than this.

This commandment appears simple, but sometimes it feels impossible. As imperfect people, we might doubt our ability to love and even question how God could love us. But in truth, this is what we were made for. To love and be loved by Jesus, fragmented life and all. Truly loving God comes from a heart of worship. A heart bowed down to the King of Kings. How do we cultivate this within?

Worship is not performance, but a genuine posture. We might spend quiet time absorbing God's word, talk to him like a close friend, sing a new song. We might take a walk and observe creation in awe. Write a letter, a poem! Whatever expression of worship we choose, let it come from a place of deep love, for this is the most important commandment we could ever fulfill.

Compassionate Creator, our hearts are completely yours. Help us to love you fully, every day, always. Amen.

DAY

54 Zephaniah 3:17

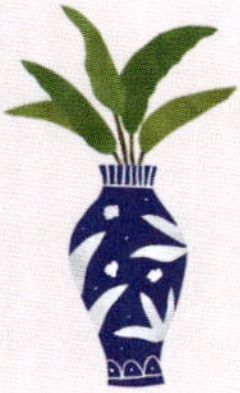

"The Lord your God is with you, the Mighty Warrior who saves. He will take great delight in you; in his love he will no longer rebuke you, but will rejoice over you with singing." (NIV)

When we think of the word "mighty," we often associate it with muscles or power. But God's might is depicted differently. Divine might is more about God's character than a show of force. It is gentle, yet powerful; compassionate, yet strong.

We often see gentleness and power as opposites. Assuming that strength must be loud or forceful to be real. But God's might flips that perspective around. Scripture shows us a kind of power that isn't fragile or domineering but deeply secure. God's strength is not lesser because it is tender. God challenges our typical understanding of power and strength, while also tenderly inviting us to trust in Christ's goodness and love.

In a world that often feels dark and overwhelming, it's easy to forget that God is mighty and on our side. But Zephaniah 3:17 reminds us that our God is not just a powerful God, but a loving and personal one who takes delight in us, cares for us, and rejoices with singing over us.

Mighty Warrior, help us acknowledge that you are still on the throne. We align ourselves with the promises of your Word and ask that you help us submit ourselves to your might. Amen.

Philippians 2:13

DAY
55

"For God is working in you, giving you the desire
and the power to do what pleases him." (NLT)

How do we learn to see ourselves accurately, neither inflating our egos, nor doubting that we can have an impact in our world?

Philippians 2:13 declares God is at work in and among us; an assurance which engenders humility. Our talents, resources, and all other good things are gifts from God. They are given simply because God loves us and desires our good, not because we tried hard enough or are superior to anyone else. All that we do, we do by the grace of God.

Along with this humility comes confidence. We may struggle to find the courage to step forward into something new, but God's empowering presence is with us. God does not promise that we will never fail, make mistakes, or experience regret, but God does enable and equip us to keep pursuing beauty and goodness. We need not rely on our own power; our Creator strengthens us for the opportunities He calls us into.

May we be filled with confidence,
Jesus, as we seek to walk the
good road you invite us on
and do the good work you
have for us to do. Amen.

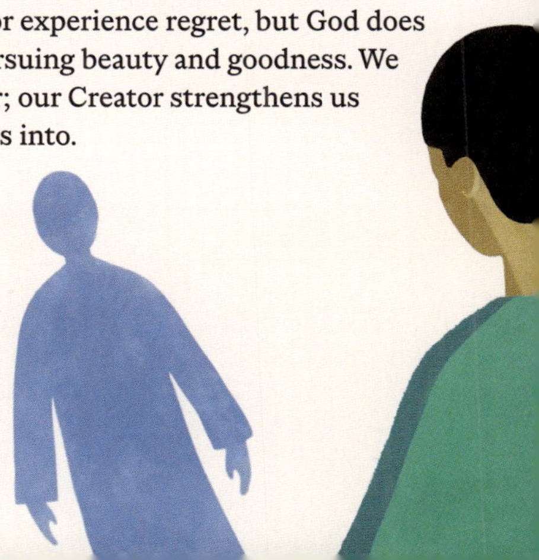

DAY

56 Proverbs 3:9–10

"Honor the Lord with your wealth and with the best part of everything you produce. Then he will fill your barns with grain, and your vats will overflow with good wine." (NLT)

The accumulation of wealth is a major fixation of our world. Books, podcasts, and finance gurus urge us to diversify our portfolios, pick up a side hustle, and make smart investments. The message seems clear—our power and value are linked to what we own and how much.

But in reality, ownership is an illusion. None of us is really "self-made". All we have is a gift from God, entrusted into our care for us to use for God's glory. We are stewards of our resources, not their source. Stewardship means treating these blessings with respect, not taking them for granted but sharing them generously. This posture becomes a reflection of God's generosity and an expression of trust that God will continue to provide.

To hoard or abuse our wealth is to ignore God's presence in it. God makes the harvests grow; God puts the very air in our lungs. Let us use the blessings we have been given to better our communities and our world, honoring our Creator with each action.

Let us praise you, oh God from whom all blessings flow. May we faithfully steward what you entrust to us for the glory of your Kingdom. Amen.

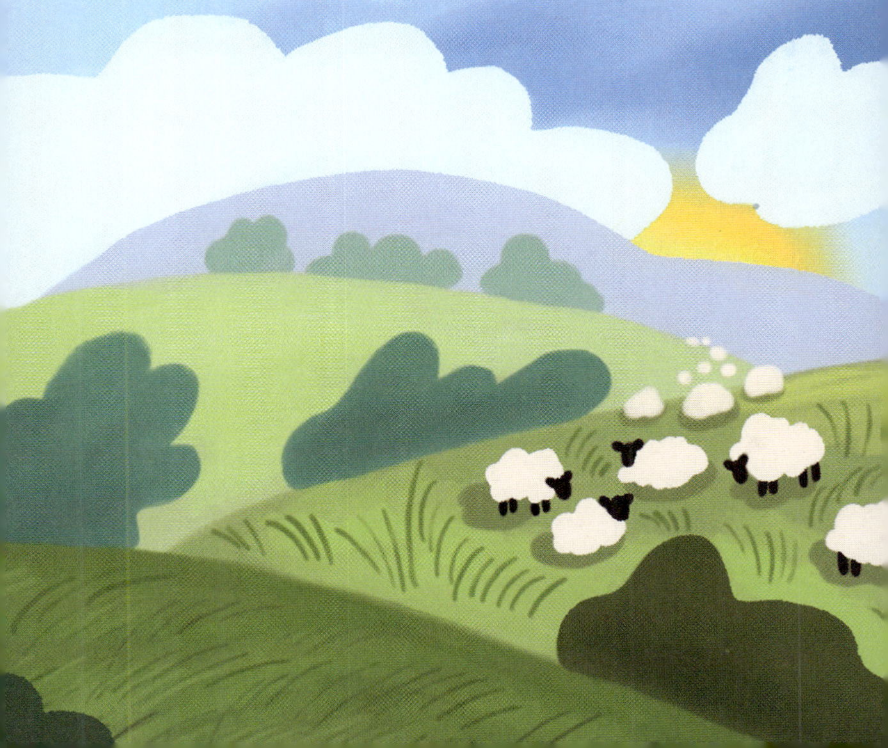

DAY

57 2 Corinthians 12:9–10

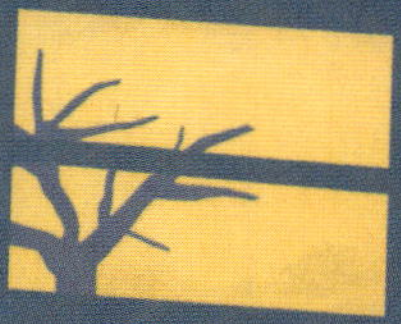

"Each time he said, 'My grace is all you need. My power works best in weakness.' So now I am glad to boast about my weaknesses, so that the power of Christ can work through me. That's why I take pleasure in my weaknesses, and in the insults, hardships, persecutions, and troubles that I suffer for Christ. For when I am weak, then I am strong." (NLT)

Perfectionism whispers that we are never enough—that we must strive harder, do better, and prove our worth. It measures our value in achievements, leaving no room for failure, no space for grace. But scripture tells a different story. God does not ask for perfection, but for trust.

The Kingdom of Heaven is not built on immaculate performances but on surrendered hearts. When we cling to control, we miss the the freedom born of reliance on Jesus. Our weakness is not a flaw, it's a feature—a door through which God's power enters. Like a cracked vessel letting light shine through, our imperfections make room for God's presence and strength in ways our striving never could.

When we release the need to be enough on our own, we step into a life no longer ruled by fear of failure but by the assurance of love that does not waver. This is the invitation—to rest, to trust, to let go. To know that in our weakness, we are held and sustained.

Jesus, free us from the weight of perfectionism and teach us to rest in your grace. Amen.

John 16:22

DAY
58

"So you have sorrow now, but I will see you again; then you will rejoice, and no one can rob you of that joy." (NLT)

Some days, sorrow settles deep, burdens press hard, and the weight of this world feels too much to bear. Jesus never tells us to ignore this pain. He never asks us to pretend. Instead, he speaks honestly: there will be times of grief, but these will, in time, be replaced by an even deeper joy.

Grief and joy pass through the same heart, one giving way to the other like the ebb and flow of the tide. Sorrow is real—loss comes, disappointments wound, some prayers seem unanswered. But no feeling lasts forever. Just as night gives way to morning, so too does suffering yield to joy. Not a shallow happiness that fades with circumstance, but a joy rooted in something deeper: the presence of God, steady and sure.

Jesus does not promise that we will never weep, but he does promise that we will not weep eternally. Even in our darkest nights, he is near, witnessing every tear and whispering that this is not the end of the story. Joy will return—not because life is perfect, but because he is present.

God, help us to hold on to your joy, even when life feels heavy. Amen.

DAY

59 Matthew 18:21–22

"Then Peter came to him and asked, 'Lord, how often should I forgive someone who sins against me? Seven times?' 'No, not seven times,' Jesus replied, 'but seventy times seven!'" (NLT)

When those we rely on let us down, we feel cut to the quick. And when the let-downs keep happening, we question how many more chances we should give. The disciple Peter clearly felt this way, asking Jesus when enough is enough. His question demonstrates a perception of forgiveness as a temporary obligation rather than an eternal offering.

Jesus tells us there is no limit to forgiving our trespassers. Forgiveness is not a one-time pass but a continual choice. It can be difficult to choose mercy instead of vengeance. But if Jesus can forgive us before we even ask, how much more should we extend grace to others? When Peter throws the number seven out, Jesus multiplies it by seventy to imply that forgiveness is an eternal gift.

Instead of letting hurts fester, we can be freed from resentment by extending forgiveness every day. In this process, our hearts begin to soften, and reconciliation becomes possible. When we choose to forgive, we become more like Jesus, who forgave it all. May we choose the merciful path and let the trespasses go.

God, give us hearts that extend endless forgiveness. Help us to forgive just as you have forgiven us. Amen.

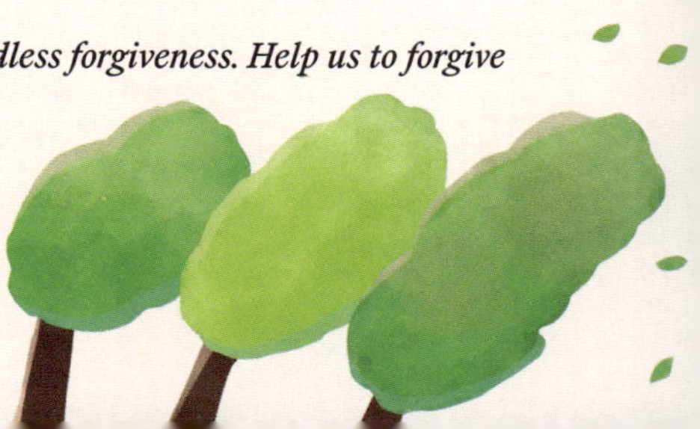

1 Samuel 3:10

DAY
60

"And the Lord came and called as before, 'Samuel! Samuel!' And Samuel replied, 'Speak, your servant is listening.'" (NLT)

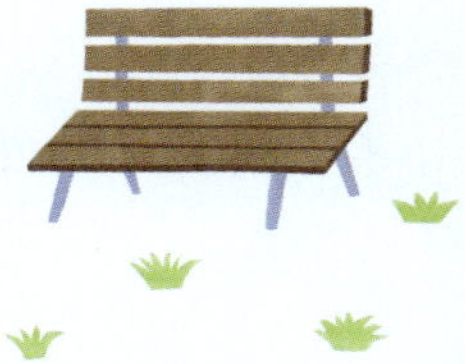

More and more, attention is a fleeting thing. In the era of "second screen" media, many of us have a divided focus, watching movies while scrolling on our phones. We're easily distracted, and with so many voices competing for our attention, it's easy to understand why. What grabs us? What gets dismissed? And how do we differentiate between noise and deliberate address?

When God speaks, it is always with intention. The divine voice commands power—the very universe was *spoken* into creation. Therefore, if we desire to be attentive to how Jesus is calling us, our listening must also be intentional.

Intentional listening can mean setting aside dedicated time for prayer and reflection. But it is also adopting an awareness and openness to the moments in which God's voice breaks into the unexpected. It comes by working to reclaim our attention and resisting the constant state of distraction. Only then will we be alert enough to hear the call that comes in the quiet.

Help us to resist the cacophony, God. When you call us, may we answer you as Samuel did: "Speak, your servant is listening." Amen.

DAY

61 Matthew 25:40

"And the King will say, 'I tell you the truth, when you did it to one of the least of these my brothers and sisters, you were doing it to me!'" (NLT)

We might feel stuck discerning big questions of calling and life direction. We wonder what our next faithful step might be.

In this story, Jesus says that what truly matters is how we treat the most vulnerable people among us: people who need nutritious food, clean water, a sense of welcome in a new place, warm clothing, healthcare, or remembrance and friendship during imprisonment.

Trusting in God to guide us, our call to act is clear. We are invited into a ministry of kindness, paying special attention to the people who are not shown kindness by our world.

We are invited to empathize with the "least of these," seeing them as our family in Christ. We are called to care. God invites us to serve in tangible ways, give generously, and listen to and learn from all sorts of people.

God, help us see all people as worthy of your love and care. Show us your own face in the ones we're tempted to write off. Help us treat them as we would treat you. Amen.

Philippians 2:3–5

DAY
62

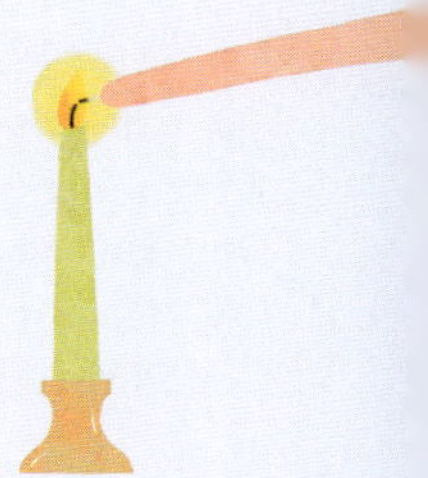

"Don't be selfish; don't try to impress others. Be humble, thinking of others as better than yourselves. Don't look out only for your own interests, but take an interest in others, too. You must have the same attitude that Christ Jesus had." (NLT)

Humility is often misunderstood as a form of passivity and self-denial. In a power-obsessed culture, it seems unattainable or undesirable. But in Philippians, Paul urges believers to imitate Jesus' humility which led him to be born human and throw himself into the complexities of earthly life for the good of creation.

The humility Jesus displays is the opposite of how we tend to characterize it. Confident in his power, he considered the needs of others. Knowing he had everything he needed in the Father, he offered himself as a sacrifice. Jesus' humility is a posture of power that comes from a complete and total trust in God.

We don't have to demonstrate might to come out on top; we can trust that God will set things right. This is the template for humility we are called to—knowing who we are and the power we have in Christ, moving in the world with care and consideration for others.

God, teach us to be humble like Jesus. Give us eyes to see the people around us as you see them, and to care for their wants, needs, and hopes in the world. Amen.

DAY

63 Luke 17:20–21

"One day the Pharisees asked Jesus, 'When will the Kingdom of God come?' Jesus replied, 'The Kingdom of God can't be detected by visible signs. You won't be able to say, "Here it is!" or "It's over there!" For the Kingdom of God is already among you.'" (NLT)

Imagine waking up with a new, rare ability to see a spectrum of color not normally visible to the human eye. What more would we notice? Would the sunrises hold more power? Would describing our favorite artwork be more challenging?

Reckoning with the reality of God's Kingdom feels similar. When the Pharisees asked Jesus about God's Kingdom, they likely anticipated the world would look dramatically different when that Kingdom came. Yet, true to form, Jesus defies expectations, pointing to the God at work in the here and now.

Sometimes when we hyperfocus on historic timelines or world-altering events, we miss the glimpses of the Kingdom already in our midst. There are sacred spaces all around us. We have the privilege of looking at the Bible with the context of the Resurrection. Through his life, death and resurrection, Jesus restored our relationship with the Kingdom of God. We know that the total restoration of humanity God promises will be incredible. But even in our day-to-day, faith allows us to see glimpses of the Kingdom amongst us.

God, remind us that your Kingdom is among us and at work. Like new rays of light, show us that it is here. Amen.

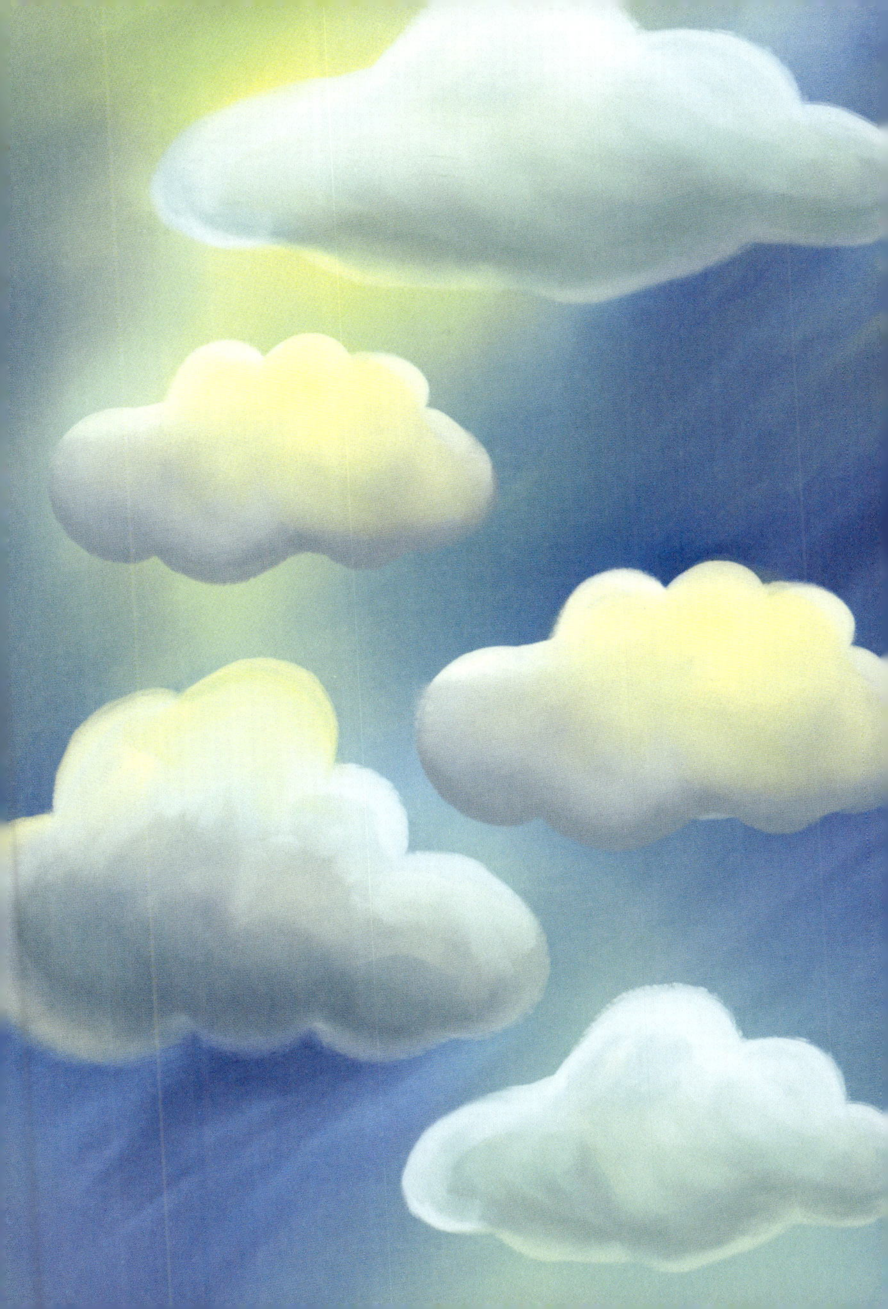

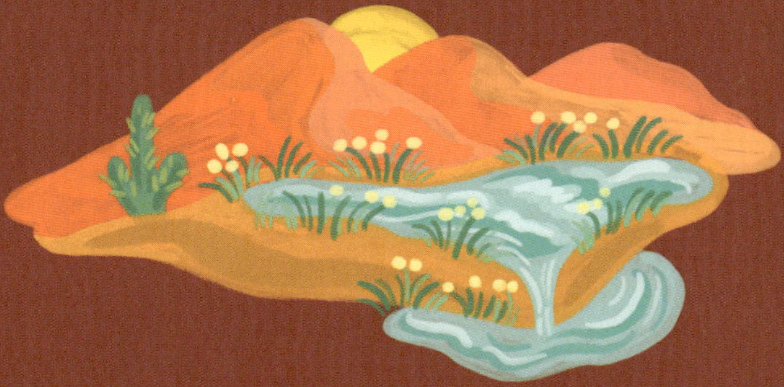

Isaiah 55:1

DAY
64

"Is anyone thirsty? Come and drink—even if you have no money! Come, take your choice of wine or milk—it's all free!" (NLT)

In our world of industry and competition, it can be easy to think we must earn our place—prove our worth, show our strength, bring something valuable to the table. But God invites us into something different. God throws a banquet not for the worthy, but for the weary, spread by the hands of a God who delights in welcoming the empty-handed.

We do not have to come polished. We do not have to come strong. The table is not set for those who have it all together, but for those who hunger and thirst—for those who know their need. How often do we hesitate, waiting until we feel more presentable, more faithful, more deserving? But grace has never asked for perfection. It simply asks that we come.

Jesus is the great welcomer, not requiring our best selves, only our true selves. The One who gathers the broken, fills the hungry with good things, calls the weary to rest, is waiting, arms open. There is nothing we must bring, we only have to acknowledge we are thirsty and come.

God, help us to receive your grace and come before you just as we are, without hesitation. You quench our thirst. Amen.

DAY
65 Psalm 139:13–14

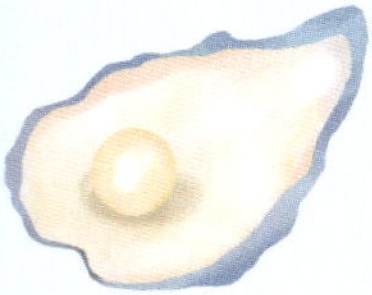

"You made all the delicate, inner parts of my body and knit me together in my mother's womb. Thank you for making me so wonderfully complex! Your workmanship is marvelous—how well I know it." (NLT)

If we ponder how we were formed, we will see divine creations and not meaningless accidents. We are God's carefully molded children, not an empty amalgamation of atoms. Consider how every bone, muscle, tissue, and cell has been spun together to make up our frame—the human design is extraordinarily intentional.

God sees each of us as eternally valuable; everyone is crafted in God's image, and therefore, there are no mistakes. What would we see if we looked at ourselves through divine eyes? A breathtaking masterpiece, a perfect piece of God's very visage.

Instead of believing the anthem of nothingness, we must remember that the Maker of the galaxies weaved our bodies together with the utmost care and attention, the crowning work of creation. Whenever we feel insignificant, it only takes a moment to pause, put our hand on our chest, and feel the rhythmic hum of our heartbeat as we take a deep breath and remember in the core of ourselves, how miraculously God made us.

Maker of the Universe, you have made us with such praiseworthy beauty and thoughtfulness, it is unfathomable to comprehend! We know your workmanship is unmatchable. Amen.

Matthew 20:13–15

DAY
66

"He answered one of them, 'Friend, I haven't been unfair! Didn't you agree to work all day for the usual wage? Take your money and go. I wanted to pay this last worker the same as you. Is it against the law for me to do what I want with my money? Should you be jealous because I am kind to others?'" (NLT)

We live in a culture fixated on status and rank, in which love and approval are quantified through likes, shares, and follows. Such evaluation places us all in competition. It can be isolating and anxiety-inducing. Opinions turn on a dime; we may live in fear of being seen as a darling one day and a disaster the next.

Jesus takes this concern with status and turns it on its head. Expectations to be first, or best, or most valuable, are not part of God's Kingdom. All are welcome and cherished in the Kingdom of Heaven.

If we're honest, our preoccupation with rank and evaluation stems from a deeper anxiety—we worry we are not enough. But God's mercy and compassion are available to everyone, even those the world has deemed unworthy. The gift of the Kingdom of God is one of inclusion. Our culture may emphasize our differences from one another, but our Creator unites us. God's love is not something we can earn, but something graciously given.

God, help us release the drive to prove ourselves to the world and instead abide in you. Amen.

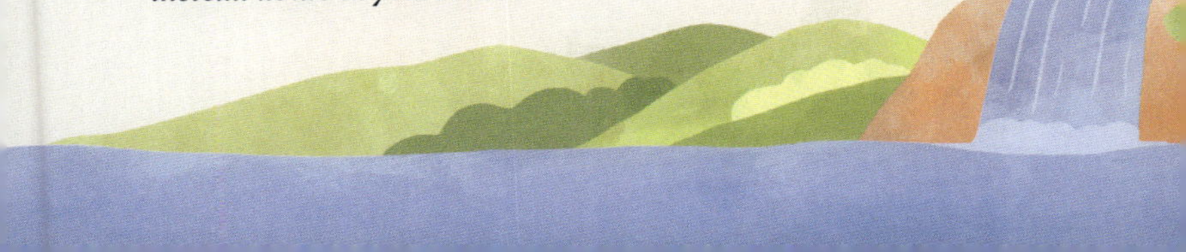

DAY

67 Isaiah 40:29,31

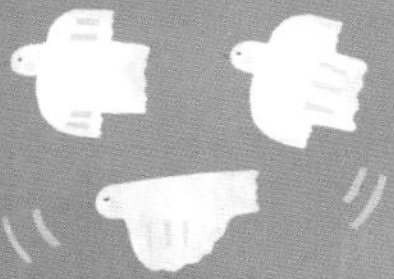

"He gives strength to the weary and increases the power of the weak ... those who hope in the Lord will renew their strength. They will soar on wings like eagles; they will run and not grow weary, they will walk and not be faint." (NIV)

Weight settles on us in weary seasons. The journey itself can feel too much to bear. Our hearts feel heavy and our steps slow. But amidst it all, there is a promise that stands firm: God gives strength to the weary.

This isn't a quick fix—it's a deep renewal that reaches the core of who we are. We're strengthened not by our own effort, but by the ongoing source of replenishment that is God's strength. With that strength, we can be confident that we will overcome our challenges. We will soar, we will run, and we will walk, knowing the Creator sustains us with every step forward.

On our own, we all grow tired and weak eventually. Yet, God promises to renew the strength of all who place their hope in Him. This hope isn't passive, a naive or simple wish. Hope is a person to connect with and that person is Jesus.

Lord, we come before you, acknowledging our weariness and weakness. Help us place our hope in you, trusting that you will renew our strength and help us rise above it. Amen.

Hebrews 4:9–10

DAY 68

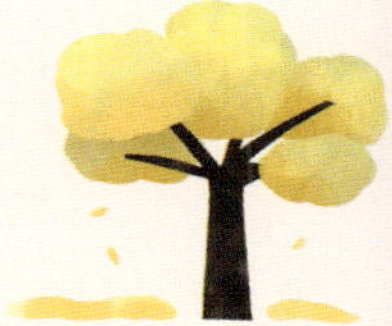

"So there is a special rest still waiting for the people of God. For all who have entered into God's rest have rested from their labors, just as God did after creating the world." (NLT)

After creating the universe, God rested. Our Creator set an example and asked creation to follow it. This call goes beyond the simple rest of sleep. Sabbath is a waking rest for our souls.

To participate in God's rest takes preparation and dedication, but it is far from stressful. In our busy lives, setting aside a day free of labor and lists is countercultural. But the benefits of a well-rested person lead to peace and increased flourishing.

Not every Sabbath looks the same. Everyone has their own patterns of enjoying rest, feeling renewed, and connecting to God. A day of rest with our Creator can be filled with peaceful conversations, nourishing food, refreshing nature, and much more, just as we see in Jesus' ministry. What matters is that we find the patterns that work for us and follow God's example, viewing rest not as an extravagance but as a necessity.

Rest allows for our souls and minds to shed stress. We gain indescribable peace during time with our Creator as God reminds us what truly matters. And when we make time for resting in Jesus, an overflow of joy and blessings fills our lives.

Jesus, we ask for your special rest, and thank you for modeling the way. Amen.

DAY

69 Psalm 118:24

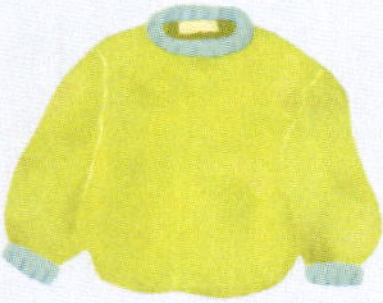

"This is the day the Lord has made.
We will rejoice and be glad in it." (NLT)

As children, some birthday gifts bring more delight than others. Roller skates? Joy. New art set? Bliss. A warm winter coat? Crickets.

Even as parents try to drum up enthusiasm, it can be hard for a child to feel much more than disappointment over such a practical gift. Until the weather turns bitterly cold, and suddenly that disregarded coat becomes the warm cocoon, enabling her to stay cozy while building a snowman or flying kites on a crisp winter day. What once seemed dull became a cherished gift—a gift she hadn't known she would need.

Each day is a gift, created and placed in our hands by God. Some feel immediately joyful, filled with beauty and abundance. We hardly need scripture to urge us to rejoice in these. The joy comes naturally, appreciating gifts that deliver uncomplicated happiness. Others are not what we would have chosen. But the value of a gift is not always seen at first glance. It unfolds with time, revealing grace we might not yet recognize. Ultimately, we rejoice in the day because we trust the goodness of the Giver.

Jesus, help us to receive this day with trust and joy, knowing that you give good gifts. Amen.

Titus 2:7

DAY
70

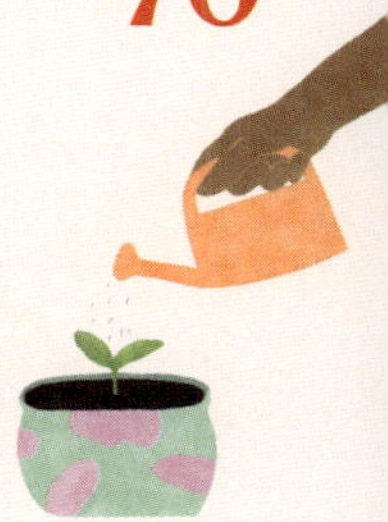

"And you yourself must be an example to them by doing good works of every kind. Let everything you do reflect the integrity and seriousness of your teaching." (NLT)

The Bible is chock-full of teachings on theology and spirituality. While this wisdom can feel heady or theoretical, it contains profoundly practical advice as well. Titus 2:7 is a prime example of a deeply applicable bit of wisdom: leaders should lead by example.

We're all too familiar with hypocrisy in leadership. We see people in power who espouse standards and morals that they themselves don't adhere to. Sometimes, this discrepancy comes from a lack of personal integrity. Other times, it results from setting standards that are impossible for anyone to meet. As leaders, we ought to ask ourselves whose expectations and teachings we are promoting, our own or God's?

The kind of leadership modeled in the Bible and called out in Titus is one that does good works with and for others. It's servant-hearted rather than controlling. When we put in the work as leaders, it strengthens the message of our leadership.

Lord Jesus, help us to lead by example. Give us eyes to examine ourselves honestly, and show us the path that leads others to do your work on earth alongside us. Amen.

DAY

71 Luke 8:23–24

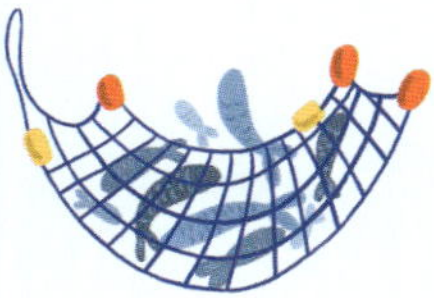

"And a windstorm came down on the lake, and they were filling with water and were in danger. And they went and woke him, saying, 'Master, Master, we are perishing!' And he awoke and rebuked the wind and the raging waves, and they ceased, and there was a calm." (ESV)

No one wants to be in the eye of a storm. Caught at the very center of the chaos, our focus narrows to what swirls around us. Our world is likewise tumultuous. Storms rain down, making the future seem precarious. Scripture assures us that even in such moments, a mere word from Jesus restores peace and serenity. Jesus calms the storm.

But here in Luke, two storms rage: one born of roaring winds and crashing waters, and another thundering inside the disciples themselves—an internal storm of fear, anger, and anxiety.

When circumstances seem fraught, our first response is typically to exert control and regain our footing. But if our efforts prove unsuccessful, waves of panic, frustration, and worry stir within us. We find ourselves floundering for some semblance of equilibrium. Jesus also calms this storm. Our God is always in control. When things seem bleak or overwhelming, we need not rely on ourselves.

Jesus, you invite us to put our faith in you. The stillness you brought to the wind and sea is available to us, too. Amen.

DAY
72

Acts 9:3-6

"As he neared Damascus on his journey, suddenly a light from heaven flashed around him. He fell to the ground and heard a voice say to him, 'Saul, Saul, why do you persecute me?' 'Who are you, Lord?' Saul asked. 'I am Jesus, whom you are persecuting,' he replied. 'Now get up and go into the city, and you will be told what you must do.'" (NIV)

When we imagine living out our faith, we may think we aren't ready yet. We don't feel wise enough, good enough, faithful enough. We couldn't possibly be prepared to serve God's plans.

Saul, soon-to-be Paul, reminds us that this is untrue. God meets us where we are, even when we're going down the wrong road. A relationship with Jesus—a life of faith—is available to us here and now, in our present imperfections. Left to our own devices, we will always be imperfect. The only way to grow is to draw close to the One who restores and renews us.

God sees our mistakes and shortcomings. *And* God has a purpose and plan for each of us. We don't need to hide our imperfections or put off partnering with God until some future, better day. We can meet Jesus right now and trust that he will guide us forward.

Loving God, we're meeting you where we are, bruises and blunders and all. Correct us where we err and enlighten us to your purposes. Amen.

DAY
73 Titus 3:5

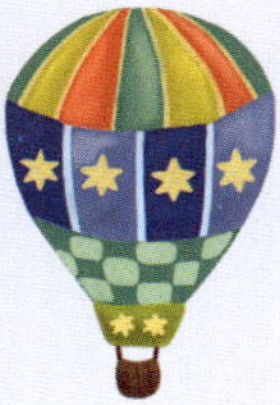

"He saved us, not because of the righteous things we had done, but because of his mercy. He washed away our sins, giving us a new birth and new life through the Holy Spirit." (NLT)

When do we feel most relaxed? Usually not when stressing over our performance. Nor do we feel calm when we get worked up about what we did wrong. But when we remember Jesus' overwhelming mercy is there to embrace us, we can unclench our shoulders, release the stress, and clear our heads and hearts.

Titus 3 proclaims our salvation does not rest on our righteousness, but God's alone. We are invited to fully relax in the merciful Spirit. We are no longer obligated to stay weighed down by the distress and demands of a world that never rests, but can enter into a place of steady peace, knowing that no remnant of our sins remains to stain our conscience any longer.

We have been given fresh rebirth and a new way of living through the counsel of the Holy Spirit. What more do we need to have peace of mind? The very God who formed the universe is residing in our chests and telling each of us that we can finally enjoy true rest by abiding.

God of rest, when we are tempted to be stirred up by stress, help us to lean into you and relax with your Spirit. Amen.

Psalm 27:14

DAY
74

"Wait patiently for the Lord. Be brave and courageous. Yes, wait patiently for the Lord." (NLT)

What do we envision when we think of courage? Perhaps the word conjures to mind images of knights and adventurers—superheroes and the seemingly invincible. As we stare down the barrel of our responsibilities, burdens, and anxieties, summoning courage can feel like a monumental task.

We often speak of courage as boldly charging ahead, come what may. To be courageous, we say, is to have no fear, to wait for no one. Through this lens, one with courage simply rises to the challenge by their own sheer will. And as we sit daunted, unsure, and exhausted, we may be inclined to believe that bravery is simply not for us.

However, scripture paints a different picture. Where we associate courage with advancing, the Bible links it with waiting. Courage is born out not through self-reliance, but by allowing God to move and shape us. We can be strong and courageous precisely because God is with us. Jesus goes before us, preparing our paths and guiding our steps. True courage is an expression of trust and faith.

God, give us hope that engenders courage and confidence. If the Creator of the universe is for us, who could stand against us? Amen.

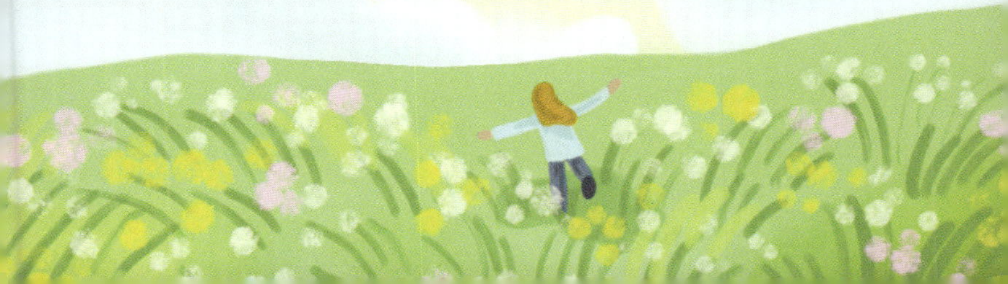

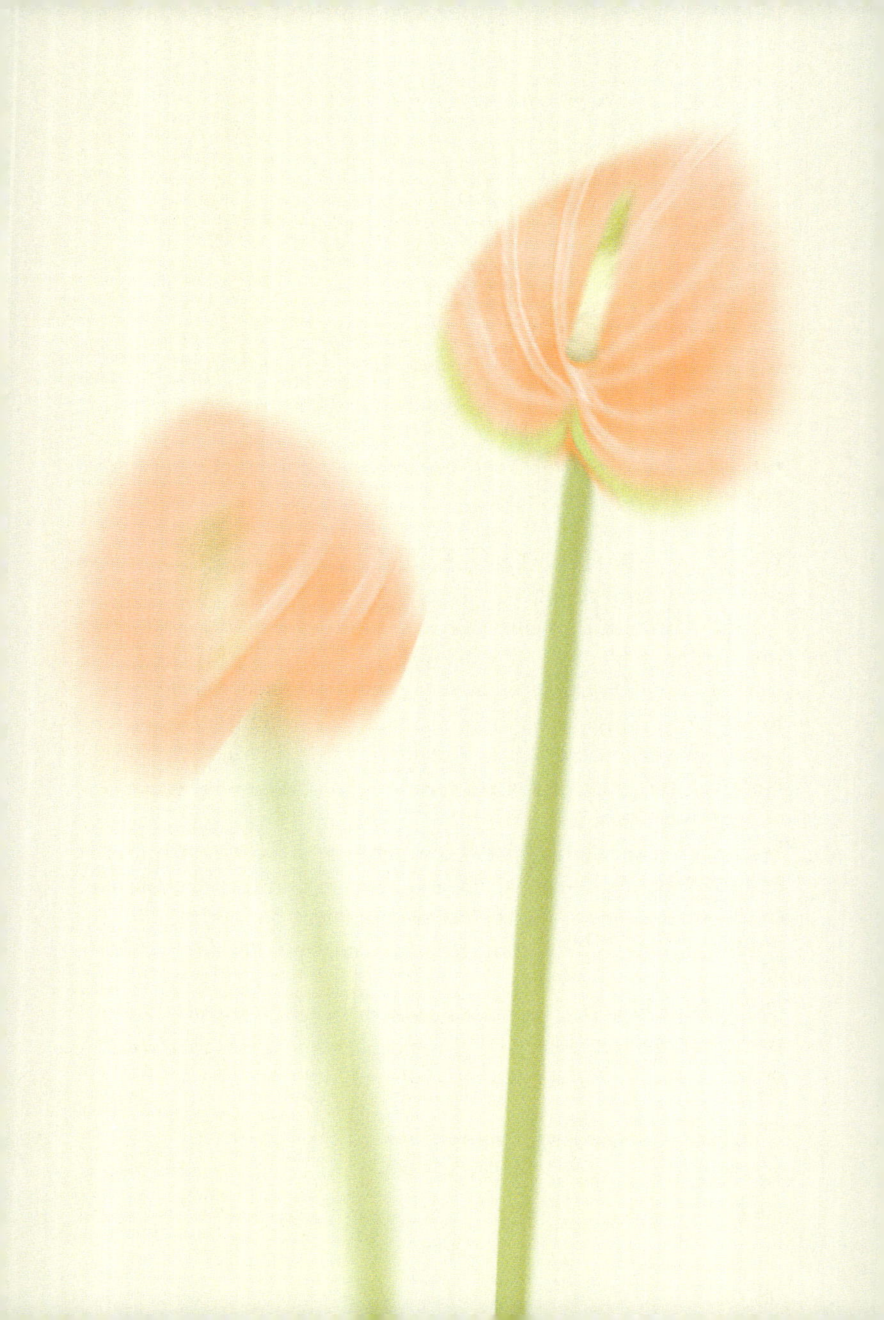

Romans 12:2

DAY
75

"Do not conform to the pattern of this world, but be transformed by the renewing of your mind. Then you will be able to test and approve what God's will is—his good, pleasing and perfect will." (NIV)

Romans 12:2 urges us not to be conformed to this age. This call begs the question, what are the dominant ways of being that mark our time and place? What mindsets and practices are we warned not to conform to?

We live in a society that has long revered "rugged individualism;" one of God's countercultural ways is to value the good of the whole community. As we are transformed, we learn to see ourselves as interconnected with other humans in our communities and around the world, as well as with the animals, plants, waters, and soils that comprise our broader ecological communities.

We also live in a time in which greed and aggression seem to get people ahead. Jesus invites us to become gentler, more attentive, more inclusive, and more generous. Facing communities full of inequality, Christ can help us build just communities.

Discerning God's will calls for transformation. Following that will invites us into nonconformity. We might feel out of step with our broader society, but we are walking a good path.

God, may we live in your countercultural ways. Show us what is good and beautiful, peaceful and just. Open us up to transformation. Amen.

DAY 76 Psalm 94:19

"When doubts filled my mind, your comfort gave me renewed hope and cheer." (NLT)

It isn't hard to drum up a list of things we'd like to change about ourselves. In our most vulnerable moments, the voices of self-loathing can take center stage. Whispers that we are worthless, that our mistakes define us, ring in our ears. We wonder why we're here, what we could possibly bring to the table.

Scripture interrupts this clamor of negative thought to declare the truth: Jesus is welcoming us to him. We each have a part to play in the divine plan for this world. Where we may see lack or insignificance, Jesus sees a treasured child. When obstacles seem insurmountable, the Holy Spirit moves within us, reminding us that anything is possible through Christ.

When we put our faith in the hands of the Spirit—when we allow God, not the world, to tell us who we are—we make room for the transformative and beautiful work God intends for the whole of creation. We adopt a divine mindset that stands assured that restoration, renewal, and refinement are real, and that doubts and darkness will not have the final say.

Soothe our doubts and insecurities, Jesus. Fill us with renewed hope and cheer. May we see ourselves through your eyes. Amen.

Romans 5:8

DAY
77

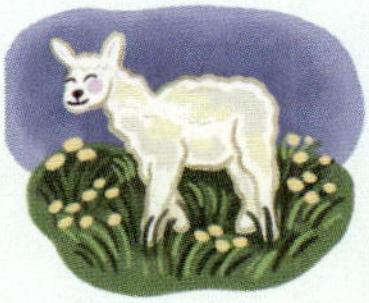

"But God showed his great love for us by sending Christ to die for us while we were still sinners." (NLT)

One of the most beautiful parts of the story of Jesus is that his sacrifice was for everyone. Not just a select few followers or do-gooders, but for every single person. Jesus didn't wait until everyone had begun to follow him; his sacrifice happened while few believed in him, in a time that was rife with corruption.

It's easy to fall into a pattern of thinking that Jesus' sacrifice is a reward, that we need to earn it in some way. But that's simply not the case. Divine grace reaches us regardless of our response and our actions! It's a reflection of who Jesus is: the son of God incarnate who cares deeply about every single person to ever walk the earth. The gift is great and has everything to do with who Jesus is, rather than who we are.

We, as followers of Jesus, have the opportunity to reflect that character of care back into the world around us, regardless of the world's response.

Jesus, grant us the eyes to see all of humanity as you do. Teach us to consider others, caring for them regardless of whether we feel they deserve it. Amen.

DAY

78 James 5:16

“The prayer of a righteous person is powerful and effective.” (NIV)

Prayer is one of the most powerful tools God gives us. But often, we treat it like a routine or obligation, instead of something that makes a difference. James 5:16 reminds us that prayer is real and it has power.

Prayer aligns our hearts with God’s will. When we pray, we’re not merely asking for our desires, but seeking God’s perspective and trusting the divine plan. Prayer helps us listen, reflect, and grow closer to Jesus. It also invites God to act. Despite being the sovereign and omniscient Creator of all things, God chooses to partner with us. When we pray, we actively welcome Jesus to intervene in our lives and the lives of those around us.

Ultimately, prayer strengthens our faith. Seeing God answer our prayers—whether small or large—reminds us of God’s faithfulness and deepens our trust in the One who is always righteous and just. The power of prayer lies in its ability to draw us closer to God, align us with God’s will, and see the power of restoration at work in our lives.

Lord, thank you for giving us access to you through prayer. Teach us to rely on you in all things, knowing you hear and respond. Amen.

Revelation 21:4

DAY
79

"He will wipe every tear from their eyes, and there will be no more death or sorrow or crying or pain. All these things are gone forever." (NLT)

We might feel, at times, as though our lives are composed of one long string of losses. We feel overwhelmed by suffering in our own lives and relationships, in our broader communities, and in our world as a whole, and wonder if it will ever end. Like countless human hearts before us, we cry out, "How long, oh Lord?"

In Revelation 21:4, Jesus responds to our heartbroken cries with a compassionate and emphatic "not forever." Our mourning, crying, and pain will not continue indefinitely. Even death will be no more. These things will have an end.

We believe in a God who draws near to us, soothes our weary spirits, and wipes every tear from our eyes. God will bring comfort and healing, even if we cannot see it yet. Life is marked by pain, but this pain will not last forever.

Jesus, help us cling to your promise that you have defeated even death itself. Be with us in our grief and comfort us in our sadness. Amen.

DAY

80 Psalm 100:4

"Enter his gates with thanksgiving; go into his courts with praise. Give thanks to him and praise his name." (NLT)

Thanksgiving is a means of drawing near to Jesus. It is not mere sentiment, but a posture of the heart—opening our eyes to his presence and filling our lips with praise. We do not wait for extraordinary moments to give thanks. Gratitude belongs in the ordinary, in the rhythm of each day, in the simple awareness that every breath, every kindness, every provision comes from God. The resilient weed emerging from a crack in the sidewalk, a smile from a stranger, the text from a friend that comes in a moment of discouragement.

As we give thanks, our hearts awaken to the depth of God's goodness. We see more clearly, rejoice more freely, and love more fully. Thanksgiving shifts our gaze from what we lack to the abundance before us. It reminds us that we are held, provided for, and sustained by a God whose faithfulness never wavers.

When we cultivate and practice gratitude, we step more fully into God's gift of abundant joy—walking through the gates with praise, into the courts of God's presence, into the eternal home that has been prepared for us.

God, help our hearts rejoice in you, and notice the abundance of gifts we receive today. Amen.

Colossians 1:11

DAY 81

"Being strengthened with all power according to his glorious might so that you may have great endurance and patience." (NIV)

The Colossian church was a community facing pressures from the outside and confusion from within. False teachings began to creep in, and believers were tempted to lean on their own understanding or worldly wisdom instead of trusting in the sufficiency of Christ. In his letter, Paul doesn't urge them to figure it out alone. Instead, he prays that they would be strengthened by God's power.

That same encouragement speaks to us today. We too live in a world full of noise—cultural pressure, shifting values, and misleading ideas about what strength is. Like them, we need a strength that helps us endure hard seasons, stay grounded in truth, and practice patience when things don't move as quickly as we'd like.

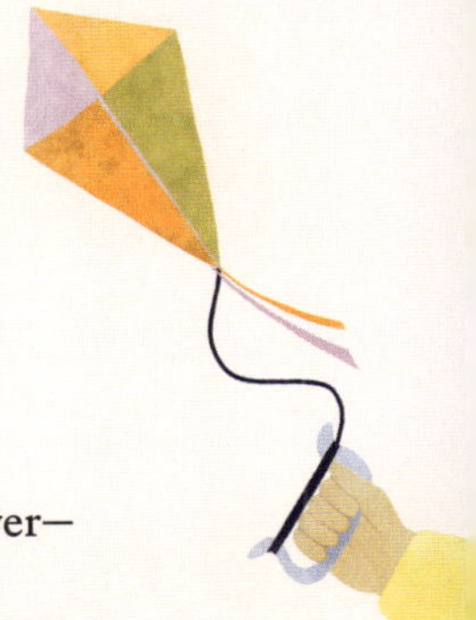

This kind of strength isn't about grit or willpower—it's spiritual resilience that comes from God's glorious might. It's the kind of strength that keeps us going, not because we're strong, but because God is.

Lord, help us rely on you in everything, especially when life feels heavy. Give us endurance, patience, and faith that hold fast. Amen.

DAY

82 Jeremiah 29:11

"'For I know the plans I have for you,' says the Lord. 'They are plans for good and not for disaster, to give you a future and a hope.'" (NLT)

"What do you want to be when you grow up?" This constant refrain echoes from childhood through young adulthood. From the moment we can talk, we are encouraged to plan what we want to study, what kind of person we want to marry, whether we want children, and how many. We diligently sketch out our future in bold lines, imagining how things should unfold.

But then, the unexpected comes—a door closes, a dream we cherished slips from our grasp. Disappointment settles in, heavy and unbidden. We think: this was not the plan.

Jesus does not ask us to pretend that these losses do not hurt. Instead, we are invited to bring them fully into the presence of the One who sees beyond what we can understand. What feels like an ending may, in time, be revealed as a beginning. The path ahead may look different than we imagined, but God is leading us, journeying with us into an uncharted future. And where God leads, goodness and mercy will follow. So we go forward with hope.

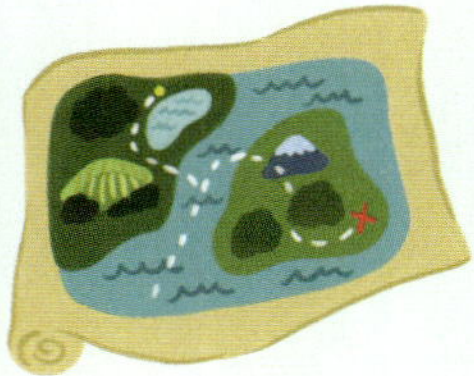

God, when our plans falter, help us trust that your ways are higher, and your goodness never fails. Amen.

James 4:6

DAY

83

“And he gives grace generously. As the Scriptures say, ‘God opposes the proud but gives grace to the humble.’” (NLT)

Pride has never produced fruit in humanity, but has led to many falls. Consider the first, when Adam and Eve rebelled against God because they thought they knew best. The good news is, God is generous to give us grace when we choose humility.

The underlying lie of pride says that we should be at the center of our lives, not God. We cling to pride out of fear of being looked over. On the contrary, the wisdom of humility says that serving is better than being served. It moves us to give up our prideful tendencies and instead pursue a life that prioritizes others before ourselves.

It is contrary to our human nature to resist selfish ambition. We are told by the world to be braggadocious about our successes. But oftentimes what is counter-cultural in this world is honorable in the sight of Heaven—God’s upside-down Kingdom. When we choose to serve others with a humble heart, we walk in the character of Jesus who was the ultimate lowly servant.

God, we lay down our pride and ask that you give us a humble heart. Amen.

DAY

84 Matthew 7:24, 26–27

"Anyone who listens to my teaching and follows it is wise, like a person who builds a house on solid rock ... But anyone who hears my teaching and doesn't obey it is foolish, like a person who builds a house on sand. When the rains and floods come and the winds beat against that house, it will collapse with a mighty crash." (NLT)

Where do we turn in times of trouble? When our backs are to the wall, where do we look for rescue? Difficult seasons are a reality of life. While we experience moments of great joy and abundance, there are also torrents and tumults to endure.

Several of Jesus' parables liken faith to structure and stability. To put our faith in Jesus is to build on a sound foundation. Where we invest and focus in tranquil times will influence how we respond in instability. If we ground ourselves in the wisdom and promises of God, we can stand firm even in the downpour.

Crucially, this parable is not a message of punishment, but one of caution and encouragement. The floodwaters are not sent to chastise the foolish builder. Hardship and trial affect all of humanity. The storm reaches both the house on rock and the one on sand. The difference is in how the storm is weathered.

God, your wisdom enables us to face storms with confidence. The winds may blow and the waters rise, but we will not be washed away. Amen.

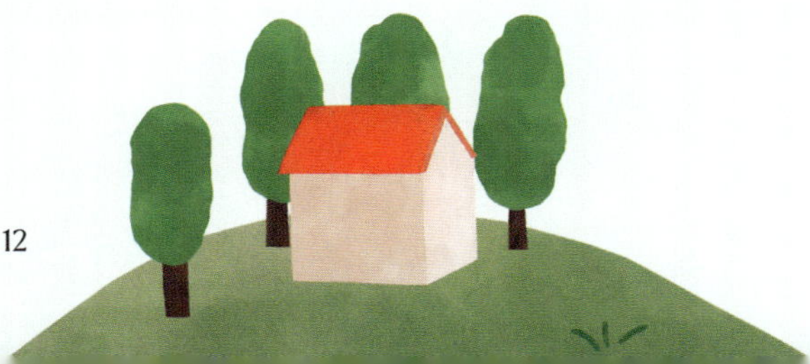

Psalm 23:6

DAY
85

"Surely goodness and mercy shall follow me all the days of my life, and I shall dwell in the house of the Lord forever." (ESV)

What does it look like to be surprised by God's goodness or arrive at sudden realizations of divine mercy?

David has a legacy of being a man after God's own heart, but he still experienced hardships. Despite the dark valleys, David saw evidence of God's goodness and mercy throughout his life. We may travel through our own dark valleys, but what if we had David's same faith in God's faithfulness?

When we dwell in the house of God, all things shine a little brighter. We are not alone—it's a chaotic and lively place. The halls echo the praises of God as believers shout, "Goodness! Mercy!" Even when our stories feel absorbed by difficulty or darkness, the testimonies of other believers are reminders that pursue us. At the end of the day, we get to the table and notice the cup has overflowed. God's banquet table shakes again, causing more to splash over as down the table someone shouts, "Goodness!" and another calls, "Mercy!"

Gracious Jesus, thank you for a dwelling place filled with beauty and redemption. We ask that we become more aware of the ways it pursues us. Amen.

Luke 1:78–79

DAY
86

"Because of God's tender mercy, the morning light from heaven is about to break upon us, to give light to those who sit in darkness and in the shadow of death, and to guide us to the path of peace." (NLT)

Peace can feel like a fantasy. Cycles of violence, systems of injustice, and ever-expanding political divisions surround us. In the face of such a world, we might lump all notions of peace in with wishes on stars—a nice idea, a childish fairytale. But scripture speaks of peace not as an ephemeral, far-off dream, but a tangible and imminent reality.

Often, we imagine peace as a veil of passivity and comfort. But this is merely a shadow of the biblical peace known as God's *shalom*. *Shalom* is creation as God intends, encompassing justice, unity, satisfaction, and joy. It is the restoration of all things, reconciling humanity to our Creator, to each other, and to our planet.

Peace does not wait for struggles to be met. God is mightier than any mayhem or unrest in this world. *Shalom* breaks through the chaos and darkness to revitalize and renew. We take part in *shalom* when we choose compassion and reconciliation—when we advocate for the silenced or oppressed.

Jesus, Prince of Peace, you've shown us what it looks like to stand in a divided and fearful world and choose unity and love. May we experience creation as it was in the beginning and will be forevermore. Amen.

DAY
87 Luke 12:24–26

"Look at the ravens. They don't plant or harvest or store food in barns, for God feeds them. And you are far more valuable to him than any birds! Can all your worries add a single moment to your life? And if worry can't accomplish a little thing like that, what's the use of worrying over bigger things?" (NLT)

Ravens are some of the smartest creatures in nature, with intelligence and mannerisms considered similar to humans. They also consume large amounts of food, hence the word "ravenous". In directing us to consider the ravens, Jesus implies two things: they are the hungriest and smartest creatures. So, why then don't they sow and reap? They don't have to worry, because God feeds them. How much more does God love to feed us, we who plant, harvest, and store!

We think that by hyperfocusing on plans, we are able to maximize time. But in actuality, we're merely causing anxiety. The mantra of things to be done repeats, and we miss the call of the ravens. Still, Jesus' words that we are incapable of adding to the time of a day, let alone our lives, hold true.

When anxiety creeps in, we can look for ravens. Their familiar caws are not hard to find. Let them be a reminder of provision and peace as they joyfully play. For God values us much more than them and will feed our every anxiety with peace.

Jesus, we thank you for reminding us that just as you provide for the birds, you provide for us too. Amen.

Matthew 23:12

DAY
88

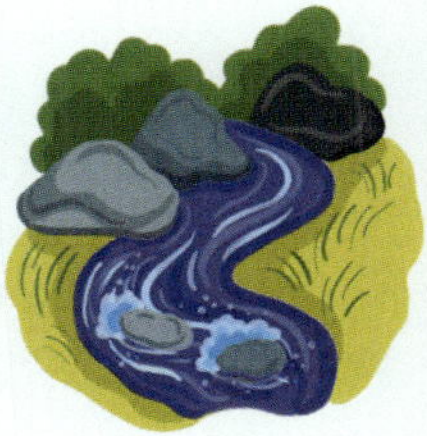

"But those who exalt themselves will be humbled, and those who humble themselves will be exalted." (NLT)

Certain people are highly visible in our faith communities. These are the people everyone knows, looks up to, and values—the people whose opinions we listen to and whose words we esteem highly.

On the flip side, other people sneak into the back of the sanctuary for church services and leave quickly afterwards, unnoticed. These are people who might cause discomfort or stand out as different. They are often ignored or otherwise devalued.

Jesus reverses our notions of who is valuable, honored, and worthy. The people we see as humble, God sees as infinitely worthy; the people we might exalt most, God wants to humble.

God invites us to see beauty and value not in stylish clothing, bubbly extroversion, powerful charisma, or an assertive leadership style, but in humility, authenticity, and simplicity. Perhaps in difference. Perhaps in serving behind the scenes. God sees the beauty of a humble heart.

God, help us see as you see. Help us see that the people among us who might be overlooked are often the wise ones we can all learn from. Teach us to see with humble eyes. Amen.

DAY 89 Acts 16:25–26

"About midnight Paul and Silas were praying and singing hymns to God, and the other prisoners were listening to them. Suddenly there was such a violent earthquake that the foundations of the prison were shaken. At once all the prison doors flew open, and everyone's chains came loose." (NIV)

Picture this: we're in a dark, damp prison cell. Our bodies are bruised and battered from the beating we've endured, our hands and feet are shackled, and there's no hope in sight. The weight of our circumstances is heavy, and fear takes control. But then the unexpected happens.

Paul and Silas found themselves in this situation. But even bruised and beaten, they worshipped. They didn't wait for things to get better. Instead, they lifted their voices in praise.

This story is an invitation for us today. When situations seem impossible, worship has the power to shake things up. More than just singing, worship is about declaring who God is. It's choosing faith when fear feels louder, and trusting that God is with us, even when everything around makes us question it. Worship can transform our situations. It may not always change our circumstances immediately, but it will change us—filling us with peace, joy, and strength to press on.

Jesus, in every trial, we can turn to you in worship. Help us to trust you more deeply and to choose worship even when it's hard. May our hearts be transformed by your presence. Amen.

Ephesians 2:10

DAY
90

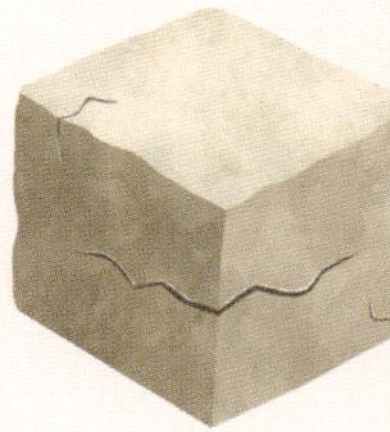

"For we are God's masterpiece. He has created us anew in Christ Jesus, so we can do the good things he planned for us long ago." (NLT)

A sculptor does not carve without vision. Every chisel stroke serves a purpose. In the same way, God is continually shaping us, refining and preparing us for the good work we are meant to do. Sometimes, that purpose is clear—a calling that stirs our hearts, a task that feels like it was made for us. Other times, we wonder if we are useful at all, uncertain where we belong. But purpose is not about striving to prove our worth. It is about trusting that God, the Master Artist, is intentionally bringing forth a beautiful plan for us, even when we cannot see the full design.

From the beginning, God has been shaping us, crafting our lives with care. This is true not only for us, but for everyone we meet. The stranger, the overlooked, the difficult—each one is shaped by the same loving hands, given a purpose we may not yet see. When we begin to view others as God's handiwork, we learn to love with kindness and curiosity, knowing God's divine artistry is at work in every life, including ours.

God, help us trust that we are created with purpose, and to see others with that same love that formed us. Amen.

DAY

91 Zechariah 7:9

"This is what the Lord of Heaven's Armies says: Judge fairly, and show mercy and kindness to one another." (NLT)

God's ways are ways of kindness. God's paths are paths of mercy. God's road is the road of truth and justice. Created as we are in God's image, we are designed to show kindness and mercy to one another, to live authentically and seek justice.

These are not small tasks. We may be tempted to try to get ahead through unkindness, insensitivity, dishonesty, and greed. After all, it seems that this is what many around us have done. But God invites us on a different path. Perhaps not a lucrative one by the world's standards, but one where our needs will be met and our deepest desires satisfied.

When we practice kindness and treat others as fellow image-bearers, we find our lives rich in friendship, purpose, belonging, and joy. We become healthy participants in interconnected communities, receiving kindness from those around us just as we have given it freely.

God, give us the courage to choose kindness in a world that frequently undervalues it. Draw us into communities marked by mercy toward all people, and especially toward the most vulnerable among us. Amen.

Psalm 143:1, 3

DAY 92

"Hear my prayer, O Lord; listen to my plea! Answer me because you are faithful and righteous ... My enemy has chased me. He has knocked me to the ground and forces me to live in darkness like those in the grave." (NLT)

Everyone gets wounded in some way; it comes with living in a rough world, ready to reopen our cuts the moment they begin to close. Incurring pain and persecution is exhausting; it drains us of energy, bringing us too close to our breaking points.

As the Psalms demonstrate, desperate times lead us to offer loud prayers for deliverance. In Psalm 143, we observe a bold demand for the Lord to listen and respond to the petitions of God's people, as is befitting of God's upright character.

The Bible constantly depicts a God who rescues us time and time again from even the deepest pits of despair. Glorious yet gentle, the Almighty acts as a Father who picks up his child after they have fallen, brushing the dust off their shoulders, and encouraging them to try again.

Scripture shows that God has been listening to us this entire time, and is ready to respond to our requests. When we are in the thick of suffering, let us come with boldness to the throne of Jesus to receive the gentle healing we need.

Lord, you are our mighty fortress and deliverer! Thank you for your willingness to heal us. Amen.

DAY
93 Psalm 121:1–2

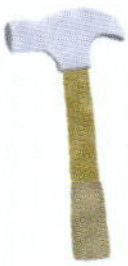

"I look up to the mountains—does my help come from there? My help comes from the Lord, who made heaven and earth!" (NLT)

Frantic and frenetic, the relentless pace of society seeps into our very thoughts and creates an expectation of instant responses. Messages swirl all around us, asserting that life is fleeting and we need to hustle. As our minds race, serenity and contentment seem out of reach. But we were not made to burn the candle at both ends. Let us instead pause and abide in the comfort of the Holy Spirit.

Stillness is a vital spiritual practice. Even so, slowing down can feel anathema. We fear falling behind or missing out. But scripture reminds us that barrelling ahead causes us to miss the beauty and wonder right in front of us. In the quiet of the night, God speaks to Samuel. Off the beaten path, Moses encounters the burning bush. Alone on a rooftop, Peter receives God's vision of inclusion and restoration. Each of these moments comes amid stillness.

Jesus, the world assures us that if we just keep moving, something good will be across the ever-furthering finish line. But, in you, goodness is available here and now. May we enter into your comfort and peace today and every day. Amen.

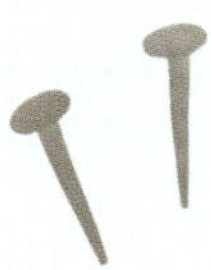

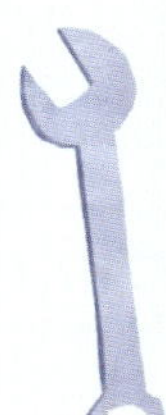

Colossians 3:9–10

DAY
94

"Don't lie to each other, for you have stripped off your old sinful nature and all its wicked deeds. Put on your new nature, and be renewed as you learn to know your Creator and become like him." (NLT)

Sometimes honesty feels scary. Will our truth be met with compassion? Will we be heard and understood? We do not know, but God invites us to try anyway.

We might suffer loss for speaking truths that weigh on our souls—loss of success, opportunity, or the familiarity of the status quo. Our relationships may change. Some may not be able to bear the weight of our honesty. And yet, speaking truly is how we strengthen and deepen relationships. When we meet honesty with empathy, our communities thrive. We open the door for our collective needs to be met.

As God renews and transforms us, we find that old habits of twisting the truth, whether to protect ourselves, to get ahead of others, no longer feel necessary or wise. Assured of our fundamental belovedness, we understand that kindness and honesty are not at odds. We learn to be our truest selves and invite others to do the same.

Jesus King, give us courage to speak and live our truth—gently but unapologetically. Help us build communities marked by the deep trust that stems from honesty. Amen.

DAY

95 1 Kings 19:11–12

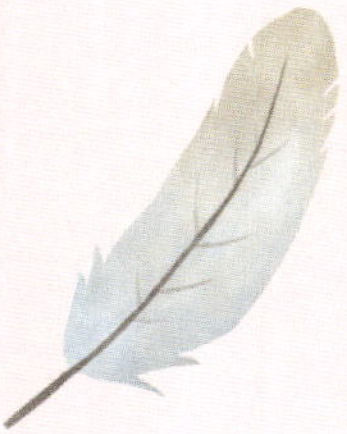

"And as Elijah stood there, the Lord passed by, and a mighty windstorm hit the mountain ... but the Lord was not in the wind. After the wind there was an earthquake, but the Lord was not in the earthquake. And after the earthquake there was a fire, but the Lord was not in the fire. And after the fire there was the sound of a gentle whisper." (NLT)

Throughout our lives, we are struck with the chaos of wind, earthquakes, and fire. The mountain that is our life rumbles and rocks fall loose. Like Elijah, we tend to look for God in the big, forceful moments. But, more often, we will see God appear in gentle, quiet ways, like a whisper.

When life feels chaotic and loud, how does God call us to respond? When we, like Elijah, feel tired and alone, we can still expect great things to happen. But we also must be patient and listen for the whispers of God.

God often enters with encouragement and hope after the chaos. Our job is to wait and follow what God asks of us both before and after. The storms may still be part of our story, but God's words are gentle and tell a greater narrative.

Gentle God, help us to stand before the winds, earthquakes and fires and still recognize your voice in the gentle whisper. Amen.

Philippians 4:8

DAY 96

“Finally, brothers and sisters, whatever is true, whatever is noble, whatever is right, whatever is pure, whatever is lovely, whatever is admirable—if anything is excellent or praiseworthy—think about such things.” (NIV)

What do we think about when we’re alone with our thoughts? Our ideas and musings have the power to induce fear or peace. Whether in the static or the dynamic moments of our lives, the thoughts that we entertain can shape who we become.

When we set our thoughts on what is true, we begin to mirror the character of Christ. Our aspirations shift from temporary desires to the eternal values found in scripture. Instead of chasing fleeting dreams or measuring ourselves by worldly standards, scripture invites us to aspire to be more like Jesus—loving, pure, and full of grace.

This focus doesn’t just change how we think; it transforms our lives. It gives us clarity in our decisions, peace in our struggles, and joy in the everyday. By fixing our minds on what is true, noble, right, and pure, we can move forward with confidence, knowing that our thoughts are aligned with God’s best for us.

Lord, help us to focus on what is true and pure. Make us more like you as you guide our thoughts to reflect your character and lead us to aspire to the good things that come from you. Amen.

DAY

97 Nahum 1:7

"The Lord is good, a refuge in times of trouble. He cares for those who trust in Him." (NIV)

A storm is a powerful natural event, formed when warm, moist air rises into cooler air, creating low pressure. This causes wind to rush in, forming powerful gusts, and resulting in rain, snow, or even lightning. It's a force that can shake the earth, uproot trees, and leave destruction in its wake. Similarly, life's storms—unexpected crises, moments of fear, or seasons of uncertainty—can feel overwhelming and chaotic. The winds of worry, the rains of doubt, and the lightning of stress can feel all-consuming.

God offers peace even as chaos rages. Nahum 1:7 reminds us that God is a refuge, a place of safety and rest. Even when life feels uncontrollable, God's presence is a steady anchor. Divine peace doesn't always remove the storm, but it provides shelter within it. No matter what chaos surrounds us, God's goodness and care are unwavering.

Lord Jesus, thank you for being our refuge. Help us find peace in your presence, even in the storms of life. Amen.

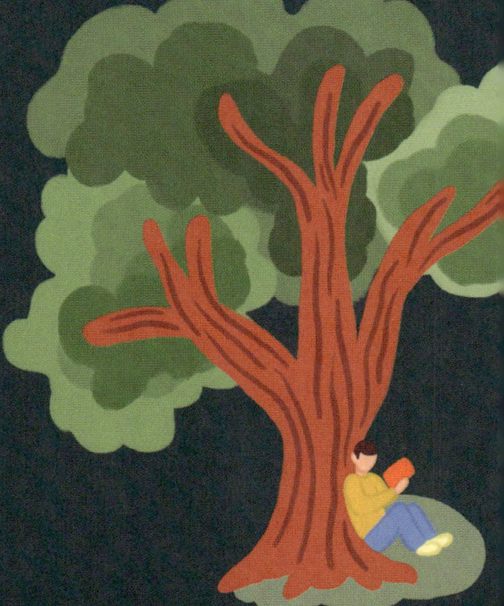

Esther 4:13-14

DAY
98

"Mordecai sent this reply to Esther ... 'Who knows if perhaps you were made queen for just such a time as this?'" (NLT)

Everyone dreams of a meaningful life. Our lifetime is a gift, and we want to use it well. If we're honest, we may not feel that our day-to-day lives are all that remarkable. We tread the waters of average responsibilities with little time available to take on the extraordinary. Or, perhaps, there is no shortage of problems to be solved, but we feel ill-equipped to tackle them.

In these moments, the doldrum and the daunting, what does it look like to live with purpose?

Our lives are filled with opportunities to live into our faith—to treat others with compassion, to stand up for justice and mercy. These may not be opportunities we planned for, but they are placed before us all the same. As simple as a conversation, as bold as taking a stand, our actions serve as an intersection of the heavenly with the ordinary.

Esther didn't set out to be a savior for her people. The circumstances confronting her seemed too perilous to face. And yet, Esther and Mordecai recognized God that was at work. God equips us for divine purposes.

Righteous God, help us to embrace opportunities to reflect your character to the world. In doing so, we are living well. Amen.

DAY 99 Matthew 6:31–33

"So do not worry, saying, 'What shall we eat?' or 'What shall we drink?' or 'What shall we wear?' But seek first His kingdom and His righteousness, and all these things will be given to you as well." (NIV)

Worry whispers to us urgently: "Will there be enough? What if this doesn't work out? How will I make it through?"

Jesus meets our anxious questions with a gentle and tender answer: "Seek me first." This soothing invitation is not an assertion that our needs don't matter. On the contrary, it is a reminder that we were never meant to carry our worries alone.

Turning worry into worship isn't about pretending our fears aren't there. It's about placing them in the hands of the One who already sees, already knows, and already cares. Worship shifts our focus. It reminds our hearts that God is not distant from our need, but present in it, working, providing, and guiding.

When the weight of "what if" starts to rise, let us pause. May we take a deep breath, lifting our eyes heavenward. Let our worries become a place of communion, not control. As we seek Jesus first, he will meet us with peace, with provision, and with himself.

Father, you see every need before we even speak it. Help us seek you above all else. Turn our worry into worship, and teach us to rest in your faithful care. Amen.

Ephesians 6:13–17

DAY
100

"Therefore put on the full armor of God ... with the belt of truth buckled around your waist, with the breastplate of righteousness in place, and with your feet fitted with the readiness that comes from the gospel of peace. In addition to all this, take up the shield of faith. ... Take the helmet of salvation and the sword of the Spirit, which is the word of God." (NIV)

We have an innate desire to guard and protect ourselves from harm, disappointment, and the ache of living in a broken world. In this, God offers us armor. Not of iron, but of spirit. Not to harden us, but to hold us.

Truth wraps around the core of who we are, reminding us that what's real is not always what's loud. Righteousness covers the heart, not shielding us from feeling, but keeping us rightly aligned. Peace is not only carried; it carries us, making trembling steps purposeful. The shield of faith teaches us where to turn when we are hit. Salvation steadies the mind with identity and belonging. The Word cuts gently through confusion, not to destroy, but to illuminate.

This armor isn't fastened in haste. It moves to the rhythm of grace, shaping who we are as we learn to trust what Jesus provides. To put on the armor of God is to become anchored, held together, not by might, but by mercy.

Heavenly Father, thank you for your divine protection and care. Help us put on full spiritual armor as we move forward in your love. Amen.

DAY 101 Exodus 20:9–10

"You have six days each week for your ordinary work, but the seventh day is a Sabbath day of rest dedicated to the Lord your God." (NLT)

It can be difficult to find time to rest. We are bombarded with constant stimulation and endless to-do lists; it seems there's no time for breaks. But rest is not only important for our physical health; it is also vital for our spiritual well-being.

Throughout the Bible, rest is characterized as God's gift to humanity. Prioritizing rest is so important to our Creator that it is one of the 10 major commandments for living as God intends. Rest enables us to slow down and reorient ourselves to the Spirit.

Jesus also prioritized rest. The Gospel of Mark recounts a time in Jesus' ministry when he and the disciples were so busy that it seemed they didn't even have time to eat. But Jesus told his disciples to come away with him to a quiet place and rest awhile (Mark 6:31). He knew that they needed time to recharge and refocus, and that rest was essential for their work and ministry.

We can rest in God's shadow, shielded from the scorching heat of life's trials. In the protective embrace of the Most High, we can find sanctuary and comfort. Amen.

Matthew 11:4–5

DAY 102

"Jesus replied, 'Go back and report to John what you hear and see: The blind receive sight, the lame walk, those who have leprosy are cleansed, the deaf hear, the dead are raised, and the good news is proclaimed to the poor.'" (NIV)

Reading through the Gospels, there is a quiet wonder in the way Jesus moves. He does not arrive with spectacle, but with compassion. There is no shouting to prove his power, but whispers through healing, through restoration, through presence. Jesus' miracles serve as signs of the Kingdom, breaking into the dust and ache of human life.

When people come with questions, Jesus does not give a defense. He gives evidence. Not of control, but of care. The blind see. The lame walk. The forgotten are remembered. The Good News is not reserved for the powerful, but offered freely to the poor in spirit.

These wonders still unfold today. In hearts awakened, in lives restored, in grief met with comfort, in emptiness filled with hope. The miraculous invites us to see with new eyes: Jesus is still at work, quietly turning what is broken into beauty, and calling us to look, listen, and trust again.

Jesus, help us to see the quiet wonders you are working all around us. Open our eyes, steady our hearts, and teach us to trust that even in silence, you are still healing, still moving, still making all things new. Amen.

DAY 103 Psalm 51:10

"Create in me a clean heart, O God. Renew a loyal spirit within me." (NLT)

A brief survey of the stories we tell and retell illustrates that we love a redemption arc. Countless movies, books, and TV shows take characters who are bad—broken, grievously flawed—and offer them a second chance. An opportunity not only to make amends but to rejoin the fold.

Looking at our own lives, it is easy to understand why these narrative beats appeal to us. Conscious of our shortcomings and mistakes, there is comfort in watching larger-than-life antagonists turn things around. Perhaps, if it's not too late for them, it's not too late for us.

Jesus assures us that this is not speculative fiction—an imagining of how things might be in some alternate world. Redemption, forgiveness, and restoration are real and available to all. Christ is relentless in his love for us, constantly working for our good and the good of the world.

We can rest easy in the knowledge that our Creator is always there to offer us a hand when we stumble. It is never too late.

We are never too far gone—through your grace and mercy, God, we are made new. Amen.

Psalm 119:35–37

DAY
104

"Lead me in the path of your commandments, for I delight in it. Incline my heart to your testimonies, and not to selfish gain! Turn my eyes from looking at worthless things; and give me life in your ways." (ESV)

Distraction is often quiet in its approach—subtle, persistent, familiar. It pulls gently, turning our attention from the sacred to the fleeting. We become consumed by schedules, drawn to comparisons, persuaded by comforts that promise rest but never satisfy. Our gaze shifts from the eternal to the immediate, and slowly, we forget what truly gives us life.

Here in Psalm 119, the psalmist writes, "Lead me ... Incline my heart ... Turn my eyes." These are not the words of one demanding control, but of one surrendering it. They speak to a longing all of us have to be realigned. To return to a way of living rooted not in ambition or noise, but in the quiet delight of Jesus.

To let go of distraction is not merely about subtracting noise, but about restoring focus. It is a return. A movement back to what is worthy, lasting, and alive. The Word becomes not a task but a path. Not a demand, but a guide.

Lord, turn our eyes from what is hollow and realign our hearts with what is holy. Draw us near to your way, where true life begins. Amen.

DAY 105 Romans 2:1

"You may think you can condemn such people, but you are just as bad, and you have no excuse! When you say they are wicked and should be punished, you are condemning yourself, for you who judge others do these very same things." (NLT)

There's an old expression, "When you point your finger at someone, three fingers are pointing back at you." Romans 2:1 offers a parallel idea: when we condemn someone, we are also condemning ourselves. Jesus, too, echoes this sentiment—"Let the one who has never sinned throw the first stone."

Humans are famously fallible. We make mistakes, and we do wrong from time to time, whether we realize it in the moment or not. We don't have the context for everyone's lives and can't fully understand why people make the decisions they do. Because of this, scripture and wisdom both tell us that we should resist judging others as much as possible. In fact, we are told it is God's role alone to judge.

The antidote for judgment is an open curiosity—a posture of asking questions, learning, and validating others' experiences. When we intentionally practice this kind of openness, we recognize our shared humanity and create opportunities for growth and healing. Everyone is beloved by God. And everyone is in need of God's grace, including us.

God, teach us not to judge. Help us to recognize the humanity in all of us, and support us in our attempts to grow with one another. Amen.

Matthew 6:1, 3–4

DAY
106

"Watch out! Don't do your good deeds publicly, to be admired by others, for you will lose the reward from your Father in heaven ... But when you give to someone in need, don't let your left hand know what your right hand is doing. Give your gifts in private, and your Father, who sees everything, will reward you." (NLT)

In the world of social media, we curate the image we put out into the world more than ever before. We can share pictures of ourselves doing good deeds, or even pretend to be doing something that we're not. We strive to make sure we "look good." In Jesus' day, religious leaders and zealots would also call attention to themselves with grandiose displays of religiosity, loudly proclaiming their virtue to curry favor with the public. While the methods of seeking attention have changed, the impulse to be applauded for our goodness remains the same.

And yet, Jesus warns us that seeking attention for our virtues often negates the good we are doing in God's eyes. Good deeds are meant to be done for the sake of goodness, not for vanity. Time and again, Jesus shows kindness and generosity in private, retreating from the fervent attention of the crowd instead of seeking more and more applause. Jesus calls us to a path of kindness and generosity for its own sake, not accolades.

Jesus, thank you for leading by example and showing us how to do good in a way that honors God. Show us how we can help those in need around us without seeking validation from others. Amen.

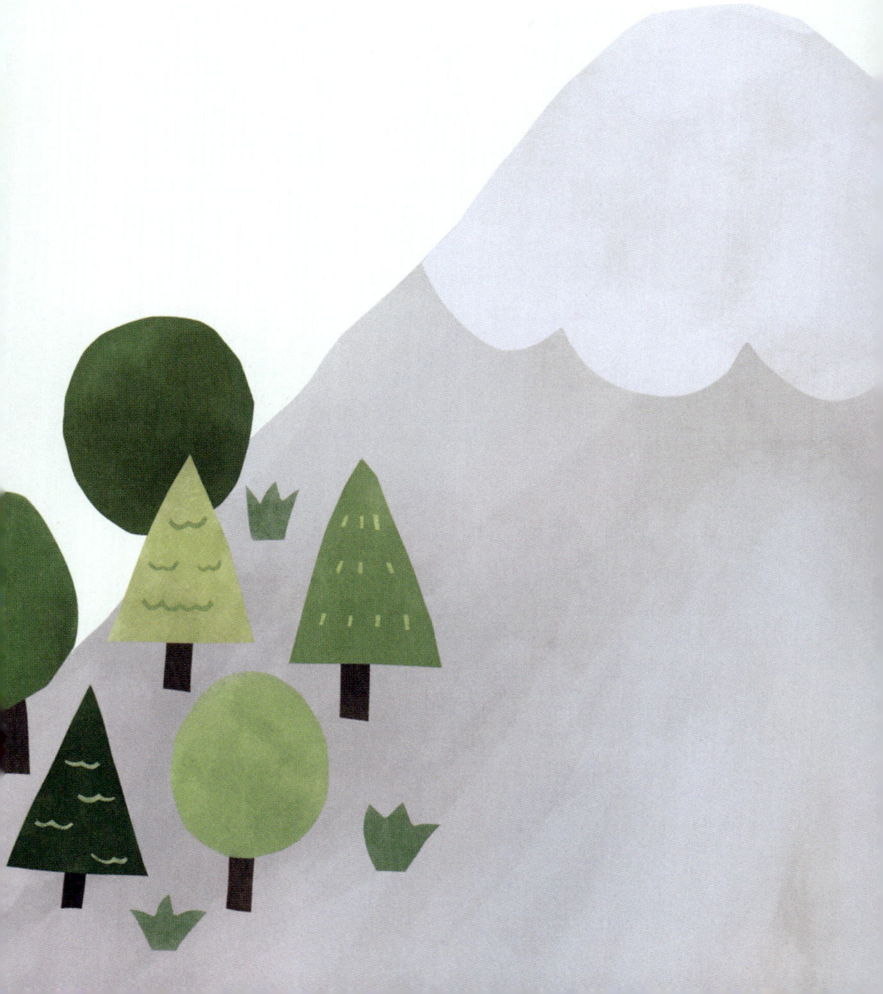

Philippians 4:13

DAY 107

"For I can do everything through Christ,
who gives me strength." (NLT)

In the quiet corners of our lives, there lies a profound and enduring source of strength—God. The Almighty is the source of hope and comfort in times of distress. In the pages of scripture, we find timeless wisdom and guidance on how to tap into this wellspring of fortitude, courage, and resilience.

Sometimes, this strength can feel hard to access. Like an athlete training to take on the next challenge, we recognize our moments of progress, and yet we feel the exhaustion born of wondering just how far we have left to go. When we reach the limits of our own strength, we can lean into Jesus. God is constantly bolstering and refining us. When life's storms rage around us, we can take refuge in God. Just as a sturdy rock provides stability amidst turbulent waters, God offers unwavering support.

We are not running away from the obstacles and difficulties of this life, but instead, we are running toward Jesus. In the serene and sacred space of reflection, we discover that finding strength from God is not a one-time endeavor but a continuous journey.

Mighty God, may we find strength in you that empowers, sustains, and uplifts. Amen.

DAY 108 Romans 8:16–17

“For his Spirit joins with our spirit to affirm that we are God’s children. And since we are his children, we are his heirs. In fact, together with Christ we are heirs of God’s glory.” (NLT)

Our days are a constant stream of ups and downs—confidence and determination ebb and flow as we go along a lifelong journey of self-discovery. Trying to define who we are can be a challenge, faced with so many competing versions of who we might be. But, when we know nothing else, this most essential aspect of our identity always remains: we are God’s beloved children.

This assurance rings out, resonating through the corridors of time, offering solace to weary hearts and hope to wandering souls. God’s love enfolds us, reminding us that we are never alone, that Jesus is our constant companion. In the face of adversity and doubt, this truth stands as an immutable beacon, guiding us through the darkest of nights and the fiercest of storms.

Our relationship with Jesus is at the core of who we are. We are heirs to a kingdom where love reigns supreme and hope knows no bounds. It is a heritage rich in promise, a legacy of faith passed down through the ages, from generation to generation.

Let us take comfort in the knowledge that we are cherished beyond measure, beloved children of a benevolent Savior who opens his arms in welcome. Amen.

DAY
Ephesians 2:8–9 109

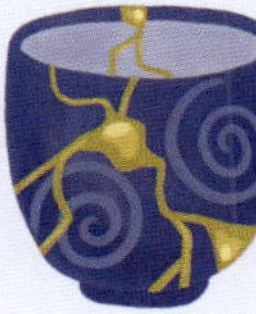

"God saved you by his grace when you believed. And you can't take credit for this; it is a gift from God. Salvation is not a reward for the good things we have done, so none of us can boast about it." (NLT)

Perfectionism is a powerful snare that binds us to the belief that our worth is contingent upon flawless execution and that any deviation is a mark of failure. It is a constant striving that breeds anxiety, fear, and a profound sense of inadequacy. It turns our inner voice into a harsh judge, not only of ourselves but of anyone who cannot live up to our rigid expectations.

Thankfully, Jesus provides a liberating alternative, grace. Grace offers acceptance and belonging, not through our efforts, but as a gift of unconditional love. God's grace recognizes that growth happens through forgiveness and learning from mistakes, not through the illusion of perfection. It fosters a spirit of compassion over judgment, understanding that we are all on a journey of becoming who we shall yet be in Christ.

This gift makes us whole. It frees us from comparison and competition, allowing us to embrace the process and find joy in the journey. We are loved and accepted not for what we do perfectly, but for who we are, imperfections and all.

Thank you, God, for the gift of your grace that welcomes us just as we are and enables us to become all we were created to be. Amen.

DAY 110 Deuteronomy 31:8

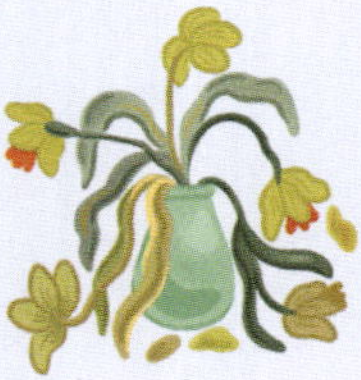

"It is the Lord who goes before you. He will be with you; he will not leave you or forsake you. Do not fear or be dismayed." (ESV)

Loss is one of the hardest experiences we face in life. Whether it's the end of a season, the death of a loved one, or the erosion of something dear, it often leaves us feeling uncertain, vulnerable, and overwhelmed. In our dismay, we may find ourselves asking, "Where is God in all of this?"

Deuteronomy 31:8 offers words of assurance to the people of Israel as they prepare to face an uncertain future. God doesn't abandon us when we walk through the hardest parts of life. God is with us, leading us through the pain, and will never leave or forsake us.

This is more than just a comforting thought. It's a call to trust in God's faithfulness, even when we can't see the way forward. As we reckon with loss, we remember that God is not distant in our grief, but walks with us through it. Jesus' presence is the source of our hope and peace, even when everything feels uncertain.

Lord, in our moments of loss, remind us of your constant presence. Help us trust that you go before us, guiding us through the pain, and that you will never leave us or forsake us. Amen.

2 Corinthians 9:8

DAY
111

"And God will generously provide all you need. Then you will always have everything you need and plenty left over to share with others." (NLT)

We all know the tension of scarcity, of feeling as though what we have will never be enough. Whether it's time, energy, resources, or strength, our instinct is to gather and protect what little we believe we have. And yet, in 2 Corinthians 9:8, Paul reassures believers that God's provision is abundant and sufficient for every need.

God promises to generously provide, so much so that we may also have plenty left over to share with others. This goes beyond material abundance; it's a spiritual and emotional sufficiency empowering us to bless those around us. God's provision is always more than enough. Divine grace overflows so that we can be instruments of generosity in a world that often feels lacking.

To trust in God's provision is to live with an open hand, resting in the certainty that Jesus will fill our hearts and lives with more than we need, so that we can give it away in love.

Lord, thank you for your abundant provision. You will always meet our needs. Empower us to share generously with others. Amen.

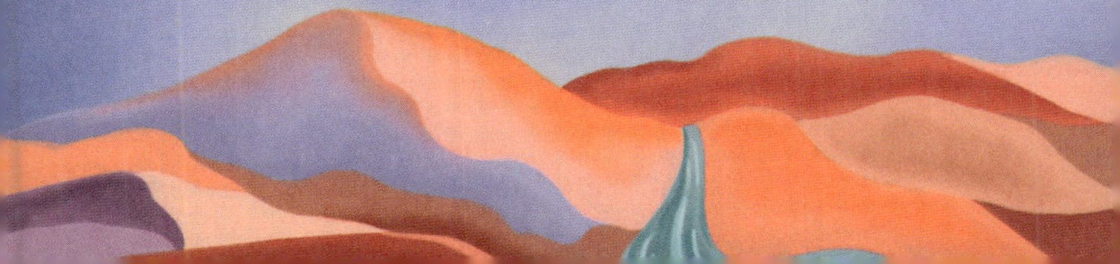

DAY

112 Hebrews 10:24–25

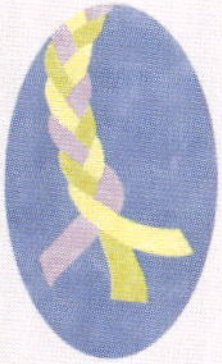

"Let us think of ways to motivate one another to acts of love and good works. And let us not neglect our meeting together, as some people do, but encourage one another, especially now that the day of his return is drawing near." (NLT)

When a loved one visits, the whole house is cleaned top to bottom, the pantry and fridge are stocked, and activities are planned. Hopefully, each member of the household will take on a role in preparing for the special someone on the way.

Our faith communities should function similarly. Jesus is the guest returning home after a long trip. We anticipate his return and work our hardest to prepare. While Jesus knows the perfect timing of his return, we often forget.

The preparation can take different forms. But when each person finds their role, we build a community that works towards the benefit of all. We remind each other of the reason for our loving actions, and our motivation is rekindled.

We continually meet together, planning good works in the name of Jesus according to each member's skills. Jesus didn't tell his disciples to wait for his return. He told them to actively pursue love in preparation. Generations later, we find ourselves doing the same—working together in acts of love and goodness.

Let us not neglect the work you have called us to do together, Jesus, as we patiently wait for you. Amen.

Psalm 127:2

DAY

113

"It is in vain that rise up early and go late to rest, eating the bread of anxious toil; for he gives to his beloved sleep." (ESV)

Sometimes we wonder what all the hard work we do is for. The psalmist writing Psalm 127 wrestled with this same question, characterizing it through vivid imagery: *eating the bread of anxious toil*. When we feel consumed by restless striving, and endless hustle is all we see ahead, we may feel that we are eating this bread.

God desires for us to pursue work that feels meaningful. *And* God invites us to rest. We are not holier when we work harder and sleep less. Rest is a precious gift from God—meant to be cherished, enjoyed, and taken seriously. Without adequate sleep, our bodies and minds do not function optimally. We are less present in our work, our relationships, and our own souls. We experience less joy and are more prone to anxiety.

We can't always control the amount of work we must do. Nonetheless, we can choose to create moments of rest; times of stillness; space to think, ponder, feel, and daydream. Jesus meets us as we do.

God, make room in our busy lives for rest. Help us know how much rest we need, and help us not to settle for less. Remind us of your dreams for us, your beloved ones. Amen.

DAY 114 1 Corinthians 12:18–20

"But our bodies have many parts, and God has put each part just where he wants it. How strange a body would be if it had only one part! Yes, there are many parts, but only one body." (NLT)

Our differences from one another serve a purpose. The gifts placed within us—our perspectives, talents, even our quirks—are not mistakes. They are intentional brushstrokes in the masterpiece God is painting.

Think of a tapestry, woven with threads of many colors and textures into an intricate design. Some threads are bold, rich in color; others are subtle, gently contributing to the overall pattern. Some are soft, some are coarse, yet every texture adds depth to the whole. At times, we may wish to be like everyone else, but if all threads were alike, the design's beauty would be diminished.

Likewise, God has crafted each of us uniquely, and our differences are the very elements that, when woven together, create something far more beautiful than we could ever imagine alone. God does not merely tolerate our differences, but delights in them. Every distinct thread, every individual life, brings joy to the Artist who carefully chose each color and texture. By embracing and celebrating the uniqueness in ourselves and others, we honor the One who lovingly designed us exactly as we are.

Jesus, help us to embrace the way you have made us and to honor the beauty of your design in others. Amen.

Proverbs 31:8–9

DAY
115

"Speak up for those who cannot speak for themselves, for the rights of all who are destitute. Speak up and judge fairly; defend the rights of the poor and needy." (NIV)

This exhortation to speak up, judge fairly, and defend the rights of the poor can sound both inspiring and intimidating. After all, when we "speak up," how will we know what to say? When attempting to "judge fairly," how can we be sure our judgment is sound? And to "defend the rights of the poor and needy"—in what way? What does such a defense look like?

The life and ministry of Jesus provide us with many examples to emulate. Jesus rebuked exploiters, showed compassion to outcasts, challenged evil in powerful institutions, and shared what little he had. He cared deeply for the vulnerable, at great cost to himself.

When we prioritize our relationship with Jesus—when we spend time in prayer, meditation, and scripture regularly—these instructions to speak, judge, and defend become easier. We begin to see with Christ's eyes. We begin to act more as he would. And with practice, it gets easier, closer to feeling like second nature.

Dear Jesus, embolden us to defend and help those in need, just as you modeled for us. Amen.

DAY
116 Psalm 103:8, 10–12

"The Lord is compassionate and merciful, slow to get angry and filled with unfailing love. ... He does not punish us for all our sins; he does not deal harshly with us, as we deserve. For his unfailing love toward those who fear him is as great as the height of the heavens above the earth. He has removed our sins as far from us as the east is from the west." (NLT)

What does it mean to be worthy? To be deserving? The world wants us to prove our worth; it says, "You get what you deserve." How different the anthem of God sounds. The beauty of the Gospel is that we can do nothing to earn our way to Heaven. Self-sufficiency is not the agent of worthiness, because our worth is built on nothing other than the gift of audacious grace.

God's love is not contingent but self-existent, not limited but endless. No amount of striving can secure it, but rather, everyone is invited to fully receive and rest in it. The Lord's gentle character is full of mercy and grace to pardon us for our sins without severe treatment. This treatment was paid in full by Jesus, who lovingly took our place.

The forgiveness we receive extends as far as extreme opposites marked on the compass, meaning endlessly. Instead of being restless about our shortcomings, we can come straight to Jesus and rest in his extensive love.

God, you are the Worthy One who makes us worthy. Help us to rest freely in your love. Amen.

James 2:17–18

DAY
117

“So you see, faith by itself isn’t enough. Unless it produces good deeds, it is dead and useless. Now someone may argue, ‘Some people have faith; others have good deeds.’ But I say, ‘How can you show me your faith if you don’t have good deeds? I will show you my faith by my good deeds.’” (NLT)

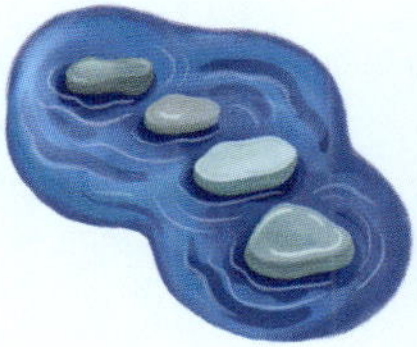

Sometimes we use the word “faith” interchangeably with “belief.” But in the Bible, faith refers less to knowledge in our heads and more to trust in the person and teachings of Jesus—trust that is evidenced by our willingness to put these teachings into practice.

James 2 tells us that acts of mercy and goodness flow naturally from a living and vibrant faith. Living faithfully looks like supplying the basic needs of people who lack essential clothing or food. It looks like showing compassion to neighbors near or far, whether or not they share our religion, culture, or ethnicity.

We may believe all the right things, but if we do not act out of empathy for our neighbors, our faith is as good as dead. We step out in faith through choosing actions of kindness and justice. And as we move in ways that honor the equality and dignity of all people as bearers of God’s image, our faith comes alive.

God, help us embody your compassionate love in our communities. Breathe life into the beliefs we hold in our hearts. Amen.

DAY 118 Romans 8:38–39

"And I am convinced that nothing can ever separate us from God's love. Neither death nor life, neither angels nor demons, neither our fears for today nor our worries about tomorrow—not even the powers of hell can separate us from God's love. ... indeed, nothing in all creation will ever be able to separate us from the love of God that is revealed in Christ Jesus our Lord." (NLT)

How might our lives and communities change if we believed in the depths of our souls that nothing could separate us from God's love? Not anything that's happening in our world. Not our doubts, anxieties, fears, mistakes, weaknesses, or regrets. Not our suffering. Not even death itself. Truly, nothing.

If we wonder whether something has separated us—if we think we've done something too bad, or wandered too far, or have experienced too much pain—we can rest assured that God's love is still there. God is near us.

This knowledge empowers us to love God, other people, and ourselves boldly. It encourages us to listen for Jesus' leading in our lives, into deeper love and fuller authenticity. It helps us get unstuck from living mired in regret, so that we can make any amends we need to make and move forward in a way that blesses our communities. God's love is right here among us.

God, thank you for your love that is truly and fully unconditional. Help us turn around and show the same kind of love to our fellow humans and our whole wounded world. Amen.

John 4:9–10

DAY **119**

"The woman was surprised, for Jews refuse to have anything to do with Samaritans. She said to Jesus, 'You are a Jew, and I am a Samaritan woman. Why are you asking me for a drink?' Jesus replied, 'If you only knew the gift God has for you and who you are speaking to, you would ask me, and I would give you living water.'" (NLT)

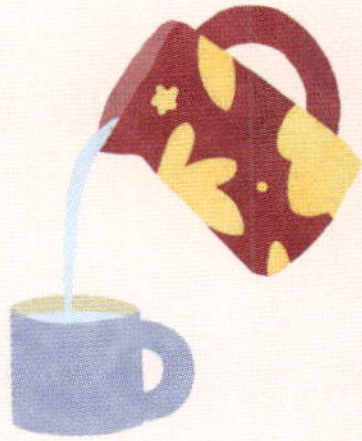

We plan our days and neatly fill our schedules, but life throws us curveballs. Like the Samaritan woman at the well, we'll be minding our business when Jesus interrupts our daily routine and asks us to engage with him. Like her, we may question such an intrusion, but if we choose to be receptive, we can experience the gift of blessing and growth from Christ.

As our carefully planned days are punctuated by the unexpected, interruptions can feel like hindrances, obstacles to overcome. But what if these detours are actually opportunities amid our ordinary routines—divine invitations offering a deeper connection, a spiritual refreshment we didn't even know we craved? Invitations to see beyond our own agendas and recognize the divine at work.

Perhaps the person who disrupts our schedule is the very one through whom God intends to bless us—to share a word of encouragement, to extend kindness, to offer us the living water, the true fulfillment only God can provide.

Lord, help us to see the interruptions in our day as divine invitations to encounter you and be blessed by others. Amen.

DAY 120 Romans 8:6

"So letting your sinful nature control your mind leads to death. But letting the Spirit control your mind leads to life and peace." (NLT)

At all hours of the day, we face a barrage of voices clamoring for our attention. We volley back and forth between doom-scrolling and distraction, trying to avoid the feeling that darkness is closing in around us.

Challenges often seem permanent. It seems assured they will have the final say, that there is no curing or eradicating them. The best we can hope for, we believe, is pain management.

The Bible tells us differently. We have been given the Holy Spirit as our advocate, a source of transformation, freedom, and strength amidst the world around us. To be filled with the Spirit is not to temporarily dull our anxieties, but to fundamentally reshape our outlook and approach.

Inundated as we are, gloom can feel all-consuming. But the peace of God, the guidance of the Holy Spirit, is everlasting and restorative. Our Creator was here long before the troubles of this world and will remain long after them. When we put our faith in the Spirit, we make room for the beautiful work God intends for the world.

Lord Jesus, let us not give in to despair. Your Spirit is our guiding light, working for our ultimate good. Amen.

DAY 121

Amos 9:14

“I will bring my exiled people of Israel back from distant lands, and they will rebuild their ruined cities and live in them again. They will plant vineyards and gardens; they will eat their crops and drink their wine.” (NLT)

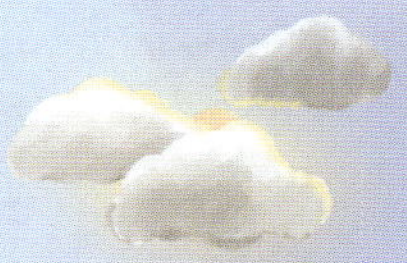

When the Israelites were exiled from their homeland, the situation felt hopeless. Their homes were destroyed, they had no political or social power, and they were scattered. However, on the edges of society, the prophets began telling a story of hope and future restoration.

God promised the Israelites they would return to their homeland, rebuild their old cities, and live abundantly. On this side of history, we know that this restoration came about 50 years after their exile. What in our lives seems so irreparably broken that we feel it could never be restored?

At times, we may feel hopeless. In moments like these, we can look back at the history of the people of God and find a thread of hope again. Even the most hopeless of situations can be turned around, and restoration is possible for God even when it feels impossible to us. Though we may be experiencing darkness, there is light ahead of us, and the only way out is through.

Christ Jesus, thank you for the way you’ve always taken care of your people. Show us how to have hope in times that feel hopeless, and remind us of your miraculous work of restoration. Amen.

DAY

122 1 Corinthians 15:58

"So, my dear brothers and sisters, be strong and immovable. Always work enthusiastically for the Lord, for you know that nothing you do for the Lord is ever useless." (NLT)

When we think about our lives, what is our driving purpose? How do we decide what to spend time on and what work is ours to do? Amidst all our goals and aspirations, followers of God are ultimately called to partner in God's divine work in the world.

The work of God in the world is multifaceted. It includes caring for the needy and outcasts, stewarding the environment, teaching people about Jesus, and so much more. We can look to the Bible for clues to understand God's heart for the world and the ways we fit into God's work. We can pray and meditate, listening to the Spirit for a unique call in our lives. However we choose to do it, finding our part in the divine work is a long-term project. Paul, in his first letter to the Corinthians, reminds us that every step in that process has value and that nothing we do for the Lord will ever be useless.

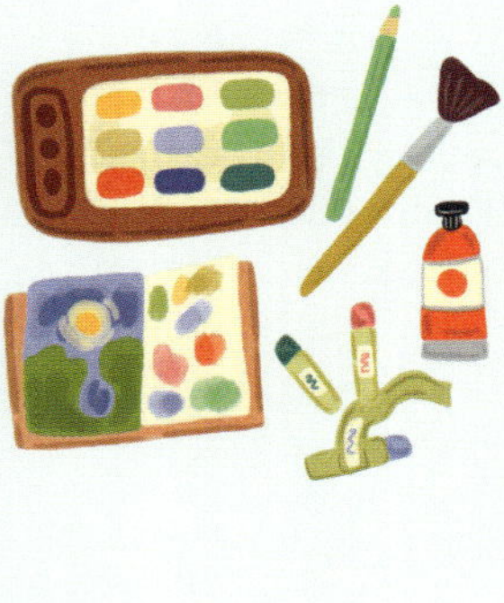

God, show us what is ours to do in the world and how we can partner with you in doing divine work. Amen.

Ecclesiastes 4:9–10, 12 DAY 123

"Two people are better off than one, for they can help each other succeed. If one person falls, the other can reach out and help. But someone who falls alone is in real trouble ... A person standing alone can be attacked and defeated, but two can stand back-to-back and conquer..." (NLT)

When we face trials, we all want someone by our side. We crave a listening ear and an advocating voice. When we fall from weight or wounds, a friend who lifts our eyes towards the beauty of God is a balm. And joy is multiplied when we invite others to celebrate our victories and answered prayers.

King Solomon, the author of Ecclesiastes, achieved wealth and power but found it to be meaningless without community. Many of us have been raised in an independent culture where self-sufficiency is encouraged. But throughout the Bible, we find stories of strengthening relationships: David and Jonathan, Naomi and Ruth, Mary and Elizabeth, and Paul and Timothy. Each of these relationships witnessed hardships, yet the Bible reiterates Solomon's declaration that humanity is stronger together.

Community is one of God's greatest blessings. Christ's sacrifice on the cross restores our communities and relationship with God. We are given the gift of the Spirit who unites us. Within this body of believers, we can find strength in divine community.

Relational God, thank you for examples of strength in relationships. When we face trials or celebrations, please bless us with friends who draw us to you. Amen.

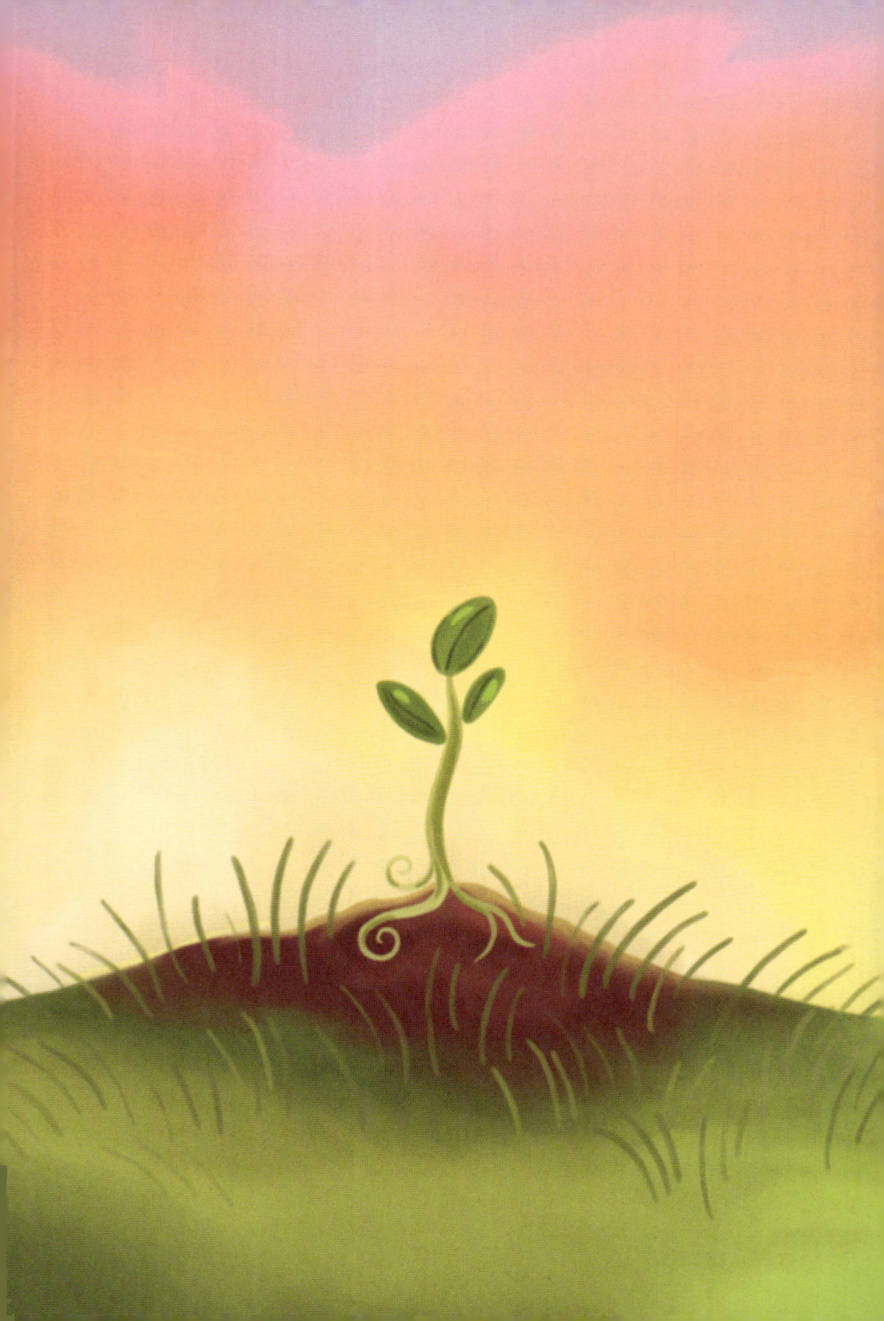

2 Timothy 1:7

"For God has not given us a spirit of fear and timidity, but of power, love, and self-discipline." (NLT)

What does it mean to live a spiritual life? A life rooted in God's Spirit might look different for each of us, just as different kinds of trees grow from the same soil but bear distinct kinds of fruit. But we may also see some similarities. 2 Timothy 1:7 suggests three markers of a Spirit-grounded life: power, love, and self-discipline.

As we seek to walk with God, we might ask ourselves: Are we walking in cowardice and timidity, shrinking back from hard conversations or from confronting inequality in our communities? Or are we walking in courage and power, boldly seeking justice so that the most vulnerable among us can flourish? Are our lives and words distorted by hatred and bigotry, or do we overflow with love that knows no borders? Are our daily choices driven entirely by self-interest, or are they shaped by self-disciplined, community-minded wisdom?

God's Spirit thrives wherever courage, power, love, and wisdom meet. As we ground ourselves in love, Jesus builds and strengthens these qualities in us.

God, may we walk in the humble confidence of knowing that you root us in good soil, that our lives may brim over with courage, love, and wisdom. Amen.

DAY

125 Romans 15:13

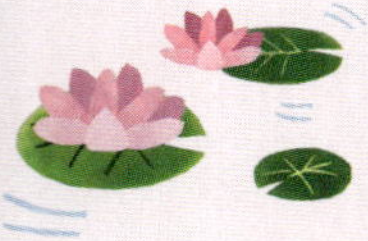

"I pray that God, the source of hope, will fill you completely with joy and peace because you trust in him. Then you will overflow with confident hope through the power of the Holy Spirit." (NLT)

We strive to live lives characterized by serenity and optimism. We answer questions of how we're doing almost automatically—we're "all good" or "doing fine." Perhaps if we say it enough, it will be true. Truthfully, most of us would not describe our lives as "overflowing with confident hope." Our fears and uncertainties pulse brightly. Peaceful joy can seem out of reach.

When circumstances feel precarious, when outcomes are unknown, anxiety abounds. How can we prepare? In a culture that preaches self-reliance and manifestation, our success can feel entirely our responsibility. Anxiety comes when we realize that our lives are not fully within our control.

It's true: we will never know everything. Sometimes, even our most careful and curated plans will fail. But for all our fallibility, we can take comfort in the knowledge that there is One who *is* in control: our God, who set the world spinning. Freeing ourselves from the shackles of worry and anxiety comes when we release our need for control and trust our Creator to care for us.

Holy Spirit, you are actively working for our betterment. You delight in our flourishing. Amen.

John 15:9–10

DAY 126

“I have loved you even as the Father has loved me. Remain in my love. When you obey my commandments, you remain in my love, just as I obey my Father’s commandments and remain in his love.” (NLT)

Sometimes God is characterized as being distant, far off in Heaven. But really, Jesus’ love for us is personal, warm, and near. This love does not merely glance at us from afar but draws us close, inviting us into intimacy and belonging.

When a child holds a parent’s hand while crossing a busy street, she stays close not out of obligation but because there is safety, care, and warmth in that grasp. Likewise, Jesus extends a hand to us, inviting us to walk near, held securely in his love. We are safest and freest when we remain close to the One whose grip is gentle yet strong, guiding us toward paths of joy.

Living in this love means continually trusting Jesus—trusting that his directives are born of genuine care for our deepest good. Obedience comes most naturally when we believe that Jesus’ guidance is truly best for us. Choosing to follow his way shows our trust in his wisdom and the kindness of his heart, affirming that the life he invites us to live moves us toward wholeness.

Jesus, help us remain close to you today, following your lead and enjoying the warmth of your loving presence. Amen.

DAY 127 Hebrews 6:19

"This hope is a strong and trustworthy anchor for our souls. It leads us through the curtain into God's inner sanctuary." (NLT)

Drifting through life without an anchor means being at the mercy of every current and gust that comes our way. What first feels like a liberating sense of weightlessness quickly turns into a yearning for something solid to hold onto when the inevitable storms of life arise. Without an anchor of purpose or belief, resilience weakens. Setbacks feel catastrophic, pulling us further out to sea with no tether to bring us back. Our journey becomes reactionary, never truly charting a course, always susceptible to being tossed about by circumstance, feeling unmoored and lost.

An anchor does more than hold a ship in place during a storm; it also provides a point of reference, preventing aimless drifting. Similarly, faith anchors us in the unchanging truths of God's Word and character, offering stability when everything around us feels shaky. It becomes our fixed point, a reliable guide in the fog of the unknown that keeps us from getting swept away. It tethers us to a hope that guides us toward the safe harbor of God's promises of deliverance and redemption.

Thank you, Jesus, for the firm and secure anchor of hope we find in faith. Help us to trust in its steadfastness through every storm. Amen.

Acts 4:32

DAY

128

"All the believers were united in heart and mind. And they felt that what they owned was not their own, so they shared everything they had." (NLT)

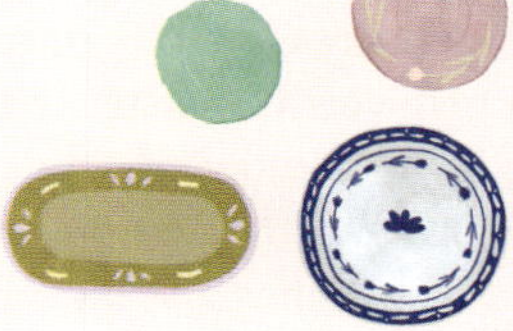

What is the purpose of a gift left in the box? It may be pristine, but it has little use. A gift enjoyed is quickly opened and put to use.

The early Church lived out the unboxed gift mentality. They witnessed Jesus' life and received the Holy Spirit—incredible gifts readily put to use. Amid community growth, their fellowship became even more intimate in both heart and mind. Nothing they had belonged to individuals—whether knowledge or physical belongings—but was shared joyfully. Seeing a need, the community came together to meet it by sending people, resources, and encouragement thousands of miles. The Spirit did mighty works among them as they gave freely.

Sharing *everything* can seem extreme. But fellowship involves a level of commitment that is uncommon. When we embrace community, our life patterns the early Church. Works of God unite our hearts and minds, the Spirit works within us, and the impulse to give grows stronger. Freely giving our talents and resources, our lives look more like the unboxed and joyfully used gift.

Holy Spirit, draw us towards where you are at work in our communities that we may experience the benefits of fellowship in you. Amen.

DAY

129 Ephesians 1:17–18

"Asking God, the glorious Father of our Lord Jesus Christ, to give you spiritual wisdom and insight so that you might grow in your knowledge of God. I pray that your hearts will be flooded with light so that you can understand the confident hope he has given to those he called—his holy people who are his rich and glorious inheritance." (NLT)

When the sun rises, it illuminates a landscape previously hidden in darkness. As dawn breaks, colors emerge, shapes take form, and paths become clear. Nothing new has been created; rather, our eyes have simply been opened to see what was always there. This is how God grants wisdom and spiritual insight: the Spirit gently lifts the veil, revealing truth, beauty, and direction we couldn't discern on our own.

Spiritual insight is a gift we receive, not a prize we earn. Wisdom isn't achieved through effort alone—it's granted by a generous God, freely given when we ask.

Asking Jesus to guide us enables us to see our lives and the lives of others more clearly. Relationships deepen, compassion grows, and choices become rooted in the steady soil of divine love rather than fleeting circumstance. Our vision sharpens, not because of our own skill, but because God delights in flooding our lives with light, illuminating the path to deeper joy and abundant life.

God, open the eyes of our hearts, granting us spiritual wisdom to see clearly and follow your loving guidance. Amen.

DAY

1 Corinthians 3:6–7 130

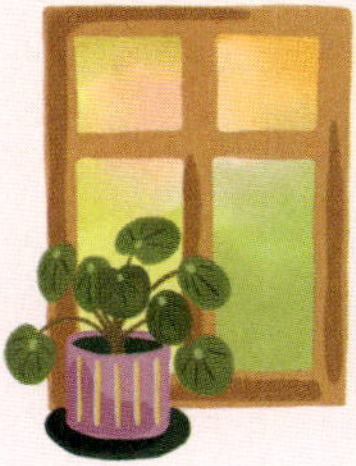

"I planted the seed in your hearts, and Apollos watered it, but it was God who made it grow. It's not important who does the planting, or who does the watering. What's important is that God makes the seed grow." (NLT)

Spiritual growth is essential for every believer. As we do life together, we develop in our faith through communities that help all to flourish. We are children of God, seed planters by the power of the Word, and in every sphere of influence we are equipped to plant this seed—scripture—into the hearts of those whose soil is ready to receive it.

In 1 Corinthians 3, Paul points to the true Gardener by reminding the people who is truly responsible for the seed's growth. We may have contributed to the process of embedding the message God wants us to give, but ultimately, we are purely helpers to the handiwork that only our Creator makes possible.

What a privilege to partake in this holy heart work, this garden -building in our inner worlds, that we who have the seed of faith planted in us can respond by spreading this seed to others! We serve a God who is fertile in love to till the soil within.

God who gardens, thank you for planting the seed of faith in us and helping us grow! May we contribute to the ripe harvest by planting seeds in return. Amen.

DAY

131 Psalm 13:2,5

"How long must I struggle with anguish in my soul, with sorrow in my heart every day? How long will my enemy have the upper hand? ... But I trust in your unfailing love. I will rejoice because you have rescued me." (NLT)

Sometimes, we feel connected and in step with God. Our prayers feel like a conversation, offering insight or connection when we need it. But some moments feel the opposite, as though God is far from us, and our prayers are unheard and unanswered.

The Psalms give us many examples of what it means to give voice to these frustrations. Reading through their prayers, we see the psalmists crying out or stubbornly waiting for God amid silence. It's okay to give God our hopes, hurts, thoughts, and emotions. We don't need to offer our prayers in a presentable package. We can bring all of ourselves, trusting that God is listening even when we don't sense it.

If we struggle to believe God is listening, we can remember the times that God has intervened in the past. We can look to the Bible or our communities for stories of God's surprising work in the world. Whatever it takes to reconnect with the reality of who Jesus is, that work is worthwhile.

God, thank you for always listening. Help us to have faith in your goodness, even when we don't understand the way your goodness is showing up in our lives. Amen.

Micah 7:18–19

DAY 132

"Where is another God like you, who pardons the guilt of the remnant, overlooking the sins of his special people? You will not stay angry with your people forever, because you delight in showing unfailing love ... You will trample our sins under your feet and throw them into the depths of the ocean!" (NLT)

We carry the weight of past mistakes like a heavy backpack. We replay conversations, relive decisions, and wonder if we've messed things up beyond repair. Our expectations—of ourselves, of others, even God—can leave us feeling disqualified or disheartened. But the Gospel flips that narrative.

We worship the God who delights in offering second chances. These aren't like the ones we sometimes receive from others—tentative, conditional, or half-hearted. They aren't reluctant moments of forgiveness but of joyful redemption. God's grace is full and free, extended without hesitation.

God is slow to anger, holds no grudges, and keeps no record of wrongs. Our Creator not only delights in showing us mercy but abounds in it—casting our sins away into the deepest waters so they can never define us again. This assurance invites us to release shame, trust in grace, and walk forward with hope. With Jesus, perfect love makes space for restoration, renewal, and the courage to move ahead. With Jesus, failure is never the end of the story. It's the place where mercy begins.

Lord, thank you for your boundless grace. May we walk in the freedom of forgiveness, embracing the second chances you offer. Amen.

DAY

133 Isaiah 55:2–3

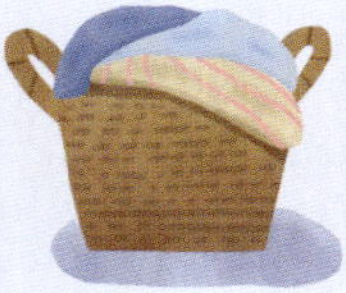

"Why spend your money on food that does not give you strength? Why pay for food that does you no good? Listen to me, and you will eat what is good. You will enjoy the finest food. Come to me with your ears wide open. Listen, and you will find life." (NLT)

We spend so much of our days chasing what doesn't satisfy. We're ruled by cravings, trends, and so-called miracle cures. We fill our schedules, striving for fullness, and still feel empty. Unexpectedly, God's invitation is not rushed. It's not buried in our busyness or lost to the sea of noise. It's clear, steady, and kind: "Come to Me. Listen. Eat what is good."

Making time for God doesn't always mean changing our whole routine. Sometimes, it's as simple as turning our hearts toward Jesus in the middle of it. The quiet in our cars. The moment before the next meeting. The pause before bed.

God is not waiting for a perfect offering—just an open ear. A heart willing to listen to the message continually shared. Even in a busy world, the Holy Voice breaks through the noise. Let our souls be nourished. May we come, just as we are. There is life here. And it is more than enough.

Generous God, help us draw near to you amid the noise and be still. Remind us that we don't need to strive for your presence. Help us to delight in you and experience the abundant life you have for us. Amen.

Philippians 3:8

DAY
134

"Indeed, I count everything as loss because of the surpassing worth of knowing Christ Jesus my Lord. For his sake I have suffered the loss of all things and count them as rubbish, in order that I may gain Christ." (ESV)

Paul previously built his life on religious achievement, status, and lineage. According to cultural and religious standards of the day, he had "made it." But after encountering Jesus, everything changed. Those former gains seemed worthless compared to Christ. What once was most important paled to the treasure of knowing Jesus personally.

How do we define success? What do we build our lives around? The only gain worth pursuing is Jesus Christ. Not because everything else is inherently bad, but because nothing else can do what he does. Jesus is the Savior of our souls and the One who holds all things together.

In Christ, we are fully known and fully loved. We no longer strive to earn our worth but rest in the finished work of the cross. Humility replaces pride, surrender overtakes control, and love becomes the highest aim. Knowing Jesus reorients our priorities and reshapes our desires. When he becomes our greatest treasure, everything else falls into its rightful place.

Jesus, teach us to count everything as loss in light of your surpassing worth. We want to know you, not just in theory, but in the day-to-day moments of our lives. Amen.

DAY

135 Psalm 136:26

"Give thanks to the God of heaven. His faithful love endures forever." (NLT)

Sometimes it can be difficult to believe we are loved. Shame over our mistakes overwhelms us; memories of being mistreated, undervalued, or forgotten replay in our minds. It's at our lowest moments that we feel the most unlovable. How much could the God of Heaven—the Creator of the universe—care about us?

Although these insecurities may feel true, the real truth is that God delights in us. Love is at the very heart of who God is. Scripture declares that God *is* love. This love is infused into all of creation. And humanity, made in the image of God, holds an especially important place in God's affection.

The world highlights our flaws and failings. We internalize weaknesses, not as opportunities to grow, but as strikes against our value. According to this worldview, love is something we must earn. The Bible tells us otherwise.

Our Creator knows us completely—from our best attributes to our areas of weakness. Amid our imperfections, God pours out love through Jesus. This love is not conditional, transactional, or temporary. We can face down our limitations unafraid, confident that the God of Heaven loves us and desires to help us thrive.

Compassionate God, wrap us up in your loving embrace. Amen.

Genesis 1:26–27

DAY 136

"Then God said, 'Let us make human beings in our image, to be like us. They will reign over the fish in the sea, the birds in the sky, the livestock, all the wild animals on the earth, and the small animals that scurry along the ground.' So God created human beings in his own image. In the image of God he created them; male and female he created them." (NLT)

There is a reason why human beings stand as the pinnacle of God's creation: we are made in the image of the Creator of the universe, which means that we reflect the divine likeness of the Lord. Knowing this, it is no wonder that people are imbued with various talents, skills, intelligence, and gifts.

Imago Dei is Latin for "image of God," a phrase used to refer to all of us. God created men and women to be counterparts of one another, though distinct in their design; both are valuable image-bearers of the same Maker.

God also gives us authority over the animals of the earth, making us stewards of creation. When we remind ourselves whose image we reflect, there is no room for questioning our worth or value—each of us is priceless in God's eyes. In this truth, our identities are established and clearly defined as beautiful representatives of the Lord.

Creator, thank you for making us in the likeness of your perfect image! What a divine privilege. We are made to represent you! Help us to reflect your glory. Amen.

DAY

137 Psalm 34:3–5

"Oh, magnify the Lord with me, and let us exalt His name together! I sought the Lord, and He answered me and delivered me from all my fears. Those who look to Him are radiant, and their faces shall never be ashamed." (ESV)

Shame feels like a heavy cloak, wrapping us in guilt and leading us to believe we're unworthy of God's love. It draws us away from our loving Creator, convincing us we're defined by our failures. But scripture tells us there is no condemnation for those in Christ Jesus. In him, we are not rejected but given radiant freedom.

When shame rises, we must intentionally remove that cloak and seek the presence of God. Psalm 34 reminds us that worship is one of the ways we do this. By magnifying the Lord, we shift our focus from our flaws to God's faithfulness. Worship recalibrates our hearts, reminding us who God is and who we are in God: beloved, redeemed, and secure. Offering this exaltation, our countenance changes. Not because we've earned freedom, but because we've received it through Jesus Christ. God answers with forgiveness, love, and grace, replacing shame with peace. By embracing our identity in Christ, we shift our focus from condemnation and guilt to healing and freedom.

Lord, release us from the cloak of shame. May we find hope and deliverance in your presence. May we glorify you and radiate your love and joy, free from the weight of shame. Amen.

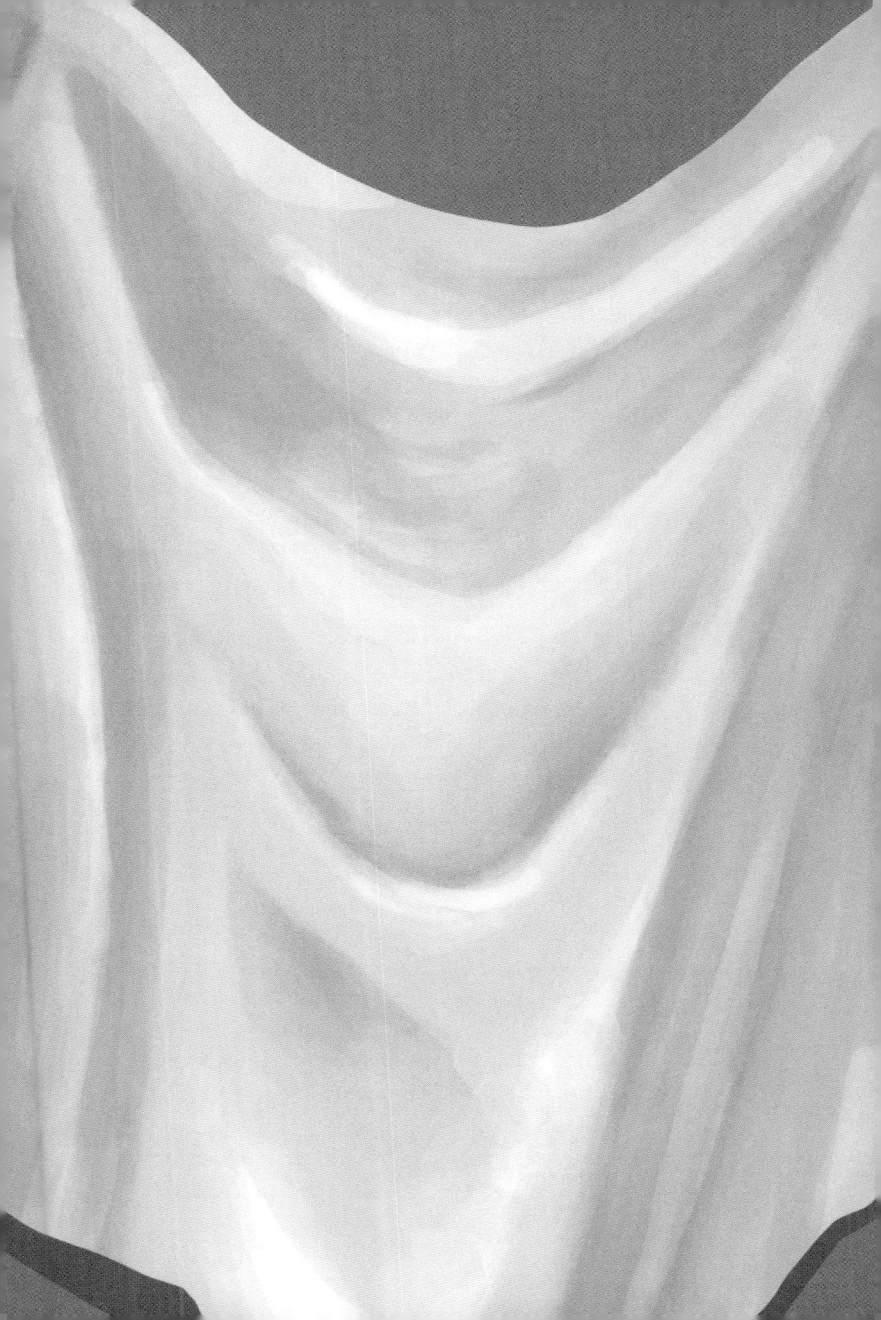

DAY

138 Revelation 3:20, 22

"Look! I stand at the door and knock. If you hear my voice and open the door, I will come in, and we will share a meal together as friends ... Anyone with ears to hear must listen to the Spirit and understand what he is saying to the churches." (NLT)

We learn to recognize a voice by listening to it often. Over time, the voices of people we love become familiar, unmistakable even among the noise. When we regularly attune ourselves to the Spirit, Jesus' voice also emerges, not as a distant authority, but as a close friend whose voice we have come to cherish.

Imagine a gathering filled with many voices, laughter spilling from every corner. Yet when a dear friend speaks, even quietly, we turn our head—we know that voice intimately. This familiarity is born from time spent together, conversations shared—laughter and quiet moments alike. Likewise, the more we listen for God, the easier it becomes to recognize God's voice, guiding us toward deeper friendship and communion.

As we mature in our faith, we realize that this familiar voice we love is also speaking to all people, shaping and guiding communities toward wholeness. We hear both personal reassurance and direction, encouragement, and wisdom that benefits the whole family of God. We trust this voice and seek to share the wisdom God imparts.

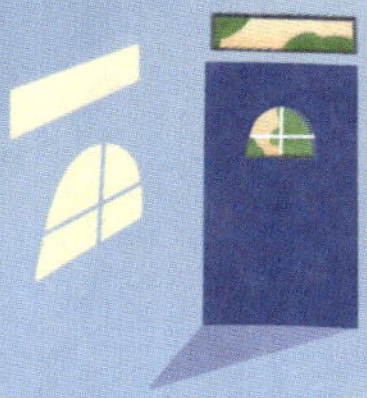

Jesus, teach us to recognize your voice, to delight in your friendship, and to follow you for the good of all your people. Amen.

Deuteronomy 6:5

DAY
139

"And you must love the Lord your God with all your heart, all your soul, and all your strength." (NLT)

There lives within us a longing to be whole. This is what integrity means: wholeness. God invites us to live in such a way that the different segments of our lives fit together as one unified whole.

In wholeness, we find freedom. No secrets, no need to hide, no fear of being found out. We experience the joy of being authentically who we are and being part of a community that loves and accepts us fully.

This is what it is like to love God with all our heart and soul and might, as Deuteronomy 6:5 instructs—to love God with the fullness of who we are. There is no aspect of ourselves that we could possibly hide from the One who creates us and sustains our every breath. God loves every aspect of who we are at our deepest, truest core, and God invites us to return this love wholeheartedly.

God, thank you for being so infinitely loving that we can be fully who we are with you, with no shame and no fear of rejection. May we love you by loving our neighbors, as Jesus taught. Amen.

DAY
140 Exodus 35:35

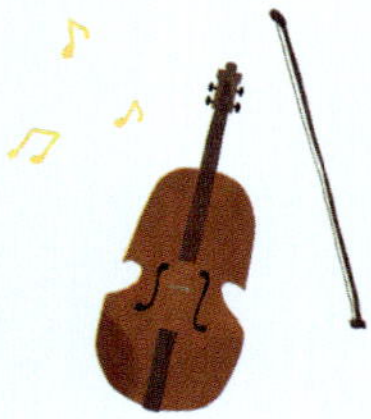

"The Lord has given them special skills as engravers, designers, embroiderers in blue, purple, and scarlet thread on fine linen cloth, and weavers. They excel as craftsmen and as designers." (NLT)

Creativity is a beautiful, vivid, and sensory response to our belief in God as the Greatest Artist. At the time of making the Tabernacle, described in Exodus 35, God equipped people with artistic gifts to build a dwelling place where the holy would commune *with* the human.

That we are the vessels by which a sanctuary worthy of the Most High would be built is unfathomable! God included skillful artists of all trades in the creative process of making a holy tent of meeting, reflecting a desire for our creativity to be an expression of our faith.

Everyone is hardwired with skills to beautify God's Kingdom, even if they aren't creative in the traditional sense. Our Creator places the utmost value on beautiful work, which reveals God's character to creation. Anything we produce can be crafted for this purpose. We have been given a spiritual gift that we are designed to thrive at—let's consider the creative avenue we feel most connected to and exercise our talents for God's glory and our joy.

Creator God, what an extraordinary blessing to be given creative skills to praise you! Inspire us for our good and your pleasure. Amen.

Luke 13:18–19

DAY
141

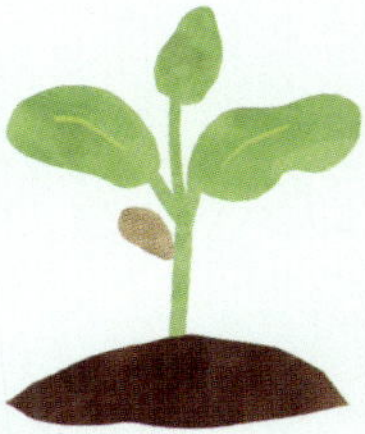

"Then Jesus said, 'What is the Kingdom of God like? How can I illustrate it? It is like a tiny mustard seed that a man planted in a garden; it grows and becomes a tree, and the birds make nests in its branches.'" (NLT)

It's difficult to shake the feeling that things in the world are not as they're meant to be. We experience loss, we suffer injustice, and we know something is wrong. But what would it mean for the world to be *right*?

Jesus describes the Kingdom of God—creation as God intends—through the imagery of a mustard seed flourishing into a great tree. The divine Kingdom is a place of growth. Here, creation is defined by compassion and care. The tree not only blossoms in its own right but also provides for the birds out of its maturation. We see the impact something seemingly small can have on all around it.

When we seek to live into the Kingdom of God, we are planting that mustard seed. Growth takes time; trees do not arise overnight. We nurture the Gospel in our hearts so that it might take root and transform the world around us. Through the work of the Holy Spirit, we glimpse a view of creation in harmony, and we anticipate the life-changing growth from God.

Jesus, the world around us is not as it should be, but we can take comfort that through you all will be made right. Amen.

DAY

142 1 Thessalonians 5:16–18

"Rejoice always, pray without ceasing, give thanks in all circumstances; for this is the will of God in Christ Jesus for you." (ESV)

What does it look like to live a life of worship every day?

In 1 Thessalonians 5:16-18, Paul paints a picture of continual worship: a life marked by joy, constant communion with God through prayer, and gratitude in every circumstance. Worship is not confined to a specific time or place; it's a posture of the heart.

Constant rejoicing means choosing joy, even when life is difficult, and focusing on God's faithfulness to carry us through those challenging moments. The invitation to pray without ceasing urges us to stay in constant communion with God and keep our hearts aligned with God's will. And giving thanks in all circumstances helps us recognize God's goodness, even in times of hardship.

When worship becomes a way of life, it transforms every moment. We default to honoring and serving God, regardless of our circumstances. We become more aware of the beauty and blessings all around us. In doing so, we fulfill God's will for us in Christ Jesus and experience his peace and presence throughout our lives.

Father God, help us to live in constant worship, finding joy, prayer, and thanksgiving in every moment. Amen.

DAY 143

Romans 8:28

"And we know that God causes everything to work together for the good of those who love God and are called according to his purpose for them." (NLT)

When life feels uncertain or painful, it can be difficult to believe God desires our good. As prayers seem unanswered, doors close, or grief settles in, we may wonder if God is truly for us.

But Romans 8:28 offers a quiet assurance: God is at work in *everything*, not just the obvious blessings, but the brokenness too. Jesus' goodness isn't limited by circumstance. Instead, he weaves all things together for the good of those who love him.

This doesn't mean everything will feel good or make immediate sense. But it does mean that nothing is wasted in God's hands. God's love is active, purposeful, and always oriented toward the divine vision of restoration and renewal.

We can take comfort in the knowledge that God's intentions toward us are always loving. Even when we don't see the full picture, we can trust the heart of the One who holds it.

God of goodness, help us trust that you are working for our good —even in the waiting, even in the unknown. Amen.

DAY

144 Psalm 92:12–14

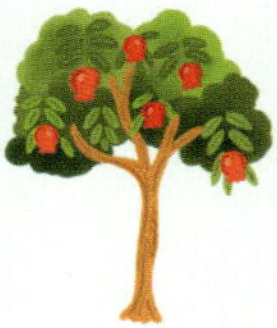

"But the godly will flourish like palm trees and grow strong like the cedars of Lebanon. For they are transplanted to the Lord's own house. They flourish in the courts of our God. Even in old age they will still produce fruit; they will remain vital and green." (NLT)

It's difficult to get our bearings when we are young. There are so many voices telling us who we should be or what we should do with our lives. Too often, we don't know which voice to listen to or what path to follow. As we grow up, a voice might begin to stand out, and a particular life path might become clear.

Throughout the noise, God has always been calling us and leading us to the path of godliness. It's a path we are all invited down, where we seek to follow and emulate God here on earth. Walking this path leads to flourishing throughout our lives. Like cedars planted in God's house, all of our needs will be cared for. This allows us to grow—we'll be known for our strength and fruit, even in our old age.

This is the path of godliness that we have been called to. Are we ready to walk down that path?

Jesus, show us how we can be more godly. Help us to grow and see fruit come from our lives, even through the end of our days. Amen.

John 21:20–22

DAY 145

“Peter turned and saw that the disciple whom Jesus loved was following them. ... When Peter saw him, he asked, ‘Lord, what about him?’ Jesus answered, ‘If I want him to remain alive until I return, what is that to you? You must follow me.’”(NIV)

Comparing ourselves to others can feel like second nature—a bad habit that we struggle to quit. “Why has God given me this hardship while this other person has it so easy?” we ask. But comparison is the thief of joy.

When we compare our journeys to another’s, we make a heap of assumptions about their life, needs, and struggles. Instead, it’s best to focus on the path God has specifically put before us, working to be faithful, wise, and generous, rather than wishing we were given a different lot in life.

The differences between us are a key part of community. Everyone has unique perspectives, experiences, and resources to offer. Because of this, we can support one another and work hand-in-hand to create a more beautiful world. This would not be possible if we were all blessed in the same way. Our paths are all unique, and that is a wonderful thing.

Jesus, thank you that while our challenges, blessings, and choices may differ, the people in our community all share the same values: to live and love well, emulating you. Help us focus on the plan you have for each of us, and help us find joy in it. Amen.

DAY 146 Psalm 19:1–2

"The heavens proclaim the glory of God. The skies display his craftsmanship. Day after day they continue to speak; night after night they make him known." (NLT)

It's impossible to comprehend the vastness of God, but creation gives us a glimpse.

The sun rises with all its life-giving beauty. Sunsets bring peace and calm into the world. Trees grow tall and strong, elegantly adorning the world in spring. Leaves fall, blanketing the ground with color in autumn.

God's workmanship is colorful, vibrant, and always changing. We can't control creation's rhythms any more than we can control God. Looking at the natural world around us, we can find comfort in the continuous movement of life because we know that God has crafted it all, down to the intricate details.

When we come face to face with this kind of beauty in the world, it reminds us we can rest because God is in control. God's perfect plans for us are beautiful and intricately crafted, and God is good.

Heavenly Creator, help us to see your handiwork in the world around us. Remind us of your careful attention to detail, and help us rest knowing that you are in control. Amen.

James 5:7–8

DAY 147

"Be patient then, brothers and sisters, until the Lord's coming. See how the farmer waits for the land to yield its valuable crop, patiently waiting for the autumn and spring rains. You too, be patient and stand firm, because the Lord's coming is near." (NIV)

What does it mean to wait patiently? It's a bit like standing in front of the microwave, waiting for the popcorn to pop. We know it's coming—but those first few kernels take their time. We're tempted to open the door and check, to speed things up ourselves. But deep down, we know that if we wait just a little longer, the rest will come in due time.

Patience with God's timing is much the same. We know things are happening, even when we don't see immediate results. Like the farmer who trusts the seasons to bring about the harvest, we must trust God's process, even when we feel like we're standing still. The popcorn doesn't pop until it's ready, and God's timing will unfold when it's right for us.

Let us stand firm in our faith, knowing that just because we can't see progress doesn't mean God isn't working.

Lord Jesus, help us trust your timing and stay patient as you work behind the scenes. Amen.

DAY 148 Psalm 55:22

"Give your burdens to the Lord, and he will take care of you. He will not permit the godly to slip and fall." (NLT)

Stress can feel like an inescapable foe. It sneaks in like a shadow, casting doubt and uncertainty over our hearts. We're constantly on our toes as we look out for the next threat we will need to outrun or outsmart. Amid this struggle, we find solace in God's Word, and guidance, peace, and strength from the Spirit.

Our Creator invites us to unload our worries and anxieties. God is a refuge, a haven for our weary souls. Divine love and grace are everlasting, providing strength and peace amid life's challenges.

As we confront stress, we can trust that God's presence goes before us, empowering us to endure and overcome. Our Savior understands the heaviness of our burdens; Jesus invites us to lay them at his feet. Prayer is a direct line of communication to the Almighty, in which we can pour out our hearts and receive comfort and assurance in return. We can acknowledge our fears, rather than burying them away, and bring them before God.

Jesus, we know that we are not meant to carry the strain of anxiety alone. We give thanks that you are ever present, ready to guide us through life's storms. Amen.

Deuteronomy 13:4

DAY
149

“It is the Lord your God you must follow, and him you must revere. Keep his commands and obey him; serve him and hold fast to him.” (NIV)

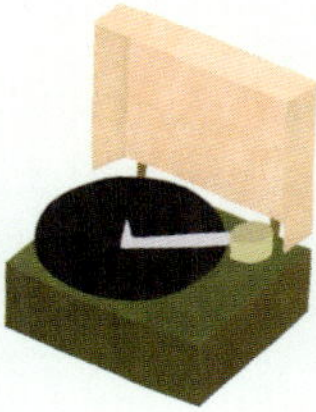

To “heed” means to pay close attention and respond thoughtfully. It’s more than just following rules; it’s about embracing the heart behind the call. God doesn’t just want us to obey but to hold fast and draw near to His heart. Are we just checking boxes, or are we truly seeking to grow closer to our Lord?

Think of it like tuning a guitar. When we adjust the strings, we’re not just mindlessly tightening—we’re seeking the right pitch, a harmonious sound. In the same way, when we heed God’s call, it’s not about following a list of commands but creating a life in tune with God’s will. Jesus calls us to revere and serve him, not out of duty, but for our betterment.

Obedience is no longer about earning favor; it’s a response to the grace God has already shown us. When we heed Jesus’ voice, we don’t just live better lives—we live in harmony with his Kingdom work. Like an orchestra playing together, hearts aligned with God bring peace, purpose, and joy to the greater song He’s composing through creation.

Father, help us tune our hearts to you, living in faithful obedience, not out of obligation but out of love for you. Amen.

DAY

150 Ephesians 5:14–16

"This is why it is said: 'Wake up, sleeper, rise from the dead, and Christ will shine on you.' Be very careful, then, how you live—not as unwise but as wise, making the most of every opportunity, because the days are evil." (NIV)

Seizing every day with alertness, care, and wisdom can seem overwhelming. The pressures of our lives, as well as our empathy for the suffering of others around the world, can leave us feeling beaten down. We might try to cope by emotionally tuning out and coasting along, instead of making the most of each day.

But apathy will not give us true peace, nor will it help us live out our faith. Apathy is often a form of anxiety; beneath our attempts to numb, we may feel restless and uneasy. "Shutting down" is a temporary solution, not a cure.

God isn't apathetic to us, our lives, the state of our world, to the suffering and wrongdoing and hurt. We shouldn't be either.

When we focus on the things that lie within our control—the responsibilities God has given us—we realize we don't need to fix everything, and we can't. By narrowing our scope to issues we can directly impact, seizing the day becomes easier. Moreover, our small actions help calm the restlessness in our hearts.

Jesus, thank you for being a respite in the midst of our overwhelm. Show us how we can resist apathy and take action. Amen.

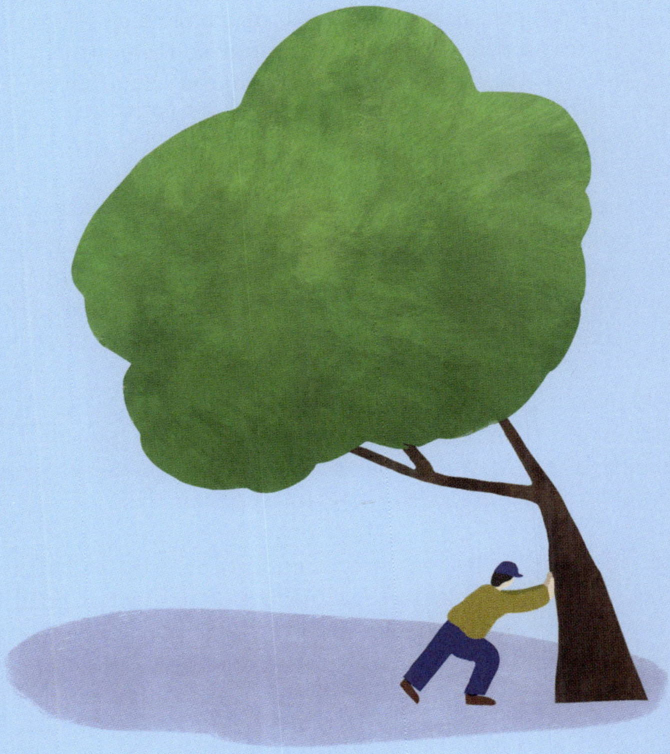

DAY
151 John 10:28–29

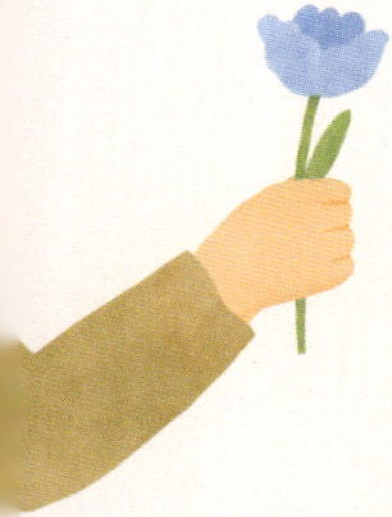

"I give them eternal life, and they will never perish, and no one will snatch them out of my hand. My Father, who has given them to me, is greater than all, and no one is able to snatch them out of the Father's hand." (ESV)

Jesus, our Shepherd, speaks over us with unmatched love and fierce protection. "I give them eternal life," he promises, but this is not just any life. It's a life rooted in his promise, never fading, never falling apart. Every moment, every breath, is held securely in our Savior's hands.

The One who spoke the stars into existence, who bore the weight of our sin on the cross, now speaks over us. Jesus promises that no one, not even the fiercest enemy, can ever take us from his grasp. We are his. Always.

When the world feels uncertain, when fear creeps in, he holds us. No matter how broken we feel, no matter how lost or small we think we are, we are held by the hands of the One who loves us with a love that will never let go. God is bigger than anything that could ever threaten us. No power, no fear, no circumstance, no past or future, can ever separate us from the Creator's grasp.

Father, thank you for sending your Son to hold us, to give us life, and to protect us always. We rest in Jesus' hands, knowing that come what may he will never let us go. Amen.

Psalm 42:3, 5

DAY 152

"My tears have been my food day and night while people say to me all day long, 'Where is your God?' ... Why, my soul, are you downcast? Why so disturbed within me? Put your hope in God, for I will yet praise him, my Savior and my God." (NIV)

It can be easy to assume that emotions like sorrow or grief come from a lack of faith. After all, if we're grieving a loved one's death, perhaps that means we're unsure about their relationship with God. If we're feeling downtrodden, could that mean we're failing to trust in God's plan? Not at all.

Scripture shows us that grief is a valid and normal part of our lives. God doesn't view our emotions as "negative" or sinful, and Jesus doesn't leave us to experience these hard feelings alone.

Jesus is with us in suffering and loss. He joins us in our experiences, and when we share our hearts with him, we find ourselves steadied. Gratitude isn't something we weaponize to prevent sorrow. Rather, gratitude is often the natural result of sharing our sorrows with Christ. And with that divine comfort soothing our hearts, we are inspired to show that same empathy to others, holding space for them in their grief.

Thank you for holding us amid painful moments, God. Open our eyes to how we can be a comfort to others, just as you have been to us. Amen.

DAY

153 Psalm 77:2–3

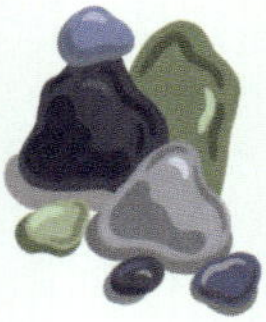

"When I was in deep trouble, I searched for the Lord. All night long I prayed, with hands lifted toward heaven, but my soul was not comforted. I think of God, and I moan, overwhelmed with longing for his help." (NLT)

The raw honesty of the Psalms reveals that faith isn't the absence of doubt, but often its companion. The writer of Psalm 77 doesn't pretend to have all the answers. Instead, they bring their confusion, questions, and longings directly to God. The confession of their doubt is not a failure of faith but a testament to faith's complexity.

Sometimes we lift our voices and stretch out our hands to God without receiving immediate relief or clarity. In such moments, we need not deny or ignore the shadows of doubt that arise. Instead, our questions can become the catalyst for our continued pursuit of God. Ongoing inquiry is itself a form of worship. Searching is an affirmation of our faith, an acknowledgement of hope, and a belief that there is something more, something true, waiting to be found.

Doubt, far from being an enemy of faith, is a pathway toward a more profound trust. God's presence isn't contingent on perfect understanding but on our persistent pursuit. It's in wrestling with our questions that our understanding of God can expand.

In our doubt and discomfort, Jesus, we reach for you, trusting that you hold us in your unwavering love. Amen.

Isaiah 30:15

DAY
154

"This is what the Sovereign Lord, the Holy One of Israel, says: 'In repentance and rest is your salvation, in quietness and trust is your strength, but you would have none of it.'" (NIV)

True strength takes multiple forms; it's not about being the loudest voice or recklessly jumping to action. To exert strength in a healthy, considerate way, we need to take our cues from Jesus.

When we take a moment to pray or reflect on the life of Jesus, we remind ourselves of the model Christ gave us for how to live. Jesus famously rebuked his own disciples' hot-headed reactions by restoring the temple servant's ear, which Simon Peter cut off. A deliberate, harm-minimizing approach is more in line with his example. To exert strength wisely means acting with conviction and wisdom instead of being rash, prideful, and reactionary.

Sometimes the best thing to do is wait, pray for guidance, and seek another's insight. In this way, restraint is a form of strength. For those naturally more inclined to react fast and loud, restraint requires a high level of self-control and wisdom. Considering consequences, being guided by our values, leaving room for God's voice to speak to us—these are aspects of true, healthy strength.

Mighty God, help us act wisely. Teach us how to use our strength deliberately. Guide us with your wisdom, and give us the willpower to make thoughtful choices. Amen.

DAY

155 John 11:33–35

“When Jesus saw her weeping, and the Jews who had come along with her also weeping, he was deeply moved in spirit and troubled. ‘Where have you laid him?’ he asked. ‘Come and see, Lord,’ they replied. Jesus wept.” (NIV)

John 11:35 is the shortest verse in the Bible, and yet so profound: “Jesus wept.” In Christ, God chose to experience all of human life alongside us. This includes sorrow, lament, and grief.

At times, grief can feel nearly unbearable. We may be tempted to push it down, for fear of being completely overcome, unable to unearth ourselves and feel joy ever again.

But God doesn’t want us to neglect our deepest emotional wounds. Instead, the way forward is *through*. When we allow ourselves to feel deeply, to let grief move our hearts, to weep as Jesus wept, we can begin to heal.

Jesus has experienced all emotions; none are inherently sinful. We are allowed to grieve. We are allowed to lament. And we aren’t alone: he is with us in our sorrow.

Jesus, thank you for joining us in the fullness of human life, with all of its heartbreak and disappointment. Illuminate the ways we can support our loved ones in their lament, just as you support us. Amen.

Hebrews 13:6

DAY 156

"So we can confidently say, 'The Lord is my helper; I will not fear; what can man do to me?'" (ESV)

When worry whispers louder than peace, we must remember: God is our helper. Our Creator is not a distant deity or a figurehead too far to reach. God is with us, now, today, in every fear, in every moment of uncertainty.

Jesus, the One who healed the broken, who embraced the outcasts, promises that we don't face the weight of fear alone. His love covers us, his presence surrounds. His power is more than enough to carry us through whatever we're facing.

When we feel small, weak, and afraid, scripture assures us Jesus is active, not sitting idly by. He enters the depths of our pain and says, "I am here." What can the world do to us when the God of all creation is standing by our side?

There is nothing that can overcome the strength of God's love. God has already overcome what we fear, has already silenced the lies that want to steal our peace. Worry not, because Jesus is with us. And in his hands, we are safe.

Jesus, thank you for being our helper. When fear creeps in, remind us that you are here, and we need not worry. We place our trust in your never-ending care. Amen.

DAY

157 2 Peter 3:8-9

" ... A day is like a thousand years to the Lord, and a thousand years is like a day. The Lord isn't really being slow about his promise, as some people think. No, he is being patient for your sake. He does not want anyone to be destroyed, but wants everyone to repent." (NLT)

Sometimes, our lives seem to move at a snail's pace. We feel like we've traveled miles when it's only been a city block. When we feel stuck, everything in us screams to go faster. God's response can seem even slower when we come across these unexpected delays.

Thankfully, 2 Peter 3:8-9 reminds us God is all-knowing and faithful. We may not see all the details, but God sees the perfection in the plan and has far more patience than us. While we only see the traffic, God is clearing the roadblocks ahead, doing the work of a thousand days in a few hours. At breakneck speeds, it can all seem a blur out the window, but in the slowness, we can sit long enough to see the architecture and art lost to freeway noise.

Still, it can be hard to see God's goodness in life's delays. But we know that divine promises will not come back void. Our God assures us that our future is secure, and all of creation has the opportunity to experience the joy we have received!

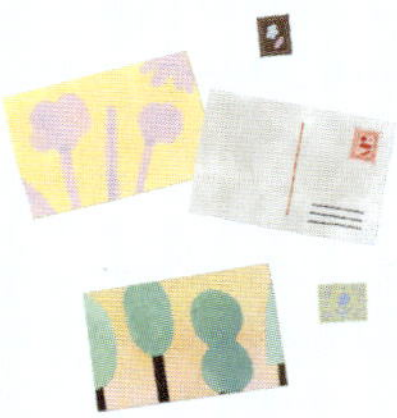

Good God, thank you for keeping your promises. Help our patience to reflect yours and bring more awareness to the beauty around us. Amen.

DAY

Psalm 139:1-4 158

"You have searched me, Lord, and you know me. You know when I sit and when I rise; you perceive my thoughts from afar. You discern my going out and my lying down; you are familiar with all my ways. Before a word is on my tongue you, Lord, know it completely." (NIV)

Being known can be terrifying. It requires vulnerability. We may feel tempted to run from true connection because it requires us to uncover our deepest insecurities, hopes, and longings. We may even close ourselves off from others for fear that they will abandon us out of shame.

But true, rich connection is worth the discomfort—and even pain—of opening ourselves up to others. Deep, authentic friendships make life richer, more joyful, and easier, offering us the support of a loving community. To have such a community, we must find a way to be vulnerable, to allow people to truly know us. It requires bravery, as we know we may be hurt again and again. How can we muster the courage?

God has searched our innermost thoughts and knows our hearts better than anyone. And yet, God still accepts us—better yet, *loves* us. And when we take time to feel God's ever-present love, we can feel encouraged to open up to others.

Compassionate Christ, thank you for your relentless love and acceptance. Give us the courage to allow others to know us, the bravery to truly connect and be known. Amen.

DAY

159 Proverbs 3:3–4

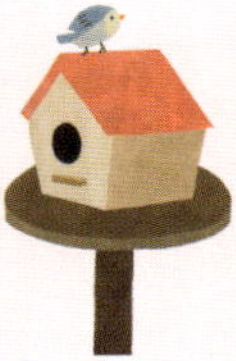

"Never let loyalty and kindness leave you! Tie them around your neck as a reminder. Write them deep within your heart. Then you will find favor with both God and people, and you will earn a good reputation." (NLT)

In a harsh world, where people are often overlooked and misunderstood, God calls us to embrace loyalty and kindness, not as something we do but as something that defines who we are. Biblical kindness isn't just about being nice. It's about reflecting God's heart, loving others even when it's hard, forgiving when it feels impossible, and showing grace when no one deserves it. Radical kindness sees the unseen, heals the broken, and reaches out when no one else will.

But kindness doesn't stand alone—it walks hand in hand with loyalty. Together, they form a picture of faithful love that shows up and stays, even when the world tells us to walk away. It's a covenant, a bond that mirrors the way God engages with us—with a love that never lets go.

Imagine the impact of living this way—radically kind and deeply loyal, even when it costs us. God promises that when we live like this, we will experience transformation. The grace and kindness bestowed upon us by our Creator spread through us to every corner of the earth.

Jesus, help us live with radical kindness, so that your love shines through us and changes the spaces around us. Amen.

John 15:1–2

DAY
160

"I am the true vine, and my Father is the gardener. He cuts off every branch in me that bears no fruit, while every branch that does bear fruit he prunes so that it will be even more fruitful." (NIV)

To live healthy, fruitful lives, trees need to be pruned. Likewise, we need pruning. God invited us to leave behind what no longer serves us, making room for something better to grow. To do this, we have to part with a belief or habit that feels essential to our way of life, our survival, our identity.

This can be a painful process. Learning new things takes serious effort, and the first step is to unlearn what holds us back. We may have difficulty parsing out those elements and then even more difficulty replacing those ingrained habits with new ones.

But Jesus is with us as we experience the growing pains. He is not only the Pruner but the Gardener, taking steps to help us flourish. When we feel his presence alongside us, we find it easier to move forward and grow, knowing that we will eventually be healthier and happier for it.

Jesus, what sorts of things are holding us back? Open our eyes to what we need to prune, and give us the courage to learn and do better. Amen.

DAY

161 Isaiah 40:26

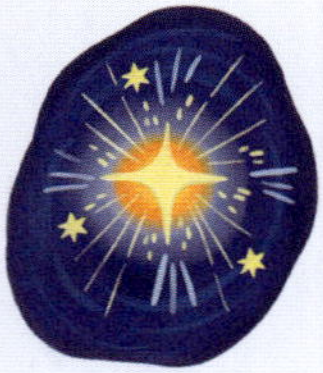

"Lift up your eyes and look to the heavens: Who created all these? He who brings out the starry host one by one and calls forth each of them by name. Because of his great power and mighty strength, not one of them is missing." (NIV)

Beauty can seem like a luxury. With all life's responsibilities and challenges, we may feel like we don't have time to stop and admire the beauty around us. What purpose does it serve? Beauty doesn't feed us, shelter us, or keep us safe.

But the beauty of God's creation does nourish our souls and provide reprieve for our hearts, if we pay attention to it. Beauty helps keep us grounded and helps us feel connected to God's larger, mysterious plan. Amid mundane hardships, beauty revives our sense of life, of joy, and gives us the strength to keep going.

Beauty matters. If it didn't, God wouldn't have bothered imbuing it into creation. The world holds an immense beauty upon beauty, into the deepest depths of the universe. If we take a moment and pay attention, we'll see God's beauty everywhere.

Blessed Creator, thank you for the abundant beauty you've given the world. Please help us appreciate this blessing and be encouraged by it. Amen.

Romans 8:18

DAY
162

"Yet what we suffer now is nothing compared to the glory he will reveal to us later." (NLT)

When the path ahead is shrouded in darkness and the landscape looks bleak, scripture invites us to lift our gaze toward the horizon of God's future promises. Imagine standing on a windswept plain, the ground rough and barren beneath our feet. But in the distance, a faint glow begins to paint the sky with hues of dawn. That distant light, that promise of a new day, doesn't negate the difficulty of our current position, but it shifts our perspective. It whispers of hope, of renewal, of a beauty that will eventually break through.

Pain, disappointment, and uncertainty can cloud our vision. Yet no matter the darkness we face, it will not diminish God's assurance that a brighter future is dawning. Journeying through hardship with hope isn't about denying the hurt; it's about recognizing its temporary nature, that in Christ, even death is a prelude to resurrection.

We can hold onto the promise of a glorious, eternal tomorrow—a life in which there is no longer any mourning, sorrow, tears, or pain, only complete joy and restoration.

Strengthen our hearts, God, to hold fast to the hope of the glory, the anticipation of a better tomorrow that awaits us. Amen.

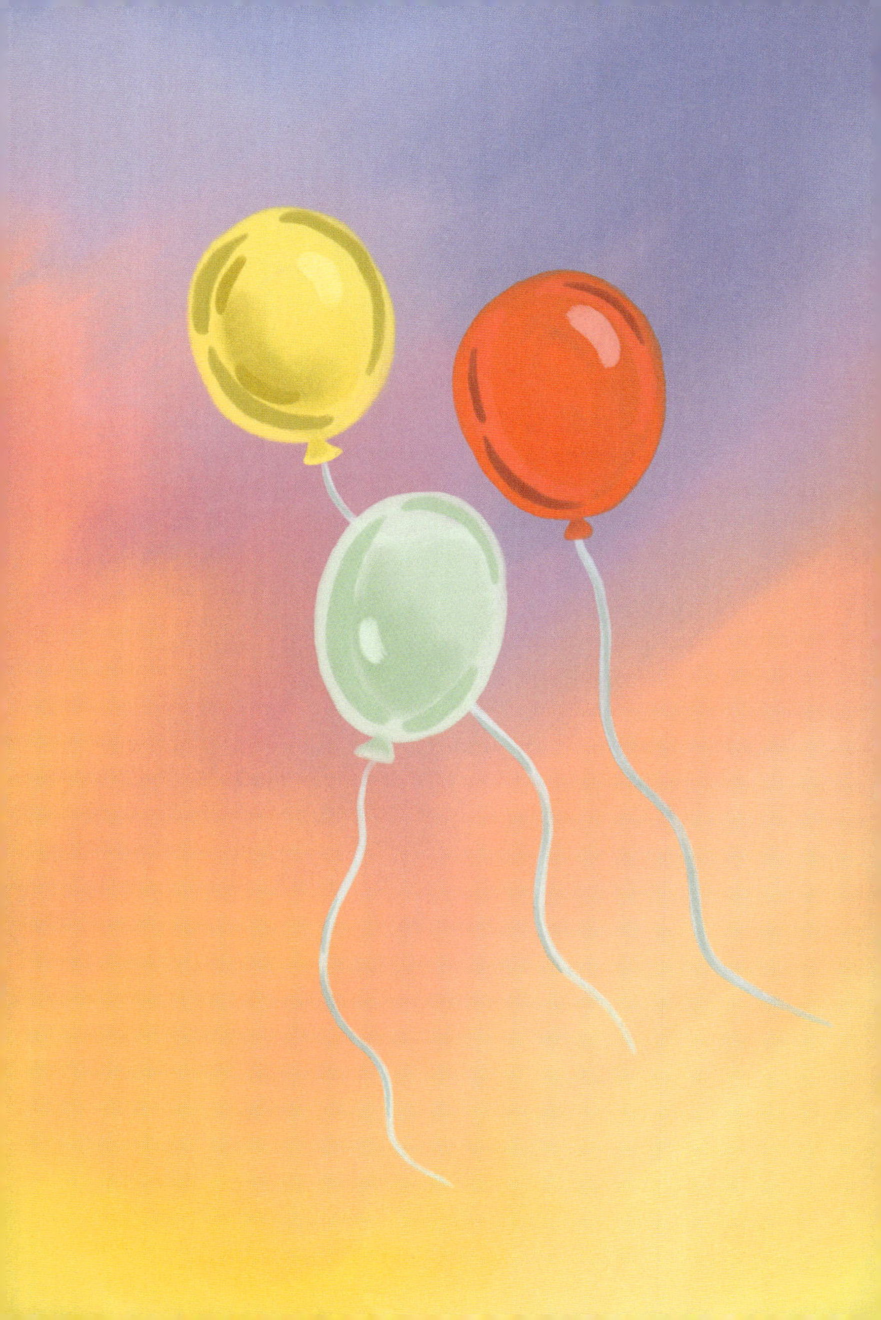

1 John 3:1

DAY
163

"See how very much our Father loves us, for he calls us his children, and that is what we are! But the people who belong to this world don't recognize that we are God's children because they don't know him." (NLT)

Why is it often easier to dissect our flaws, to drown ourselves in a chorus of self-criticism, than to marinate in God's unconditional love? As we replay our mistakes, we are harsh judges of our every misstep. We magnify our imperfections and whisper doubts into our own ears.

Tragically, we can feel more comfortable with the negativity of our inner critic than we are with hearing scripture's repeated profession of God's love. Love that isn't a prize for perfection but rather a freely offered gift sounds suspect to us. Foreign. Undeserved. Too good to be true.

Yet, this is the love God offers—a love that precedes our actions, a love that forgives all our flaws. Our mistakes, failures, and rejections do not have to define us if we allow God's voice of love to be the loudest one we hear. This divine love extended to us on a Cross that punches through the grave invites us to die to all our guilt and shame and instead rise anew out of our true identity as children of God.

Help us, Jesus, to truly believe we are your beloved children and to silence the voices of self-condemnation with the truth of your unfailing love. Amen.

DAY

164 Romans 15:4

"Such things were written in the Scriptures long ago to teach us. And the Scriptures give us hope and encouragement as we wait patiently for God's promises to be fulfilled." (NLT)

In moments of transition, we often find ourselves holding our breath, waiting for clarity or direction. Usually, what we are seeking is security—something to hold onto in the uncertainty. While this may not come right away, God has already given us something steadier: His promises. Those promises offer real hope and encouragement even when the next step isn't fully in view. Scripture assures us, God's promises are not conditional or uncertain—they are steadfast and sure.

God's Word is a guarantee. Scripture teaches us that even in times of waiting, God's promises are already working in us. Jesus doesn't just offer us an end goal, but gives us patience and encouragement along the way. As we trust in these promises, we are filled with hope, knowing that God's perfect plan is unfolding here and now.

Leaning on Jesus during times of transition is not just about the future but about the peace, encouragement, and patience given to us now. Moving forward is not always dependent on clarity. Instead, God offers something far better: peace.

Jesus, remind us daily of your promises. Fill us with your peace and patience as we wait for your plan to unfold. Amen.

Mark 6:34

DAY
165

"Jesus saw the huge crowd as he stepped from the boat, and he had compassion on them because they were like sheep without a shepherd. So he began teaching them many things." (NLT)

The best teachers are those who patiently encourage us, listen carefully, and illuminate what once seemed difficult. Their joy isn't in simply transferring knowledge but in watching us grow, discover, and flourish into the people God made us to be. How much more does Jesus, the gentle Teacher, delight in guiding our hearts toward abundant life?

After Jesus fed the masses, he saw the crowds gathering and had compassion. He saw the people's lack of direction and knew they needed wisdom that only he could provide. He taught out of deep love, gently guiding hearts toward truth.

Jesus knows the places of confusion, question, and doubt in our hearts. Patiently and compassionately, he teaches us—not just doctrines or rules, but about his character and how to live lives marked by grace, wisdom, and love. When we open ourselves to his teaching, we find rest in weariness and purpose in uncertainty. His lessons shape us not only for our own good but also for the healing and blessing of the world around us.

Jesus, help us to learn from you with an open heart, trusting your gentle wisdom to shape our lives. Amen.

DAY

166 Psalm 62:8

"O my people, trust in him at all times. Pour out your heart to him, for God is our refuge." (NLT)

Trust isn't easy to rebuild once it's been broken. Having been hurt once, we feel tempted to close ourselves off, insulating ourselves from further disappointment. However, without working to reestablish trust, we find ourselves isolated or jaded. The difficult reality of life is that people will fail us, our loved ones included. And because God's timing doesn't always align with our expectations, sometimes it can feel like God has failed us and broken our trust. We have a choice: to let go of trust completely or do the challenging work of repair and learn to trust again.

Rebuilding trust requires vulnerability. It requires "pouring your heart out" in the Psalmist's words. Uncomfortable as they can seem, trust and vulnerability have something to offer us. They offer us a chance for mutuality and the opportunity for deeper love. Jesus is trustworthy, and the community of Jesus can reflect that trustworthiness, too.

God, teach us how to trust again. Amen.

Isaiah 33:6

DAY
167

“In that day he will be your sure foundation, providing a rich store of salvation, wisdom, and knowledge. The fear of the Lord will be your treasure.” (NLT)

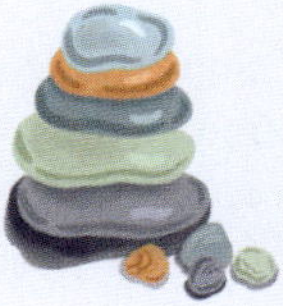

Picture an ancient ruin, thousands of years old. There are solid stone floors and maybe a few walls standing, but the roof is gone. If we were to stumble upon it, it wouldn’t seem significant, but with knowledge of its legacy, it’s a treasure.

The Israelites had forgotten the history of God’s goodness, making ruins of their legacy. As they looked at the disarray before them, they attempted to build something new, established on other powers and gods. They lost the understanding of the treasure in God-centered life.

But hope was not lost. Isaiah prophesied restoration, knowing a Messiah was coming. Jesus sacrificed everything, even to the point of death, to restabilize our relationship with God. In this fulfilled promise, we see the treasure returned.

When we balance our lives on Jesus, we can be assured of stability. Instead of placing trust in walls that will crumble or roofs that cave in, we know that our hope is in the foundation that remains even in the ruins. Like Isaiah, we trust in God who builds us a rich store of salvation, knowledge, and wisdom.

Jesus, we thank you for your sacrifice, which gave us the treasure of salvation. Amen.

DAY 168 Luke 17:3

"So watch yourselves. If your brother or sister sins against you, rebuke them; and if they repent, forgive them." (NIV)

What is forgiveness? Is it a return to the status quo, to how things were before? Can we forge new relationships with people after they've hurt us?

Despite what we may believe, forgiveness is compatible with having boundaries—that is, negotiating a new way to interact with each other. For our relationships to thrive, we need boundaries—clear ideas of what types of behavior we are willing to receive from others—and what behavior we will remove ourselves from. We can forgive those who have hurt us, have compassion for their circumstances and context, and still not give them unconditional access to us.

To have boundaries that are kind, rather than punitive, we need to communicate. If someone has hurt us, we need to tell them directly. We can't expect an apology without identifying the harm. And then we should forgive, just as God forgives us. From there, we can decide on the healthiest way forward: a restored relationship, or a new one that looks a bit different.

Jesus, please give us a compassionate heart to navigate challenging relationships with grace, and please give us the discernment to know when a change in boundaries is needed. Amen.

Psalm 139:16

DAY 169

“You saw me before I was born. Every day of my life was recorded in your book. Every moment was laid out before a single day had passed.” (NLT)

Psalm 139:16 presents a powerful declaration of God’s sovereign knowledge and control over our lives. God saw us even before we were born. More than passive awareness, God actively knew us before our existence, before our first breath. Our lives are not an afterthought; they were carefully planned before any of them came to pass.

We must be careful not to judge our story before God reveals His hand. If we are in Christ, the script is sure. What our eyes cannot see, what our ears cannot hear, and what our hearts cannot imagine now, our God is preparing for us. Even in seasons when we feel lost, confused, or directionless, this truth remains: God has written our story, and every page is under divine guidance.

This truth should shift how we walk through life. No moment is wasted, and no season is without purpose. God’s hand is on us from the very beginning, and God remains present throughout, sovereign over every moment.

Father, we trust in your perfect plan for our lives. Thank you for holding our story in your hands. Amen.

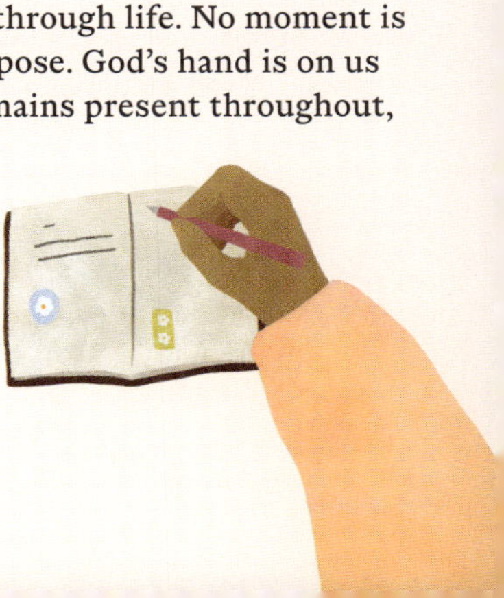

DAY

170 Hebrews 11:1

"Faith shows the reality of what we hope for; it is the evidence of things we cannot see." (NLT)

Faith magnifies the reality of hope. It channels the vast brilliance of God into a singular point and ignites hope into a flame. Through faith, we stand in wonder at a process we cannot see apart from the evidence of the flame.

In the in-between moments of our lives, between the grand joys and the painful sorrows, faith can feel abstract. It's much easier to point to the flames of faith in our triumphs. But when things feel quiet and ordinary, what does faith look like then?

Our faith magnifies God's story in our lives and the Spirit within us. When we place our faith in Jesus, we can rest even when we cannot see because we know God is at work. Should we ever doubt, we have a Bible filled with incredible stories of faith, as Hebrews 11 reminds us. When we struggle to see flames of faith in our own lives, we can look to the fires of hope that have continually burned through the work of God's light.

Faithful God, encourage us with the hope of the unseen that we may strengthen our faith in you even in the in-between. Amen.

Psalm 145:1-2

DAY
171

"I will exalt you, my God the King, and praise your name forever and ever. Every day I will praise you and extol your name forever and ever." (NLT)

What would it look like to live a life characterized by endlessly praising God? A life where every single moment, every breath, is consumed by the worship of the One who holds the universe in balance? Psalm 145:1-2 calls us into this kind of existence—a life where we are living in perpetual adoration of God.

The psalmist declares a forever praise—a commitment to honor and exalt God forever and ever. It's a heart posture for every day, a longing to continually bless God's name. Praise is not just an event—it's a way of life. It's waking up with gratitude, moving through our days with awe, and falling asleep in worship.

What would it look like for us to embrace this lifestyle? What if every day, no matter the circumstances, we chose to praise Jesus' name, to continually remind ourselves of his goodness and greatness? When we choose to live in constant praise, we align ourselves with God's will and invite the divine presence to saturate every corner of our lives.

Gracious God, stir in us a heart of endless praise. May our every moment be a reflection of your glory and goodness. Amen.

DAY 172 John 13:34–35

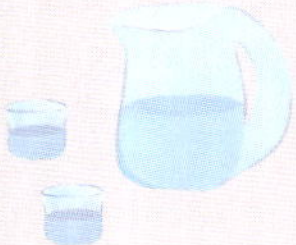

"So now I am giving you a new commandment: Love each other. Just as I have loved you, you should love each other. Your love for one another will prove to the world that you are my disciples." (NLT)

Just before his death, Jesus instructed his followers on how they should live in his absence. In short, they should love one another.

As God's beloved ones, we are not only invited to receive the boundless love of Jesus but also to walk in it ourselves. We strive to imitate Jesus' ways of empathizing with all, tearing down barriers that keep people apart, and making a way for reconciliation and life-giving community across diversity.

Loving one another is not easy, but it is God's holy invitation to us. It is the body and blood of Christ, the communion we share. It brings joy and color into our worlds, making our lives meaningful.

As God's people, we are not to be known by who or what we oppose, condemn, call sinful, or hate. We are not to be known by who or what we are not. We are to be known by how we love.

God, may we be part of faith communities marked by your committed, sincere, wholehearted, borderless love. May we find that our relationships, neighborhoods, and cities thrive as we do so. Amen.

Colossians 3:12

DAY 173

"Since God chose you to be the holy people he loves, you must clothe yourselves with tenderhearted mercy, kindness, humility, gentleness, and patience" (NLT)

In a dog-eat-dog world that seems to reward aggression and sharp edges, gentleness can seem like an ill-advised attribute. At best, we might deem it a quiet background note in a symphony of otherwise stronger traits. Yet, overlooking the untapped potential of this expression of Christ's character, made available to us through the Holy Spirit, is detrimental.

A gentle touch can soothe a troubled heart. A gentle word in the face of provocation can diffuse rising tension. Before ever-growing chaos, a gentle spirit can create a safe space for vulnerability and solidarity. Bearing the ability to disarm anger, build bridges where walls exist, and nurture growth where harshness withers, gentleness isn't passivity. It's an expression of the grace of Christ. It's choosing to respond with quiet strength rather than loud force, with understanding rather than reaction, to foster connection rather than to draw lines of separation.

Let us celebrate and adopt a posture of gentleness, not as a sign of frailty but as the seedbed of peace, a balm for wounded spirits, and a reflection of the transformative love of Jesus.

Clothe us with your gentleness, God, that we may reflect your tender love in all we do. Amen.

DAY
174 Romans 8:31

"What shall we say about such wonderful things as these? If God is for us, who can ever be against us?" (NLT)

The great lie—whispered first in Eden and rehearsed often in our minds today—is that God is against us. We are prone to interpret our trials as symptoms of God's indifference, condemnation, or wrath. That leads us to find shelter in false defenses, like self-preservation and isolation. The scripture confronts this lie with remarkable clarity: *God is for us.*

This statement of fact has weighty implications. If the Creator of all things—who holds all space, time, and matter—is on our side, who or what can we possibly fear? What obstacle poses any threat? With God, there is no form of failure, mistreatment, or suffering that can overcome us. Every inch of darkness is eclipsed by divine light.

To know that God is with us is to live with courage and hope amidst uncertainty. We will no doubt endure suffering on this side of Heaven, but it is by acknowledging God's solidarity with us that we can move through life at peace. Jesus is for us—singing over us, walking alongside us, and moving on our behalf. He is for us.

Lord, help us to live each day in the confidence that you are for us. Amen.

DAY

James 1:2–4

175

"Consider it pure joy, my brothers and sisters, whenever you face trials of many kinds, because you know that the testing of your faith produces perseverance. Let perseverance finish its work so that you may be mature and complete, not lacking anything." (NIV)

To meet suffering or disappointment with joy seems paradoxical and impossible. James is not calling us to escape, downplay, or sanitize our suffering, but to consciously adopt a gaze that looks beyond present pain to what God might be doing in us. This is, definitionally, *perseverance*.

In one form or another, sages throughout history have concluded "the obstacle is the way." Christians have been a people that have suffered and persevered. It is our birthright and witness to be people of joy amidst suffering.

Trials represent opportunities. Every disappointment, challenge, and unanswered prayer stretches our faith, chiseling away at our self-reliance to reveal the likeness of Christ. Perseverance is not just about enduring for the sake of enduring; it is about *becoming*. It is the way by which God teaches us dependence and offers us peace beyond our circumstances. Through the refining fire of trials, we are made whole.

Lord, help us to trust you in every trial, knowing that you are shaping us into who we are meant to be. Amen.

DAY 176 Psalm 37:23–24

"The Lord directs the steps of the godly. He delights in every detail of their lives. Though they stumble, they will never fall, for the Lord holds them by the hand." (NLT)

We so desperately desire security in a life that presents us with constant uncertainty. What do we do when the future feels fragile? When plans change and expectations are dashed, we may be tempted to grip our hands tight and protect ourselves from further disappointment.

But in Psalm 37, we are reminded that it is God's care that secures our steps, not our control. The Lord directs us with delight, even if the destination feels distant to us. Every detail of our lives matters to our Creator. Even when we stumble, we are not left to falter. We are upheld by a steady, unseen hand.

Trusting God with our future means learning to release what we cannot know and rest in what we do: that we are never alone, never out of sight. This trust does not erase uncertainty, but it transforms how we walk through it. We move forward not because the path is easy, but because the One who guides us is faithful.

May this truth meet us in our doubts and provide confidence in Jesus' care over our lives. Amen.

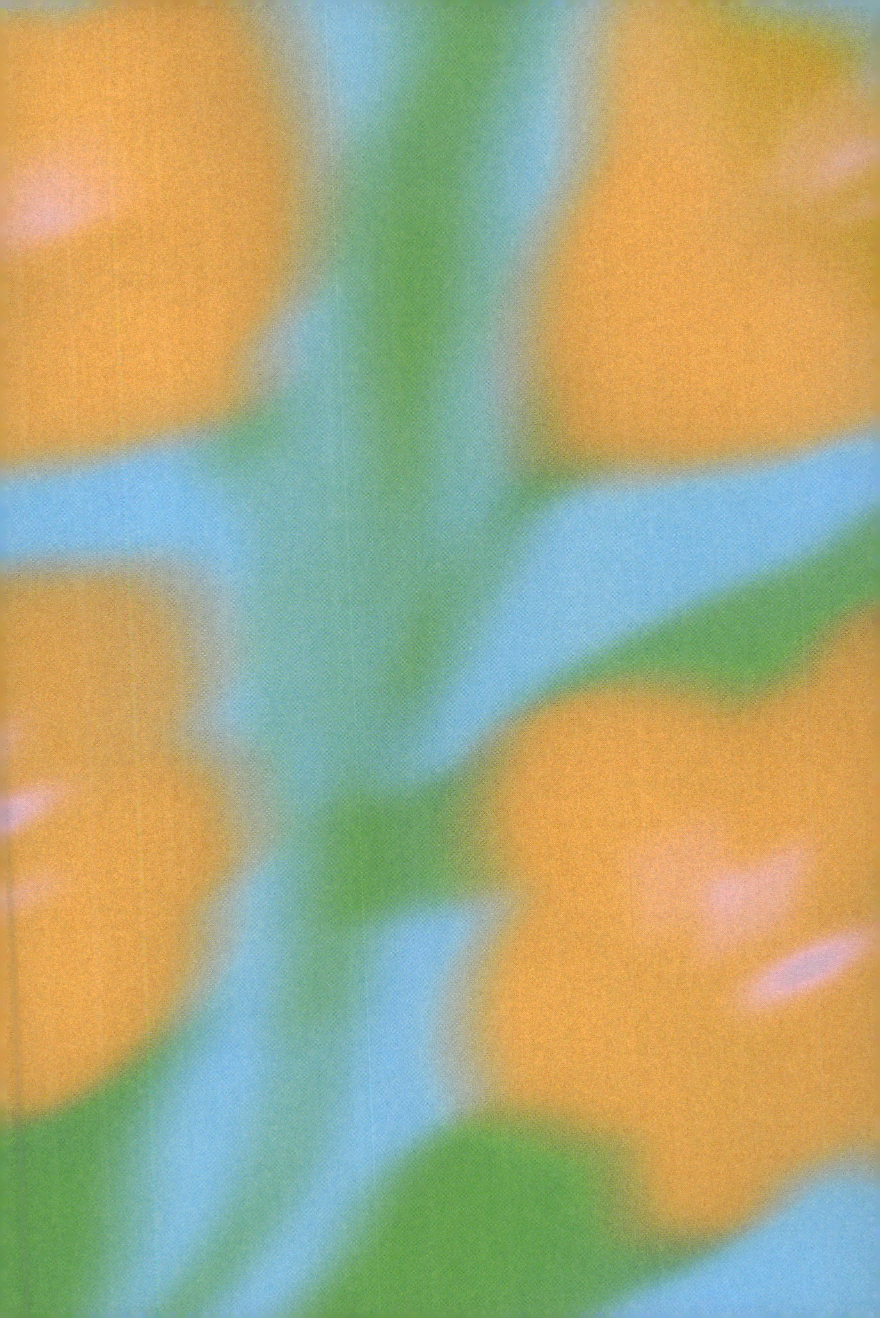

DAY

177 Romans 8:1–2

"So now there is no condemnation for those who belong to Christ Jesus. And because you belong to him, the power of the life-giving Spirit has freed you from the power of sin that leads to death." (NLT)

Shame holds us in secretive captivity. It convinces us that our worth is conditional and that our past is too heavy to carry into the presence of God. As it takes its hold, freedom can feel like a far-off promise, reserved for someone more disciplined—someone more deserving.

But scripture breaks through this illusion. In Christ, we are not held by condemnation; we are held by grace. Belonging to him does not begin with perfection. It begins with release. Romans 8 declares that we are freed by a Spirit that gives life. Not momentary relief, but true liberation from shame, fear, and the patterns that once defined us.

Freedom in Christ is not about striving harder. It is about resting deeper in the truth that we are already loved, already known, already rescued.

May we live from this place. May our freedom be more than a concept; it is a way of being, grounded in grace. Amen.

John 8:12

DAY

178

“Jesus spoke to the people once more and said, ‘I am the light of the world. If you follow me, you won’t have to walk in darkness, because you will have the light that leads to life.’” (NLT)

What does Jesus mean when he says he’s the Light of the World? Light banishes the darkness. It offers security and confidence by illuminating what’s around us. It offers a glimpse at the road ahead. Light brings life.

Jesus came into a chaotic world, teaching about the heart and ways of God. He exposed corruption among the religious and political leaders. He drew near to people with dark outlooks on their lives. He gave sight to the blind. He brought life to the people around him.

The invitation of Jesus is to walk with him throughout our lives. When we feel weary or unsure, we need not fear. He will show us the path ahead of us. He will expose and cast out the darkness in and around us. He offers security. Jesus brings more and more life.

This is what it means for Jesus to be the Light of the world.

God, thank you for Jesus and the light he provides to the world. Help us to walk with Jesus, so we won’t have to walk in darkness again. Amen.

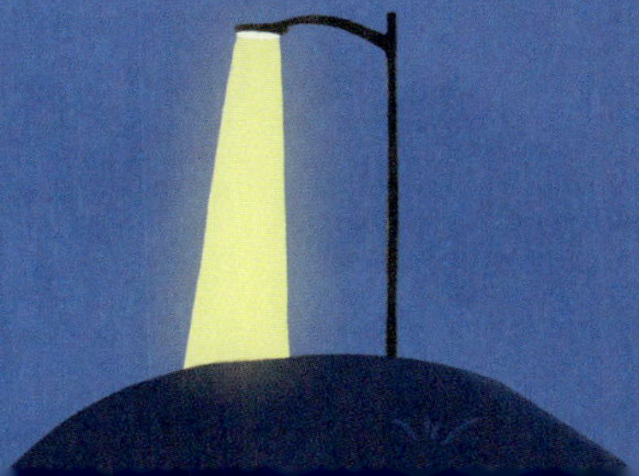

DAY 179 Matthew 6:25–27

"Therefore I tell you, do not worry about your life, what you will eat or drink; or about your body, what you will wear. ... Look at the birds of the air; they do not sow or reap or store away in barns, and yet your heavenly Father feeds them. Are you not much more valuable than they? Can any one of you by worrying add a single hour to your life?" (NIV)

Whether by biological wiring or social reinforcement, worry is the hallmark of our lives. We are urged to plan, prepare, and control every outcome, rehearsing contingency plans for when our expectations are unmet. Jesus' way is different. He invites us—the stewards of the earth with unmatched intelligence—to imitate nothing less than birds—those odd, colorful things always fluttering above us, hardly noticeable.

Without savings accounts or any certainty about the day ahead of them, birds simply go about their lives foraging, eating, building nests, flocking together, and singing. They wake each morning not in fear but in freedom, sustained by a God who never forgets them.

To Jesus, bird-watching can be a spiritual discipline. If God cares for the smallest sparrow, how much more does our Creator care for you? If God is so meticulous, thorough, intentional, and gracious to clothe the flowers and feed the birds, we can trust for the same with our own lives.

Lord, teach us to release our worries and rest in your faithful provision. Amen.

Psalm 91:4

DAY
180

"He will cover you with his feathers, and under his wings you will find refuge; his faithfulness will be your shield and rampart." (NIV)

There is a rich, impenetrable safety in God's presence. Like a mother bird covering her young, God spreads His wings over us, shielding us from harm, surrounding us with perfect faithfulness. In a world that often feels unpredictable and unsafe, we can hold this image as a picture of reassurance—God is not distant or watching from afar. Our Father is covering us, protecting us, holding us close.

Amidst the inevitable disappointments, uncertainties, and sufferings of life, it's tempting to believe we are alone. That we must fend for ourselves. But God invites us to take refuge not in our own capacities and control, but in His. Divine faithfulness is not fragile. It is not like human promises, prone to failure or change. It is a shield, a fortress, a covering that will not break.

When the burdens of life weigh heavily on us, we remember where we dwell—not in fear, but under the shadow of the Almighty. What would it look like to trust God's covering today, to rest in the shelter of divine love? We are not abandoned. We are hidden beneath God's wings.

Lord Jesus, help us to trust in your protection and rest in the shelter of your unfailing love. Amen.

DAY

181 1 Timothy 6:6–8

"Yet true godliness with contentment is itself great wealth. After all, we brought nothing with us when we came into the world, and we can't take anything with us when we leave it. So if we have enough food and clothing, let us be content." (NLT)

How much more just and peaceful would our world be if powerful nations were content with what they had and did not invade others' lands, extract their resources, and oppress their people? How much healthier and more joyful would our own lives be if we practiced contentment rather than acquisitiveness?

Our world holds enough food, water, and other resources to meet everyone's needs, but greed keeps some struggling to make ends meet while others hoard unnecessary excess. Contentment is the antidote. We brought nothing into this world, and we will take nothing out of it. Accumulating material possessions is meaningless. Instead, God invites us to invest in love, to build communities where everyone's needs are met. In this, we find lasting joy.

In Jesus' eyes, simple lives are beautiful ones. We can resist the urge to keep acquiring more; if we have food and clothing, and if we live in interconnected relationships where we care for one another and are cared for in turn, we have everything we need.

God, may contentment take root deeply in our lives and communities. May it spread outward to make peace in our world. Amen.

Galatians 5:6

DAY 182

“For when we place our faith in Christ Jesus, there is no benefit in being circumcised or being uncircumcised. What is important is faith expressing itself in love.” (NLT)

Faith is not a mere moment of belief or a ritual completed. It is a living, breathing expression of what we believe and who we follow. The apostle Paul reminds us that outward signs of piety and devotion are not the end-all be-all—what matters is faith expressing itself in love.

True faith is not a one-time decision, but a continual way of being. While sacraments and spiritual practices have deep significance, they are not what saves us. Our faith is revealed through the way we live, in the grace we extend, and the love we pour out.

Faith is not a static mark upon us, like a tattoo, but a cloak we choose to wear each day—clothing ourselves in kindness, patience, and mercy. Each act of love, no matter how small, is a participation in God’s ongoing work of restoration.

When we live out our faith, we make the world a little more like the Kingdom of God. Every interaction becomes an opportunity to reflect goodness, to bring healing, and to extend the same love we have received.

Holy Spirit, move us to extend our faith beyond mere belief, embodying divine love in action. Amen.

DAY

183 Galatians 5:13

"For you have been called to live in freedom, my brothers and sisters. But do not use your freedom to satisfy your sinful nature. Instead, use your freedom to serve one another in love." (NLT)

Freedom, as God gives it, is expansive and dignifying. It releases us from what once held us and gently redirects us toward one another.

"For you have been called to live in freedom," Paul writes. But not the kind of freedom that isolates or hoards. Not freedom that demands space without offering presence.

Instead, freedom finds its truest expression in love.

To serve one another in love is not to diminish ourselves; it is to embody the heart of Christ. A love that reaches for others. A love that holds dignity in its hands. A love that does not grasp for power but makes room at the table.

This is the paradox of the Kingdom: the freest among us are those who serve not from obligation, but from overflow. They are not coerced into compassion but compelled by grace.

So we ask: What would it look like to use our freedom to build, bless, and uplift? What kind of world might unfold if we believed that love and service were not in conflict but in rhythm?

God, we know that true freedom doesn't end with us, it moves through us. Let it move through you today. Amen.

Ecclesiastes 3:1,4–5

DAY 184

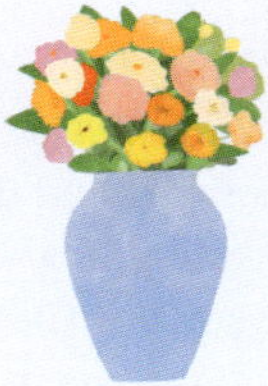

"For everything there is a season, a time for every activity under heaven. A time to cry and a time to laugh. A time to grieve and a time to dance. A time to scatter stones and a time to gather stones. A time to embrace and a time to turn away." (NLT)

Rainy days give way to sunny days. Leaves fall from the trees. Animals go into hibernation. Spring comes again.

All throughout the natural world, there are seasons and rhythms to life. We've learned to embrace these changes, marking them with holidays and festivals, with seasonal clothing, and food. There's a deep acceptance of the beginnings and endings of these seasons, and all that comes with them. So too do we experience seasons in our lives.

Happy days give way to sad days. Work demands more attention. Family has more needs to be met. We exchange staying at home for going out into the world and exploring.

Human beings are complex. We have more than one path to walk down. Not everything will happen at once. We must have patience and move towards acceptance of the season of life we're in. Though we may be tempted to prioritize one season over another, the invitation God displays to us in nature is that each has its purpose and belongs at its right time.

Christ Jesus, teach us to accept the season we're in. May we flourish in the fullness of the rhythm of life. Amen.

DAY

185 Luke 21:1-4

"While Jesus was in the Temple, he watched the rich people dropping their gifts in the collection box. Then a poor widow came by and dropped in two small coins. 'I tell you the truth,' Jesus said, 'this poor widow has given more than all the rest of them. For they have given a tiny part of their surplus, but she, poor as she is, has given everything she has.'" (NLT)

There is something musical about the sound of coins clinking together. Even though much of our currency is virtual, a handful of coins still makes a child feel rich.

In an era when coins were the primary currency, what one had could be measured by the sound it made. In Luke 21:1-4, Jesus was preaching at the Temple to the sounds of offerings ebbing and flowing when a widow's two coins caught his attention. Her giving wasn't a cacophony of coins, but quiet and humble. She gave her best because she had hope in the words Jesus preached.

At times, we may feel like the sound of our offerings isn't loud enough to please God. Our meager best may be all that we have to survive on, but God still values our giving. The widow's best was all she had. Yet, Jesus multiplied its sound not by adding more coins but through the sound of his voice ringing truth and praise over her efforts. And like the widow, we can humbly give everything over knowing that it will be used in the house of God.

Jesus, take our best and use it for your good. Amen.

1 John 3:17–18

DAY
186

“If anyone has material possessions and sees a brother or sister in need but has no pity on them, how can the love of God be in that person? Dear children, let us not love with words or speech but with actions and in truth.” (NIV)

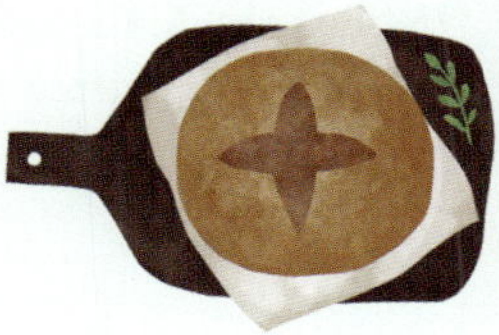

Love is more than a feeling: it’s an action. If we say we love someone but don’t take steps to care for them, do we truly love them?

Jesus didn’t just love us in theory, but in practice. When we know Christ, we’re compelled to emulate his generosity, to share what we have. We can share in many ways: by donating to charity, preparing a meal for new parents, volunteering at a food bank, visiting lonely residents at a nursing home, or sitting with someone as they mourn a loved one.

In this way, the love we live out in action intertwines with the love displayed through words: prayer. Praying for someone is a beautiful form of intercession, but we should also remember: it could very well be that we are the instruments of help God is using. What steps can we take to tangibly help the same people we pray for?

God, thank you for the blessings you’ve given us, large and small. Open our eyes to the ways we can share our abundance. Amen.

DAY

187 Psalm 4:8

"In peace I will lie down and sleep, for you alone, O Lord, will keep me safe." (NLT)

True rest requires more than the absence of noise or exhaustion—it comes from deep, unshakable trust in God. The unrest of our lives and minds can run us ragged, eroding our ability to be at ease and sleep. We may find ourselves awake at night, gripped with worry—replaying today's conversations, bracing for tomorrow's stress, and altogether unable to be still. David's song in Psalm 4 beckons us to surrender.

Peace is not something we accidentally stumble upon. It is something we receive when we entrust ourselves to the One who never sleeps, who is our source of safety and refuge. Peace does not derive from perfect circumstances but from the presence of God.

Tonight, as we lay our heads down, may we release our fears to God. Let Jesus' presence be our shelter; Jesus' love, our security; his faithfulness, our rest.

Lord, quiet our hearts and help us trust in your perfect peace, for you alone are our refuge. Amen.

Colossians 2:7

DAY 188

"Let your roots grow down into him, and let your lives be built on him. Then your faith will grow strong in the truth you were taught, and you will overflow with thankfulness." (NLT)

The Book of Colossians is a letter written to a church wrestling with doubt. In a new and rapidly growing faith community, rooting their hope and trust in the right places was critical. Paul encourages them to root themselves in Jesus no matter the circumstances and to build their faith so that truth a nd thanksgiving will flourish.

Whatever the circumstances in which doubt arises, we too can find encouragement in Paul's words. When we walk with Jesus, doubts will come creeping in, especially where roots are shallow. Paul doesn't dismiss doubt but encourages believers to lean into what we have been taught.

Fellow believers encourage us in our lives with Jesus. Many have traveled the same bumpy soil. Like a forest, their outstretched roots can be the guide for growing towards the deeper waters of faith and truth. And, it is those same believers who celebrate with us in thanksgiving as we navigate doubts.

As we journey with you, Jesus, we thank you for listening to our doubts and providing spiritual mentors to remind us of your truth. Amen.

DAY 189 Proverbs 15:31–32

"If you listen to constructive criticism, you will be at home among the wise. If you reject discipline, you only harm yourself; but if you listen to correction, you grow in understanding." (NLT)

Humans are naturally hardwired to learn. We start from our earliest moments, exploring the world around us and constantly discovering something new. But earthly knowledge has a different ambition than heavenly knowledge. We are trained to strive for high performance and secure reputations, but in the spiritual world, learning works differently.

Pride tells us we don't need the feedback of others. We may start to attribute success only to self, without recognizing the divine help we received along the way to get us where we are. When we shut ourselves out from receiving formative counsel, we miss out on growth that has the power to transform our lives. Instead, when we heed Spirit-led instruction from others, we invite new understanding to shape us.

We are always learning. If we open ourselves up to guidance with a heart willing to grow, we find a place among the wise who mean to bless us with a teachable spirit.

Dear Lord, give us humble spirits that are willing to learn from you and the people you want us to encounter. Amen.

John 10:14–15

DAY
190

"I am the good shepherd. I know my own, and my own know me, just as the Father knows me, and I know the Father. And I lay down my life for the sheep." (NLT)

As shepherds nurture and guide their sheep, so Jesus gathers, nourishes, and cares for us. And like a good shepherd who will not let even one sheep remain separate from the rest, Jesus seeks and finds us, restoring our relationships and providing belonging.

This is an image of community: the flock thrives together, and as shepherds in the plural but the design copy is singlular makes sure of that. It is also an image of intimacy. Just as a shepherd knows each of their sheep and each sheep knows its shepherds voice, so God invites us to know and be known by God.

Perhaps the endless hustle of grind culture would have no appeal for us if we knew we were taken care of by a shepherd willing to lay down his life for us. Perhaps our need to accumulate possessions and succeed by whatever standards human-made systems have set before us loses its taste in our mouths when we live in this kind of close, loving relationship with our Good Shepherd, Jesus.

God, lead us into green pastures and beside still waters. Restore our souls, our energy, our inner knowing, our community. Thank you for knowing and loving us, for walking with us so closely. Amen.

DAY

191 Matthew 5:43–44

"You have heard that it was said, 'You shall love your neighbor and hate your enemy.' But I say to you: Love your enemies and pray for those who persecute you."(NLT)

Jesus issues us a challenging invitation: Love everyone. Even our enemies. Even the people we have been raised to despise, the ones our people look down on.

Depending on our environment and upbringing, this might include people of a particular race, ethnicity, or gender; it might be immigrants or refugees, single parents, unhoused people, or drug users. We often find ourselves rushing to make judgments. But God calls us instead to simply love and pray.

As we learn to love the people we assumed to be our enemies, we gain compassion for all sorts of people and even for the difficult parts of our own pasts and personalities. We begin to see others through God's eyes, recognizing their value and individuality. We release all judgment to God, and we rest in love.

God, help us seek our neighbors' well-being as much as our own, even and especially the neighbors we have been taught to dislike or distrust. Help us see them as fellow imperfect humans doing their best in a difficult world. Help us offer kindness where we can and leave the judgment to you. Amen.

Psalm 32:8

DAY
192

"The Lord says, 'I will guide you along the best pathway for your life. I will advise you and watch over you.'" (NLT)

Each day, we face countless choices—some mundane, others significant. Every choice opens up a new set of options, with even more choices. Often, we desire to know the outcome of each path before we choose it—frantically seeking advice from friends or so-called experts, thinking that if we do enough research and planning, our lives will unfold seamlessly. Yet God, who sees beyond what we can perceive, offers something even better: to be our guide and companion along the way.

God offers us insight grounded in limitless perspective. God sees around the corners we cannot and knows the paths our feet have not yet trod.

God's wisdom is always available, ready to illuminate our next turn whenever we pause to ask. Though we rarely receive a detailed map of the whole journey in advance, we have the gift of a compass in the form of God's loving presence and unwavering trustworthiness to give us direction and point the way forward.

As we walk with Jesus, we find peace, not by knowing every detail of our path, but by knowing the One who guides us.

Christ the Lord, grant us the faith to trust your guidance, knowing your wisdom goes beyond our limited perspective. Amen.

DAY

193 Deuteronomy 16:15

"For seven days celebrate the festival to the Lord your God at the place the Lord will choose. For the Lord your God will bless you in all your harvest and in all the work of your hands, and your joy will be complete." (NIV)

God calls us to celebration as a spiritual discipline. Though we don't often think of it on par with prayer, fasting, or scripture, celebration is an essential component of our life with God. Here, Israel is commanded to set aside a full week to rejoice in God, the blessings of harvest, and their own labor. Their joy was not meant to be stifled or quietly enjoyed but communally elevated.

Counterintuitively, celebration can be a challenge. We are prone to rush beyond our blessings, hurtling between tasks and days without ever pausing to *rejoice*. We pray fervently for God to provide, but when provision comes, we hardly acknowledge it. God desires for our joy to be full, not just fleeting. We cannot bear the spiritual fruit of joy without being people who *rejoice*.

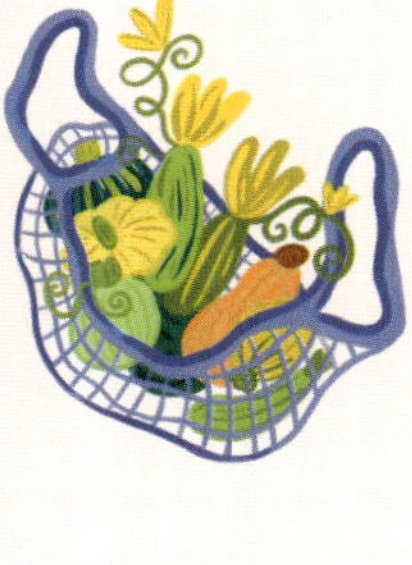

Let us take time to celebrate—not only the big triumphs but the quiet mercies. May we rejoice in what Jesus has done, and in doing so, find our joy made complete.

Lord, open our eyes to see your blessings and teach us to celebrate your goodness with a heart full of joy. Amen.

Philippians 1:9–10

DAY 194

"And this is my prayer, that your love may overflow more and more with knowledge and full insight to help you to determine what really matters, so that in the day of Christ you may be pure and blameless." (NIV)

There is no shortage of noise in our world. Many people want to claim authority over our lives, telling us how to spend our time, what choices to make, or how to manage our finances. But when we walk with Jesus, God invites us to discern for ourselves the answers to the most crucial questions of our lives. And God invites us to do this alongside fellow ordinary people who are also seeking good ways of living.

What really matters? What makes our lives pure and blameless? God provides wisdom as we seek to live faithfully. We gain clarity through studying scripture, praying, and engaging in honest conversations among communities marked by mutual care. We do not need other people to tell us what to do, but to come alongside us in a posture of love, openness, listening, and wisdom, as we seek to do the same for them. Jesus invites us to seek insight and to walk on the road of love— love that grows deeper and wider. A love that overflows toward all people.

God, please sharpen our discernment to know what is most important in this life and help us to pursue these things wholeheartedly, guided always by your love. Amen.

DAY 195 1 Samuel 17:45

"David said to the Philistine, 'You come against me with sword and spear and javelin, but I come against you in the name of the Lord Almighty, the God of the armies of Israel, whom you have defied.'" (NIV)

Life is full of intimidating challenges. They can seem pretty insurmountable. Our fear might say, "Why strive for a different outcome? I already know I won't succeed."

But just because loss seems inevitable doesn't mean it is. Our obstacles or enemies may feel larger than life, overwhelming in power, but we have more support, tools, and resources than we realize. We are not alone. We are not helpless.

Jesus is with us in our hardest, scariest moments. His closeness encourages us in the face of hardship. We can look for the resources he has given us through the Holy Spirit to succeed and endure. We can take comfort in the community that he has blessed us with, the friends who surround and support us.

At the end of the day, the darkest circumstances cannot rob us of God's love. We have the greatest of allies on our side.

Almighty God, thank you for the many ways you fight for us and alongside us. Give us the wisdom to see your sovereignty in the midst of overwhelming odds and the peace of being comforted by it. Amen.

John 7:37–38

DAY

196

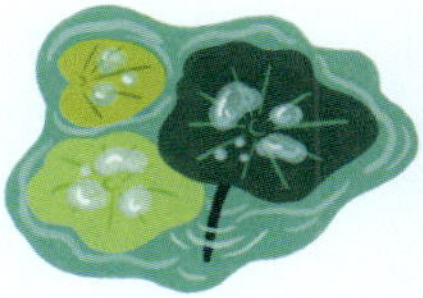

"On the last day, the climax of the festival, Jesus stood and shouted to the crowds, 'Anyone who is thirsty may come to me! Anyone who believes in me may come and drink! For the Scriptures declare, Rivers of living water will flow from his heart.'" (NLT)

Most of us go through times when our spirit feels empty or dry. Even then, Jesus is still with us. He is still crying out, "Let anyone who is thirsty come to me."

Jesus does not judge, condemn, or blame people who are spiritually thirsty—those who know that their spirits need some kind of encouragement or sustenance. His invitation is simple: "Come to me. You are welcome here."

Jesus reminds us that life is about more than the daily routines of work, childcare, cooking, eating, cleaning, sleeping, and doing it all again. We are holistic creations—body, mind, and spirit—who need nourishment for the whole of who we are. And Jesus offers this comprehensive nourishment.

Jesus fills our cups. This invitation is for everyone; no one is too empty or too parched. Rather, the thirstier we are, the more gratitude rises up in our hearts as we receive living water.

God, may we feel our thirst and come to you for spiritual drink. May we feel our hunger and come to you for spiritual food. Thank you for receiving us without judgment. Amen.

DAY

197 Matthew 10:42

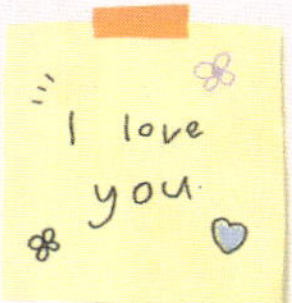

"And if you give even a cup of cold water to one of the least of my followers, you will surely be rewarded." (NLT)

Throughout Matthew 10, Jesus paints a sweeping, intense picture of ministry for his disciples, but he ends by drawing their attention to a rather small, ordinary act: the giving of a cup of water. He reminds us that no act of kindness is ever wasted when done in love and in his name.

Our world valorizes and encourages us towards that which is grand, notable, and idealized. Naturally, we internalize the assumption that the significance of our actions is tied to size or scale, even acts of service or love. But the way of Jesus does not follow this logic. In the Kingdom of God, it is the unseen kindness, the quiet generosity, the thankless expression of servanthood that is rewarded. It is simple, ordinary faithfulness that serves the greatest purpose.

Jesus invites us to live attentively—to notice those who thirst physically, emotionally, and spiritually, and to offer whatever gift of presence, encouragement, or compassion we can. Nothing done in love is ever forgotten.

Lord, help us to see the sacred in the simple and to serve others with quiet faithfulness. Amen.

Psalm 63:6–7

DAY 198

"I lie awake thinking of you, meditating on you through the night. Because you are my helper, I sing for joy in the shadow of your wings." (NLT)

In recent years, there has been a lot of emphasis on gratitude in self-help and personal development circles. Studies have shown a link between the regular practice of gratitude and increased longevity and happiness. The value of gratitude is also supported scripturally, with countless petitions urging us to give thanks. But how do we tangibly practice gratitude?

One popular practice is spending five minutes making a list of things we're grateful for before going to sleep. We can write this list down before bed or, like the author of Psalm 63, lie in bed and meditate on the things we're grateful for. This prayerful gratitude offers us a chance to share our thankfulness with God and consider all God has done for us. Over time, gratitude will become a more natural rhythm.

Adopting a gratitude practice can shape the way we look at the world, reminding us of the abundance God has for us. It helps transform our perspective, renewing our minds into the person God has created us to be.

Jesus, remind us of all the good things we have to be grateful for. In the stillness of night, may we experience peace, remembering all of the things you've done for us. Amen.

DAY

199 Matthew 6:19–21

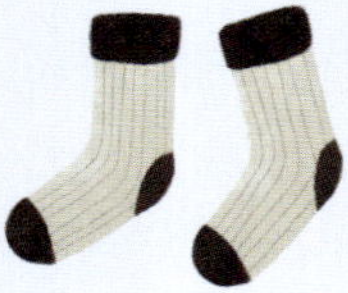

“Don’t store up treasures here on earth, where moths eat them and rust destroys them, and where thieves break in and steal. Store your treasures in heaven ... Wherever your treasure is, there the desires of your heart will also be.” (NLT)

The notion of simple living can feel unappealing. It draws to mind images of asceticism or, perhaps, a trite consolation for those without ample resources. But simplicity is not about lack—it is about clarity. When we focus our hearts on what matters most, we find a freedom that cannot be taken away.

Think of a cluttered house—disorganized, chaotic, overwhelming. At a certain point, too much stuff is a detriment. So many things mean nothing is properly cared for. Things fall into disarray or lie forgotten. The same is true in our lives. When we are pulled in too many directions, when we chase after every opportunity, we risk engaging in nothing fully. We become spread thin, distracted, unable to give our best to what is most important.

Simplicity is the art of treasuring what we have. When we clear away what is unnecessary—both in our physical spaces and in the demands we place upon ourselves—we make room for what is most valuable. We see the gifts before us with fresh eyes. We learn to cherish rather than accumulate.

Jesus, turn our hearts toward the greatest treasure we have: you. Amen.

Proverbs 2:2–5

DAY
200

"Tune your ears to wisdom, and concentrate on understanding. Cry out for insight, and ask for understanding. Search for them as you would for silver, seek them like hidden treasures. Then you will understand what it means to fear the Lord, and you will gain knowledge of God." (NLT)

Seeking wisdom can feel like tuning an old radio to the right station. On first searching, all we can hear is static as we slowly turn the dial until the sound becomes fuzzy and then clear. When we intentionally search for wisdom, it begins to sound clearer amongst the static of daily life. It shimmers amongst conversations, music, and media like the hidden treasure described in Proverbs.

To live wisely isn't to just collect wisdom. Once we have tuned into the wisdom station, we must concentrate as we cry out for understanding and insight. Hearing is different from understanding; living a wise life requires us to internalize the insights and teachings we receive.

At times, even the disciples struggled to fully comprehend what Jesus was saying. Their response was to ask Jesus questions. We also must ask questions of God and the people around us who possess the treasure of wisdom so that we can share in God's knowledge. To live wisely means continually tuning our ears to wisdom and seeking understanding.

Wise God, as we hear so many words, we cry out to you that we would be able to recognize the wisdom and understand it. Amen.

DAY 201 Psalm 18:2

"The Lord is my rock, my fortress and my deliverer; my God is my rock, in whom I take refuge, my shield and the horn of my salvation, my stronghold." (NIV)

We often say that the only constant in life is *change*. Change for the better—new opportunities, relationships, and joys, as well as change for the worse—novel diagnoses, anxieties, and sufferings. But scripture directs us to another constant: the very person of God.

In Psalm 18, David gives God the titles of *rock, fortress, shield*, and *stronghold*. Together, these indicate defense, strength, and steadfastness. These are forged not for peacetime but for war. Under assault, the rock does not move, the fortress does not cave, and the shield absorbs the blow. The presence of God is impenetrable and unshakeable. It is the chosen environment where we are delivered from crushing pressure, sin, and fear.

These declarations are not abstract but deeply personal: *my* rock, *my* fortress, *my* deliverer. In the wilderness, Hagar famously named God *El Roi* or "the God who sees me." Abraham named God *Yahweh Yireh*, or "the Lord will provide." Joshua named God *Yahweh Shalom*, or "the Lord is peace." Amidst whatever changes we face, we too give our personal titles to the God who never changes.

Lord, be our refuge when all around us shifts. Amen.

Joshua 1:8

DAY
202

"Study this Book of Instruction continually. Meditate on it day and night so you will be sure to obey everything written in it. Only then will you prosper and succeed in all you do." (NLT)

There's a difference between reading something and really studying it. We might skim through news articles or social media posts without taking a second to absorb what we just read, moving on quickly to the next article or post. Similarly, many of us read the Bible without really seeking to understand it or allowing its words to transform our lives.

If we want to engage with what we read and take it in, we have to take our time, pause, and reflect. We need to give our brains space to meditate on the words we're reading and understand how they fit into, challenge, or complement our lives. Without taking that time, we miss out on the transformative work that can happen as we learn new ways of looking at the world. When we go on a journey to truly understand, giving ourselves time to pause and reflect, we'll see a transformation work itself outward into our lives and the fruit that comes from it.

Jesus, be with us in our studying and meditations. Amen.

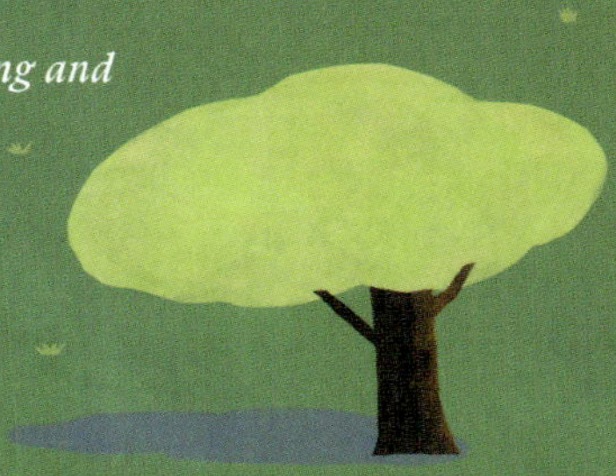

DAY

203 John 21:9-11

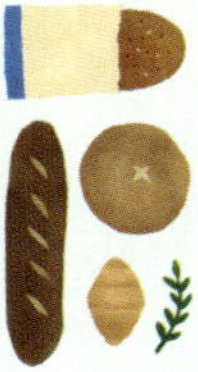

"When they got there, they found breakfast waiting for them—fish cooking over a charcoal fire, and some bread. 'Bring some of the fish you've just caught,' Jesus said. So Simon Peter went aboard and dragged the net to the shore. There were 153 large fish, and yet the net hadn't torn." (NLT)

When Jesus showed himself to his followers after his resurrection, he could have done so in any number of dramatic, supernatural ways. Instead, he helped his friends catch fish, and then made a fire and cooked them breakfast.

We may think that certain aspects of our lives are too mundane for Jesus' presence. Would God meet us in our cooking and eating, our washing dishes, our sweeping and vacuuming and tidying up? Would God speak to us in the most unglamorous aspects of our daily work?

John 21:9-11 suggests a wholehearted *yes*. Not only does God meet us in those places, but perhaps God specializes in imbuing them with significance. God loves those places. When we walk with Jesus, there is no part of our daily lives too mundane for God to breathe new life into.

God, bless us with a real sense that you are having breakfast with us, working with us, driving or taking the bus with us, caring for our kids and elders with us, infusing every moment of our days with wonder. Open our eyes to see you, providing for us and eating with us. Amen.

Psalm 138:1–2

DAY
204

"I give you thanks, O Lord, with all my heart; I will sing your praises before the gods. I bow before your holy Temple as I worship. I praise your name for your unfailing love and faithfulness; for your promises are backed by all the honor of your name." (NLT)

Our lives move at dizzying speeds. It's all too easy to lose sight of the small wonders that grace our regular rhythms. We take simple moments for granted as we fix our eyes on what we don't yet have. The practice of gratitude offers us a tranquil sanctuary—a space to pause, reflect, and find solace amid the blaring of life.

Gratitude breathes life into our hearts, infusing every beat with the melody of contentment. It is an invitation to savor the abundance bestowed upon us. As we reflect upon the blessings that grace our lives, we uncover a profound peace that transcends understanding—a peace that flows like a gentle river, nourishing the parched landscapes of our souls.

But gratitude is not confined to moments of abundance and delight; it finds its truest expression in the wilderness of trials and tribulations. With gratitude as our heavenly compass, anxiety finds solace, and worries lose their grip as we bask in the assurances of our faithful Creator. God's promises are backed; we do not give thanks in vain.

God of unending blessings, we give you thanks. May our gratitude help illuminate the world in the radiant glow of your love. Amen.

DAY 205 Psalm 56:3–4

"When I am afraid, I put my trust in you. In God, whose word I praise—in God I trust and am not afraid. What can mere mortals do to me?" (NIV)

Fear is an inevitability of life. When chaos, anxiety, and uncertainty abound, scripture details the antidote: trusting in God.

Trusting God does not mean our fears will instantly disappear. It means we choose to root ourselves in something stronger and more enduring than our fear—God's presence, promises, and Word. In the Psalms, David praises God's Word because it reminds him of what is true, even amidst threatening circumstances. It is by trusting that he overcomes his fear.

There is no shortage of concerns, but God provides us a yet greater reason not to worry: we do not face our fears alone. Jesus is with us. When we shift our gaze from that which terrifies us to the One who holds us, our hearts can begin to rest. Trust arises in us—not because we are fearless, but because God is faithful.

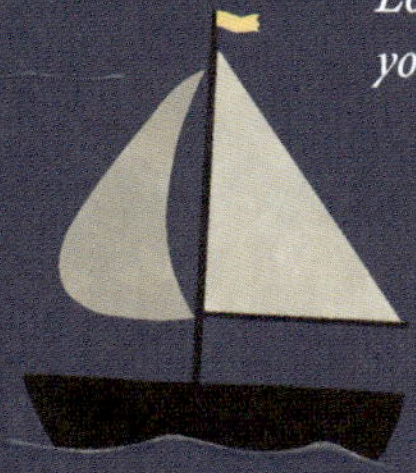

Lord Jesus, help us to trust in your Word and rest in your presence. Amen.

Jeremiah 17:7–8

DAY 206

"But blessed are those who trust in the Lord and have made the Lord their hope and confidence. They are like trees planted along a riverbank, with roots that reach deep into the water. Such trees are not bothered by the heat or worried by long months of drought. Their leaves stay green, and they never stop producing fruit." (NLT)

Very few trees are capable of bearing fruit year-round, with citrus being the main category of tree that does so. Some of the earliest evidence of citrus has been found just outside of Jerusalem. So, Jeremiah could have been referring to a citrus tree flourishing by a river as compared to desert shrubs when he spoke of the results of our trust in God.

When we find trust, hope, and confidence in God, our spiritual lives will reflect the flourishing of this tree. But spiritual flourishing isn't spontaneous and takes being planted with roots deep in flowing water. It takes three to six years before a citrus tree will bear any sort of fruit. We practice patience in the growth of our spiritual fruit.

We can find encouragement from scripture that our trust in God over time will also yield an abundance. With enough time, there will be no doubt that we are rooted in God and producing sweet and faithful fruit in every season.

Gardener God, we trust you to plant us near your flowing river that we may find spiritual flourishing in you. Amen.

DAY

207 Acts 5:27–29

"Then they brought the apostles before the high council, where the high priest confronted them. 'We gave you strict orders never again to teach in this man's name!' he said. 'Instead, you have filled all Jerusalem with your teaching about him, and you want to make us responsible for his death!' But Peter and the apostles replied, 'We must obey God rather than any human authority.'" (NLT)

The most tragic stories of human history are full of ordinary people doing evil things that cause great harm to others, all because an authority figure ordered them to. In Acts 5:27-29, we are reminded that orders from human authorities do not make an action right in God's eyes.

Sometimes people in power demand that we do things that oppose our conscience or contradict what we know God wants from us: mercy and justice, kindness and humility. In these cases, God's invitation is to resist. Just like Peter and the other apostles, we are called to obey God rather than any human authority.

In these decisive moments, our faith comes to life in a new way. Boldness arises from deep within us. We act with courage we did not know we had.

Jesus is with us in these times, guiding us on paths of love, even and especially when pursuing God's ways of love and justice for all people turns out to be risky, dangerous, or even forbidden.

God, help us step out in faith with great boldness. Raise up within us the courage to resist unjust orders. Be with us as we do so. Amen.

3 John 1:11

DAY
208

"Dear friend, do not imitate what is evil but what is good. Anyone who does what is good is from God. Anyone who does what is evil has not seen God." (NIV)

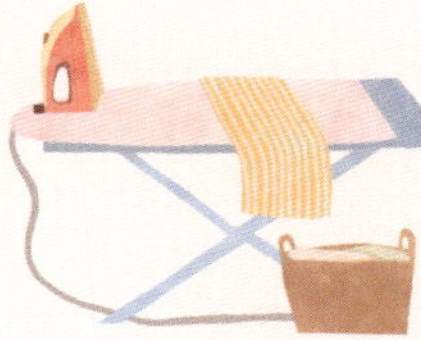

Here is a potentially uncomfortable truth: goodness—even selfless love and incredible generosity—is often found outside the confines of the Church. Meanwhile, wrongdoing, oppression, and harm can be found within our own Christian communities, poisoning what should be a holy refuge. What do we make of this?

First, it is not enough to call ourselves Christ-followers, to attend church regularly, to read scripture. We must go beyond labels, rituals, and words. We must take steps to pursue goodness and live out Christ's example of a loving, generous life.

Second, we should not be quick to judge people whose spiritual lives—or lack thereof—look different from ours. We cannot judge others' hearts; that's up to God alone. What we *can* do is evaluate actions. We can pursue and encourage goodness wherever we see it, even if the source surprises us.

God of goodness, help us take active steps to do good rather than being complacent. Help us welcome goodness wherever it comes from, for whoever does good is serving you. Amen.

DAY 209 Psalm 121:7–8

"The Lord will keep you from all harm—he will watch over your life; the Lord will watch over your coming and going both now and forevermore." (NIV)

When restlessness stirs up our hearts, scripture gives us an lifeline. God does not glance at us peripherally or momentarily; Jesus' gaze is complete and eternal. In the unseen, the mundane, and the lonely, he is there. We are safe under God's watch.

We are constantly looking out for ourselves. Rehearsing contingencies, avoiding risk, and fighting for control, we exhaust ourselves in defense of potential harm. Psalm 121 reminds us that we are already being watched over by a God who never sleeps or looks away. Every moment of our past, present, and future is seen. Our *coming and going*—our routines, transitions, seasons, and all the unfolding of life—is under the watch of God. Such keeping is not only protective—it is personal.

Lord, thank you for being our constant protector—help us to rest in the peace of your faithful watch. Amen.

1 John 4:11–12

DAY 210

“Dear friends, since God loved us that much, we surely ought to love each other. No one has ever seen God. But if we love each other, God lives in us, and his love is brought to full expression in us.” (NLT)

Love begins with God. Not as an abstract idea, but as a lived, poured-out reality. Scripture’s call for us to love each other is not merely a suggestion or command but a description of the natural outflow of being loved by God: what fills us is meant to overflow.

God’s love is not static. Like a spring bubbling up from deep underground, it moves—first toward us and then through us. When we receive it, it begins to reshape us from within. We find ourselves softened in places that had grown hard, made generous in ways we once resisted. And slowly, gradually, we become people who love—not perfectly, but sincerely.

This is the mark of God’s people. Not power. Not perfection. Love. If God’s life dwells in us, then love will be what people see. It will guide our words, temper our judgments, and widen our welcome. Love is the evidence of God’s presence among us.

As we love one another, God’s love is “brought to full expression.” The invisible God becomes visible through acts of patience, through mercy, through daily, ordinary kindness.

Jesus, let your love flow through us so fully that others see you more clearly. Amen.

DAY

211 Exodus 23:29–30

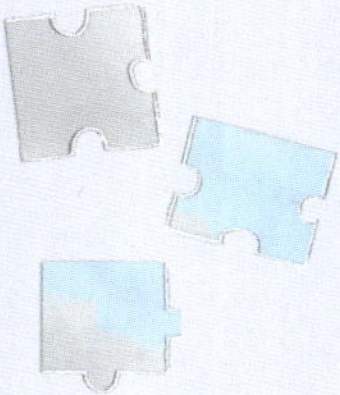

"But I will not drive them out in a single year, because the land would become desolate and the wild animals too numerous for you. Little by little I will drive them out before you, until you have increased enough to take possession of the land." (NIV)

Our culture trains us to anticipate instant gratification. We expect quick fixes, immediate results, and prompt responses, and we often assume that God, too, will comply with our timelines. But here in Exodus, God reveals an alternate pace of love: a patient, wise, and strategic love that works little by little.

God was leading the Israelites into a land of promise, but knew they were not ready to handle it all at once. There were blessings ahead—but also responsibilities, risks, and growth. So, God led them on the slow road.

Sometimes, what feels like a delay is actually divine care. God paces the journey not to frustrate us but to form us, strengthening us for the very things we're praying for. May we trust in the slow unfolding of God's promises.

Shepherding Jesus, teach us to trust your timing and to see your wisdom in every step, even when the way is slow. Amen.

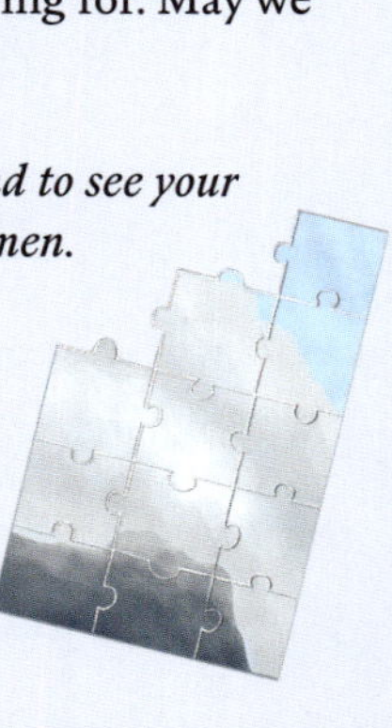

Luke 24:14–15 DAY 212

"As they walked along they were talking about everything that had happened. As they talked and discussed these things, Jesus himself suddenly came and began walking with them." (NLT)

Going for a walk with someone tends to foster a depth of conversation. On long walks, we know we have time to fill, so the conversation flows like a river. On the long road from Jerusalem to Emmaus, two travelers were caught up in discussing their thoughts and emotions over the events surrounding Jesus' death. Their conversation was fast-moving, so it took them a moment to realize a man had joined them. To the travelers, he seemed to be an ordinary stranger, and they didn't recognize that it was Jesus.

He didn't look like their friend who had conquered death and fulfilled prophesies or the brilliant angels who had announced his resurrection. Because rather than appearing in all his glory, Jesus was humble, present, and invested for miles of conversation.

Our walks with Jesus can be the same. God expresses interest in our laughter and tears in every moment of the journey. There is no need for him to appear in glory; we have a God who enjoys conversations in step with us.

Listening God, thank you for walking with us on the long roads so that we can better appreciate your presence upon arriving at our destination. Amen.

DAY

213 Isaiah 43:2

"When you go through deep waters, I will be with you. When you go through rivers of difficulty, you will not drown. When you walk through the fire of oppression, you will not be burned up; the flames will not consume you." (NLT)

"Do not fear." These are powerful words, spoken from God to humanity again and again throughout the Bible. Isaiah 43:2 is surrounded by this invitation: "Do not fear, for I have redeemed you and you belong to me," says verse 1. "Do not fear, for I am with you," declares verse 5.

Even knowing that Jesus is with us, we still experience the chaos of this world in our lives. We have no guarantee that we will not pass through stormy waters. We are not promised a life free of things so difficult they feel like trial by fire.

But God does promise to be with us through the rough waters. God says we will not be completely consumed by the flames, though we may be changed and scarred by them. Like so many before us who have lived through tumultuous times, we experience God's presence as a source of peace and confidence. God carries us through.

God, remind us of your presence with us. Even in the most violent storms, help us act out of courageous love and not fear. Build in us an inner oasis of peace. Amen.

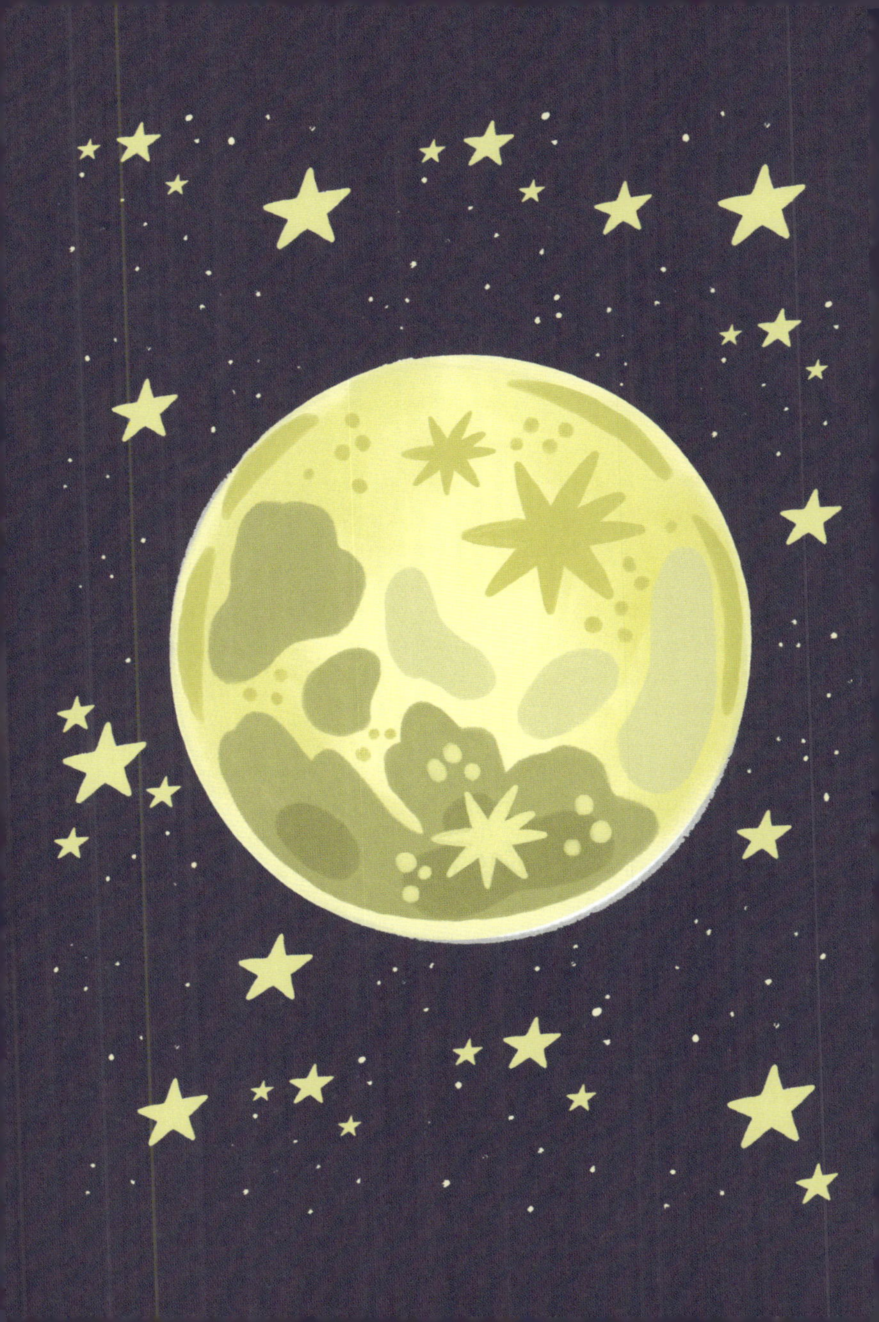

DAY
214 Psalm 37:5–6

"Commit everything you do to the Lord. Trust him, and he will help you. He will make your innocence radiate like the dawn, and the justice of your cause will shine like the noonday sun." (NLT)

When the sun rises, the whole world is at peace. The birdsong begins as the dew evaporates with the soft touches of light. If a time of day could be innocent, it's dawn.

Then, the sun hits its peak, and very little can be hidden from the light it casts. The morning dew is long gone, and flower petals have unfurled to reveal their beauty. This is the time of day for openness and justice.

When we trust in God, our lives pattern the sun. We may encounter difficulty in the darkness of night, but we also radiate innocence and justice in the light of the sun. We don't place our hope in one who is unsympathetic to our nights. Jesus faced every trouble and injustice, even death. Yet, he radiated truth, innocence, and justice, appearing as bright as a sunny day when he proclaimed victory over death! When we place our trust in Jesus, we give ourselves over to a helper who has faced it all and will still pursue justice on our behalf.

We praise you, Jesus, for your victory over death and every struggle. Like a flower, help us to bask in the light you shed today. Amen.

1 Thessalonians 3:12–13

DAY 215

"And may the Lord make your love for one another and for all people grow and overflow, just as our love for you overflows. May he, as a result, make your hearts strong, blameless, and holy as you stand before God our Father when our Lord Jesus comes again with all his holy people. Amen." (NLT)

We often conceptualize Heaven as some distant, ethereal location high above and far away. Scripture, however, describes Heaven less as a place to go and more as the transformation of this world by God. This wide-sweeping change that will eventually overtake every square inch of creation begins with us—with our transformation through Jesus—and radiates ever outward.

Paul's prayer for the increase and overflow of love isn't just about personal piety; it's about manifesting God's promised makeover for all creation, through our lives. More than a sentimental wish or dream for the future, it's a call to live as citizens of God's dawning Kingdom, a blueprint for bringing Heaven to earth.

Imagine letting the love of God guide our interactions by practicing kindness and extending mercy and forgiveness. Each word and deed so offered chips away at the darkness and brings forth the light of a renewed creation. We experience the promise of God's perfect peace and justice right here, right now.

God, empower us to embody your overflowing love so that our lives become a tangible reflection of your Kingdom here on earth. Amen.

DAY

216 Ephesians 6:18

"Pray in the Spirit at all times and on every occasion. Stay alert and be persistent in your prayers for all believers everywhere." (NLT)

There are seasons when prayer flows easily—when gratitude spills over and words rise without resistance. And there are seasons when prayer takes effort. It feels like silence, like reaching for something just out of view.

But scripture invites us into rhythm. Not perfection, not performance, but presence. "At all times, and on every occasion." It is not the length of our prayers that matters but the continual turning of our hearts towards God.

Prayer is not only what we say with our words; it is a route that we journey on. An avenue of connection to a God who desires to walk alongside us. Prayer is a practice of honesty, a rhythm that steadies us, whether in joy or despair.

To pray in all seasons is to let God into all of them, not only the polished ones. The Spirit intercedes when we cannot, speaks when we are weary, and draws near in ways deeper than words.

We remember that you, Jesus, are not waiting for the right moment to hear us. You are already here. Amen.

2 Corinthians 5:20

DAY **217**

"We are therefore Christ's ambassadors, as though God were making his appeal through us. We implore you on Christ's behalf: Be reconciled to God." (NIV)

To be an ambassador is to represent someone else, carrying their message, speaking on their behalf, and embodying their values. Paul assures us that this is our identity in Christ. We are not just believers, but *representatives* of Jesus to the world.

This is no small calling. God can interact directly with the world, but often chooses to work through us—imperfect, ordinary humans—making the divine appeal of *shalom* and reconciliation through our lives, labors, and love. The message we are given is not one of judgment but grace that implores: *Come home. Be restored. There is peace with God.*

This means every interaction is a sacred opportunity to reflect the heart of Christ. This is not an optional project but an identity. Let our lives be a personalized echo of God's longing for the world to be reconciled.

Lord, help us to live as your ambassadors—faithfully reflecting your love, grace, and invitation to a hurting world. Amen.

DAY 218 Leviticus 19:18

"Do not seek revenge or bear a grudge against a fellow Israelite, but love your neighbor as yourself. I am the Lord." (NLT)

What does it look like to love our neighbors as ourselves? Ultimately, it goes beyond mere kindness when things are easy. In the quiet tension of disagreement, in the sting of a careless word, in the frustration of misunderstanding—this is where love is tested and where it is most necessary.

It means seeking peace when it's difficult. In conflict, love listens not merely to respond, but to understand. It makes room for the other's perspective, even when our own feels urgent and justified. To love as we wish to be loved means offering the grace we long for, the patience we hope others would have with us.

The love Jesus calls us to means choosing the harder path of reconciliation over the ease of resentment or disengagement. It means remembering that those we struggle with are also loved by God, shaped in God's image, and carrying an unseen load.

God invites us to love, knowing that seeking revenge and carrying grudges is too heavy a burden for us to bear. Loving our neighbor is not only for their good but for ours as well.

God, teach us to love even in conflict—with humility, grace, and a heart that seeks peace. Amen.

Luke 4:18

DAY
219

“The Spirit of the Lord is upon me, for he has anointed me to bring Good News to the poor. He has sent me to proclaim that captives will be released, that the blind will see, that the oppressed will be set free.” (NLT)

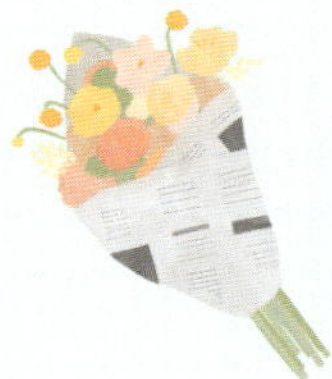

It’s easy to feel beaten down. As we read through the news and look around our neighborhoods, we see the poor getting poorer while the rich get richer. We see oppression and injustice running rampant. Sickness continues to spread.

The exhausting gloom of bad news can feel inescapable. But into this space, Jesus arrives to deliver Good News. Yes, the pain we endure now is real, but it is neither permanent nor intended.

Scripture is clear—poverty, captivity, illness, and oppression are not a part of the Kingdom of God. We can take comfort in the knowledge that our active and ever-present God is pushing back against these forces. Jesus is on the side of the weary. This Good News is both a comfort and a reassurance—a balm to our tired spirits. Beauty and restoration are promised.

Benevolent God, you see what breaks our hearts; it breaks yours, too. Preserve us amidst the darkness and shepherd us into your light. Amen.

DAY 220 Isaiah 61:1

"The Spirit of the Sovereign Lord is upon me, for the Lord has anointed me to bring good news to the poor. He has sent me to comfort the brokenhearted and to proclaim that captives will be released and prisoners will be freed." (NLT)

When we remember the lowest moments of our lives, the times when we feel crushed in spirit and broken down, what soothes our wounds? Scripture establishes Jesus as the perfect wounded healer, sent into this world to mend everyone of their brokenness through the tender comfort and freedom of his Spirit.

Isaiah 61 introduces a prophecy Jesus would later fulfill in the flesh, describing him as the deliverer who came to release captives from their chains of oppression, opening prison doors so that all people may walk through life, completely set free.

Not one person goes unnoticed by the sovereign Lord who intends for all to be restored. Jesus came for this very reason: to heal the sick, to meet the poor with living hope, and to mend the brokenhearted. Oftentimes, it is in our lowest moments that the deepest breakthrough happens. When we let God address the wounds inflicted and allow Jesus to heal our hearts, our stories transform from those of deep hurt to restored hope.

Dear Lord, you set us free. We invite you to heal every part of us, even the most painful parts we feel are too damaged. Amen.

Micah 6:8

DAY
221

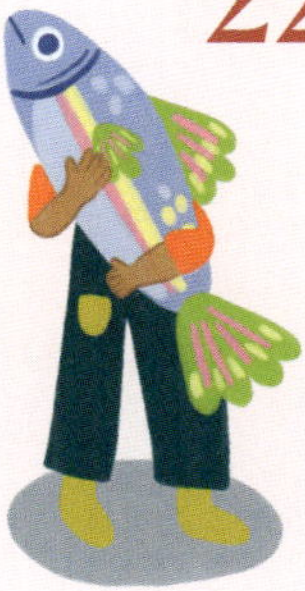

"He has shown you, O mortal, what is good.
And what does the Lord require of you?
To act justly and to love mercy and to walk
humbly with your God." (NIV)

Act justly, love mercy, and walk humbly—this is what it means to live out our faith. This is the heart of the Christian life. But it can be hard to see what the just course of action is, how to balance mercy with that justice, and how to keep a humble spirit in the midst of it all. How will we ever measure up?

Jesus lived according to these values, criticizing the Pharisees' hypocrisy, healing a blind man on the Sabbath, preventing a woman from being stoned, and feeding the hungry crowds, all while directing the credit and glory to God. When we spend time reflecting on Christ's deeds, we can better emulate them.

While we will never accomplish perfect justice, mercy, or humility, we can strive toward them as ideals. With practice and prayer, we become more well-versed in rebuking evil, caring for the sick and needy, protecting the vulnerable, and giving glory to God.

Jesus, thank you for being an example of what it means to pursue what is good. Please guide us as we pursue these ideals, and give us the patience to try again when we fall short. Amen.

DAY
222 John 15:12–13

"My command is this: Love each other as I have loved you. Greater love has no one than this: to lay down one's life for one's friends." (NIV)

Friendship isn't technically a need: we don't require it the way we require air, water, or food. But friendships are essential for a life of joy, comfort, and encouragement. Sharing our blessings and hardships is a form of intimacy, and so we need to be intentional about the friends we choose.

Shared values are the bedrock of healthy relationships. Even when our circumstances and choices differ, friends should be aligned in their guiding principles. Encouraged by the same faith, priorities, or goals, we can trust that our friends are helping us move in wise, healthy directions when we seek support or advice.

To create an environment where everyone feels comfortable asking for help, we can take a vital step: ask for help ourselves. If we aren't willing to be vulnerable, lean on others, and open up about our struggles, we can't hope to receive the greatest gift of friendship: authentic connection and community.

God, thank you for blessing us with people who love and care about us. Give us the courage to be vulnerable enough to have real connections with people who share our faith. Amen.

Hebrews 13:5

DAY 223

"Keep your lives free from the love of money and be content with what you have, because God has said, 'Never will I leave you; never will I forsake you.'" (NIV)

Contentment can feel radical in a world that urges us to reach for more. Scripture calls us to embrace peace and satisfaction, rooted not in belongings but in the presence of God. True security is not found in possessions but in the unwavering promise of Emmanuel, "God with us."

Discontentment is often the result of comparison, unmet expectations, or a fear of scarcity. We believe that happiness is found in the next purchase or achievement, yet experience proves otherwise. There is always something on the other side of "next." Being content isn't about denying our desires but anchoring them in something unshakable—God's provision and presence.

This doesn't mean life will always be easy, but we are never without what we truly need. Trusting that God provides exactly what is necessary, we are freed from the anxiety of insufficiency. We cultivate contentment by shifting our focus from what we lack to what we have and seeing possessions as tools rather than treasures.

God, you promise us, "I will never leave you nor forsake you." Help us internalize this promise and experience the true peace that comes from you, who are always enough. Amen.

DAY

224 Ecclesiastes 3:11

"Yet God has made everything beautiful for its own time. He has planted eternity in the human heart, but even so, people cannot see the whole scope of God's work from beginning to end." (NLT)

When we plant a flower, we have an idea of what will grow. For a while, all the growth of the seedling is out of our eyesight. Then it slowly sprouts, and we have hope. Later, the flower will bloom in the warmth of the sun. But if the sun disappears, flowers hide their blooms or fade away.

We are like the flowers in God's eternal garden. Much of our growth is done beneath the soil without a grasp of eternity, even though God has placed that seed in our hearts. As we draw nearer to God, we begin to sprout and grow.

Whatever phase of growth we are in, we must take hope that God has made everything beautiful for its own time. We don't know our place in the garden or what shares our soil, but God does. As the cultivator and gardener, God sees the whole plan for the eternal garden and when each flower will bloom. Our only job is to continue growing towards Jesus and opening our faces towards the sun.

Eternal Gardener, thank you for your hope that sustains us and blooms us into beauty in our time. Amen.

Colossians 3:15–16

DAY 225

“And let the peace that comes from Christ rule in your hearts. For as members of one body you are called to live in peace. And always be thankful. Let the message about Christ, in all its richness, fill your lives. Teach and counsel each other with all the wisdom he gives. Sing psalms and hymns and spiritual songs to God with thankful hearts.” (NLT)

Gratitude is not a foreign concept. From childhood, we are taught to say “thank you.” We often express gratitude for life’s blessings—family, provision, health. But how often do we give thanks for our greatest gift, the abiding presence of Jesus?

Letting Christ rule our hearts means letting him govern our thoughts and actions. True peace is not found in favorable circumstances but in the unshakable reality of Jesus with us. His presence steadies us when life feels uncertain, comforts us in sorrow, and fills us with joy beyond understanding.

We experience Jesus’ presence through his Word dwelling richly within us. When we fill our hearts with scripture, our perspective shifts; we move from worry to trust, from striving to rest, from discontentment to gratitude. God’s truth reminds us that we are loved, redeemed, and never alone. When Christ’s peace and Word fill us, gratitude naturally overflows.

Jesus, your presence is our greatest treasure. Your peace steadies us, your word guides us, and your love fills us with joy. May our hearts be ever grateful. Amen.

DAY

226 Romans 1:11–12

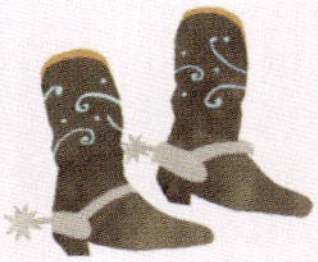

"For I long to visit you so I can bring you some spiritual gift that will help you grow strong in the Lord. When we get together, I want to encourage you in your faith, but I also want to be encouraged by yours." (NLT)

Our words matter. They can build people up or tear people down. Paul understood this, and he spent a lot of energy and ink telling the early church to take the power of their words seriously. He warned them not to gossip or lie to each other, but just as important to his message was this: to encourage one another as often as we're able.

It's easy to focus on what the Bible says we should restrict from our lives, but so much of scripture actually focuses on the transformative actions we can adopt. If we focus on using our words for encouragement, we'll unleash fewer words that can be used in negative ways.

Encouraging one another can take many forms: speaking well of someone, complimenting them, showing gratitude, sharing hopeful stories, or supporting them in need. Encouragement helps build meaningful relationships, and it gives us the energy and confidence we need to move forward in a difficult world.

Jesus, help us be an encouraging presence to the people around us. Help us be vulnerable and gracious, building up the family of God. Amen.

Genesis 16:13

DAY
227

"Thereafter, Hagar used another name to refer to the Lord, who had spoken to her. She said, 'You are the God who sees me.' She also said, 'Have I truly seen the One who sees me?'" (NLT)

In the wilderness, alone and desperate, Hagar encountered God. Cast out, unseen by those who held power over her, she was met with God's presence. After this encounter, she named God *El Roi*—"the God who sees me." Hagar, an outsider in her community, came to know that she was not invisible to God.

Do we believe we are truly seen by God? Not just our shining achievements or spiritual insights, but the whole of us—our doubts, pain, compulsions, and even our failures? Are there parts of us we readily offer to God and others we prefer to keep hidden in the shadows?

It can be tempting to try to maintain a certain image, even before God. But the God who found Hagar in the wilderness did not turn away from her pain or complexity. God saw her fully and met her with care.

To be seen by God is to be known and loved. The One who formed us sees every part of us, even the parts we would rather hide, and looks upon us with the eyes of a Creator who delights in their own handiwork.

God, thank you for seeing us fully—and loving us still. Amen.

DAY
228 Isaiah 44:22

"I have swept away your offenses like a cloud, your sins like the morning mist. Return to me, for I have redeemed you." (NIV)

Having grace for ourselves can be scary: What if we continue to do harm? If we have self-compassion, will we ever "learn our lesson"? Is extending ourselves grace a way of enabling our poor choices?

Self-punishment does not actually facilitate growth; it just keeps us mired in the past. Doing better doesn't happen overnight. Unlearning takes time. God doesn't expect us to be perfect; He just wants us to practice doing better. Having grace with ourselves is always the best way forward; it's exactly how God treats us. The Almighty washes away our sins with mercy and forgiveness. We can take comfort knowing that our slate is clean, and we can be inspired to try again.

The way we regard ourselves can also come out in how we treat others. When we practice self-compassion, we may find it easier to have patience for others. And on the flipside, we can see our grace toward others as a reminder that we also deserve that same grace.

Jesus, thank you for showing us unending forgiveness. Please soften my heart when I am weighed down by guilt and anger toward myself, and remind me that every day is new with your mercy. Amen.

Psalm 102:18

DAY
229

"Let this be recorded for future generations, so that a people not yet born will praise the Lord." (NLT)

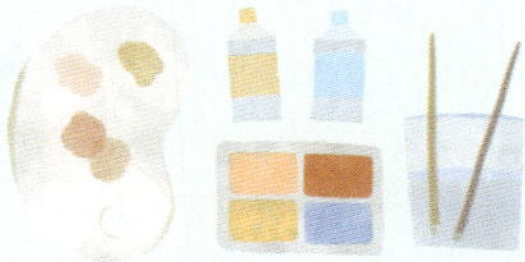

The Psalms are the hymnal of the people of Israel. They were the songs used for celebration and mourning; the music of their daily lives. For generations, these words have been offered up in worship to God.

Today, the Psalms continue to offer comfort long after the authors' names have been lost. In Psalm 102, the psalmist recognizes that these words of praise will outlast them. They cared more about the significance of the worship than their own importance. In their humility, we are better able to read their creative worship and continually bring praises to God.

If we approach creativity as a devotional practice, the posture of our hearts should mimic that of the psalmist. When we offer our worship, may we humbly pray that our creativity invokes others to worship God, both in our community and for generations to come.

God, we feel blessed and called to worship from the recorded words of the past. As we offer our worship to you, may it continue to magnify who you are for all those who encounter it. Amen.

DAY

230 Revelation 17:14

"Together they will go to war against the Lamb, but the Lamb will defeat them because he is Lord of all lords and King of all kings. And his called and chosen and faithful ones will be with him." (NLT)

History is littered with rulers fighting for dominance—kings and conquerors determined to secure power at any cost. Wars are waged, thrones are seized, and empires rise and fall in the endless pursuit of control. When we picture a victorious king, we likely imagine one of immense might—intimidating, merciless, and undefeatable in battle.

Revelation 17:14 upends our expectations. The king who triumphs over all others is not a ruthless warrior but a lamb. Jesus defies every presumption of what it means to reign. His kingdom is not built on violence, oppression, or fear, but on love, mercy, and restoration. He does not arm himself with guards and battalions to die in his defense, but instead lays down his life willingly for the world.

The bold and brash antics of the power-hungry may make a lot of noise, but their empires will ultimately be short-lived. Here, in this vision of the end and beginning of all things, scripture declares that it is Jesus, the meek lamb, who wears the crown. And his Kingdom will reign forever.

Oh, King of kings, we give thanks for your Kingdom of peace and compassion. Draw us in close to you as you work to bring that Kingdom to fruition. Amen.

1 Chronicles 16:8,12 DAY 231

"Give thanks to the Lord and proclaim his greatness. Let the whole world know what he has done. ... Remember the wonders he has performed, his miracles, and the rulings he has given." (NLT)

Our days rush by, filled with the urgent demands of the present. Sometimes, however, we need to take a moment and look back. We remember the times we felt overwhelmed yet found strength and courage we didn't know we had. We recall those spaces when we received unexpected kindness and support. We look back on those moments of peace and assurance that settled over us like a warm blanket.

These aren't random occurrences. They are threads of grace woven into the tapestry of our lives by the constant, unseen hand of God. Remembrance isn't about dwelling on the past; it's about building a foundation of trust and hope for the future. Acknowledging the blessings that have shaped us cultivates both our gratitude toward and continued reliance upon Jesus.

The best way to get to where we are going is by remembering where we've been. More importantly, reminding ourselves of the One who has carried us this far affords us the confidence and trust that this same God will lead us exactly where we need to be.

Thank you, God, for your constant presence in our lives. May remembering your past goodness fill our hearts with present gratitude and future trust. Amen.

DAY

232 Luke 15:20

"So he returned home to his father. And while he was still a long way off, his father saw him coming. Filled with love and compassion, he ran to his son, embraced him, and kissed him." (NLT)

In Luke 15, religious people grumble because Jesus "welcomes sinners and eats with them." In response, Jesus tells a series of stories to show what God is like. These stories reveal that the heart of God welcomes people who have been rejected, breaks bread with people others might consider beneath them, and affirms the humanity of all people.

The heart of God is to run toward us while we are still a long way off. No matter what, God always welcomes us home. God does not judge or hold in contempt anyone who sincerely desires to return to walking in God's ways of goodness and love.

When we make mistakes or feel far away, Jesus greets us with compassion, reminding us that God's love for us has not changed. When we take even the tiniest steps toward love, connection, community-building, and peacemaking, God runs toward us and meets us more than halfway.

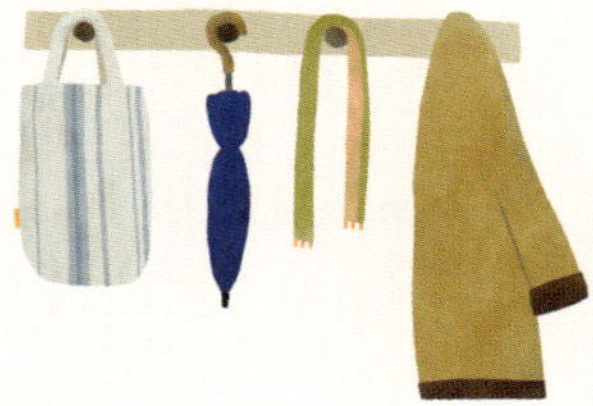

God, help us show compassion to others as you have shown it to us. Help us have compassion for ourselves as well. Thank you for running out to meet us while we are still far off. We run toward you. Amen.

2 Timothy 4:7

DAY
233

"I have fought the good fight, I have finished the race, I have kept the faith." (NIV)

It can be tempting to rush through the "messy middle" of a journey so we can reach the perfectly achieved end. But most of our lives are spent in that period of being in progress, awaiting the day a dream is fully realized or a challenge is conquered.

The outcome of a journey is often not *exactly* what we hoped for nor *precisely* as perfect as we envisioned. And the time we spend celebrating an accomplishment is overshadowed by our realization that there is yet another task to undertake, another goal to labor toward. We are constantly in progress.

But in the middle of the process, there is beauty. God's blessings never cease, even amid pain and difficulty. It is through this journey that real growth and refinement happen. The destination is only remarkable because we know how far we've come. Let's celebrate each part of life, even if we haven't fully closed a chapter or reached a goal. Each day can be full of small successes and blessings if we choose to shift our perspective.

Holy Savior, thank you for each moment of our journeys. We ask that you prompt us to see the goodness, joy, and beauty of each step. Amen.

DAY

234 Romans 12:19

"Dear friends, never take revenge. Leave that to the righteous anger of God. For the Scriptures say, 'I will take revenge; I will pay them back,' says the Lord." (NLT)

Anger can be holy, and it can also be heavy. When left unchecked, it calcifies into bitterness, robbing us of peace. When ignored, it simmers, slowly rising to a boiling point.

Scripture does not ask us to deny our anger. It asks us to entrust it to the Lord.

"Leave that to God," we are told, not because justice does not matter, but because vengeance is too weighty a burden for the human heart to bear.

To give our anger to God is not to pretend we are unbothered. It is to say: "This pain is too much for me to carry alone." It is to believe that God sees rightly, acts justly, and loves wholly, even when we cannot. It is a sacred release. A return to peace, not because wrongs are forgotten, but because our souls are not meant for retribution.

Jesus, may your presence tend to the need that anger is calling out for. Let our trust in you give us the freedom to let it go. Amen.

DAY

Mark 10:43–45

235

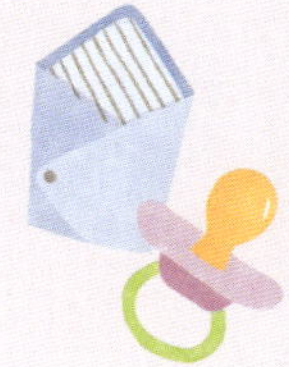

"But among you it will be different. Whoever wants to be a leader among you must be your servant, and whoever wants to be first among you must be the slave of everyone else. For even the Son of Man came not to be served but to serve others and to give his life as a ransom for many.'" (NLT)

Religious leaders in Jesus' day didn't know what to do with his radical teachings and approach to ministry. They worked from the top down, aligning with power structures and exercising authority over people. Conversely, Jesus worked ground-up, critiquing power structures and restoring people's agency and dignity.

This is the fundamental difference between the Kingdom of God and the kingdoms on earth—in the Kingdom of God, those with the least power and status on earth will be honored, and those who serve others will be considered leaders.

This friction is not exclusive to Jesus' time. Many leaders today miss the upside-down nature of God's Kingdom. According to Jesus' teachings, leaders should be servants of all, critiquing power structures that oppress. The world constantly pushes us to amass power, and an important job of spiritual leaders is to resist that pull. Let us take some time today to pray for the spiritual and religious leaders around us, that they would be leaders in the way Jesus was a leader.

God, please guide our leaders into the upside-down reality of the Kingdom of God. Amen.

DAY 236 Deuteronomy 6:6–7

"And you must commit yourselves wholeheartedly to these commands that I am giving you today. Repeat them again and again to your children. Talk about them when you are at home and when you are on the road ..." (NLT)

Faith is not intended to live only in sacred spaces. It is meant to echo through the rhythms of home: woven into meals, questions, stories, and quiet moments of connection.

The call to pass on faith is not reserved for the eloquent or the flawless. It begins with wholeheartedness—with the desire to let God's truth shape how we live and how we love. Families, biological or chosen, are shaped not just by what is taught but by what is lived. The way we speak, the way we repair, the habits we repeat, and the grace we extend to one another.

Deuteronomy offers a vision of discipleship through everyday life. It removes the barrier to entry from rigid instruction to steady presence. We can develop a faith that walks alongside, that listens, that grows over time.

Christ, may you continue to grow our bonds with loved ones, allowing that to shape our faith day by day. Amen.

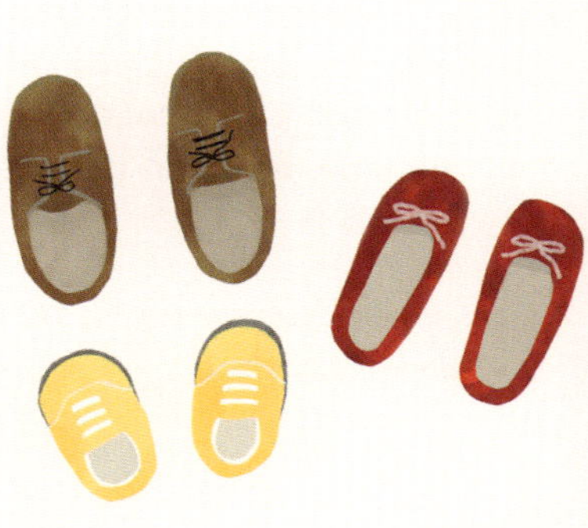

Luke 16:10–11

DAY 237

"If you are faithful in little things, you will be faithful in large ones. But if you are dishonest in little things, you won't be honest with greater responsibilities. And if you are untrustworthy about worldly wealth, who will trust you with the true riches of heaven?" (NLT)

In the Gospel of Luke, Jesus teaches that faithfulness in small things reflects our ability to steward greater things. The way we handle earthly resources—our time, responsibilities, and finances—reveals the integrity of our hearts. If we are trustworthy with little, we prove ourselves ready to handle more. But if we are careless with what we have now, why would we be entrusted with greater things?

Stewardship is not just about money; it is about how we manage all that God has given us. Every resource—our gifts, opportunities, and influence—is a trust from the Almighty. Though worldly wealth is temporary, our faithfulness in using it wisely has eternal significance. God's Kingdom is not built on greed or wastefulness but on generosity and wisdom.

Being a good steward is a daily act of faithfulness. When we are diligent in small matters, we demonstrate trust in God as the true provider. And in God's perfect timing, we are entrusted with greater opportunities to serve the Kingdom.

Whether in little or much, may we live with open hands, using all we have to honor Jesus, knowing that true riches are found in his presence and purpose. Amen.

DAY
238 Genesis 2:7

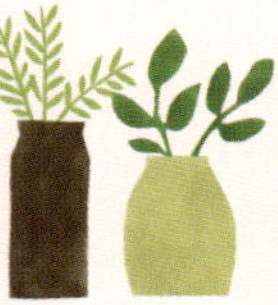

"Then the Lord God formed the man from the dust of the ground. He breathed the breath of life into the man's nostrils, and the man became a living person." (NLT)

Breathing is the most essential aspect of life. It sustains us, refreshes us, and provides a rhythm and a flow for our bodies. When all is well, our breathing fades into the background. It becomes automatic, a process that we take for granted as we fix our attention on other things. We lose sight of the wonder—the power—of breathing.

Breath is generative, not only maintaining our bodies but, biblically, the breath of God is an instrument of creation. Genesis 2 reminds us that it was through breathing that God transformed humanity from mere dust into living people.

If we pause to breathe mindfully, we are reminded of God's presence in every moment of our lives. Each inhale and exhale becomes a testimony to the provision and care of our Creator, equipping us for the moment ahead.

When the world seems uncertain, when we feel ourselves caught in the swirls of anxiety and doubt, our breathing can ground us. We pay attention to the rhythm of our lungs and reflect on God's unchanging nature, on God's unfailing love for us all.

God, you are the source of the very air in our lungs. We give thanks to you. Amen.

John 3:16

DAY
239

"For this is how God loved the world: He gave his one and only Son, so that everyone who believes in him will not perish but have eternal life." (NLT)

We often think of generosity as giving from surplus—sharing what we can spare. If we have extra time, money, or resources, we give to those without. This kind of generosity is good, but God's generosity goes far beyond human standards. As John 3:16 declares, God gives not from excess, but what is most precious—God's only Son. This is not merely a gesture of kindness but a sacrifice of infinite worth, offered for our redemption. It is an act of love for all eternity, securing life beyond what we can see and know.

God's generosity challenges us to shift our perspective. If the Creator of all things gives so freely, how much more should we reflect that generosity in our own lives? Not just in giving what we can spare but in giving of ourselves—our time, our love, our resources—even when it costs something.

When we grasp the depth of God's giving heart, gratitude naturally follows. And from gratitude flows a desire to give in return—not to earn God's love, but because we have already received it so abundantly.

May we be people who mirror your divine generosity, God. May we live open-handed in a world that often clings too tightly. Amen.

DAY 240 Psalm 16:11

"You will show me the way of life, granting me the joy of your presence and the pleasures of living with you forever." (NLT)

Sometimes we look forward to something that we think will bring us joy, only to find that the promise comes up empty. We work hard to achieve a goal, only to wonder, "Is this it?" We assume a new relationship will make us happy, only to discover that it also brings complications and difficulties.

While our lives rarely feel like a jubilant, straightforward procession from one level of happiness to another, we can rest assured that when we seek God's presence, we do find a lasting sort of joy. Psalm 16 celebrates the delight God gives. We might wonder whether God wants us to be happy. We may have been taught that the things we experience as pleasurable in our lives must be contrary to God's very serious will. If so, the psalmist invites us to think again.

The most joyful things in our lives are good gifts from God. And knowing that a Spirit of infinite love surrounds us wherever we go, staying with us through life's ups and downs, is perhaps the most joyful gift of all.

God, help us pay attention to what brings deep delight to our spirits. We receive these good gifts from you. Amen.

Job 6:11

"What strength do I have, that I should still hope? What prospects, that I should be patient?" (NIV)

Hope is a small word, and it can feel like a trite, simple concept. But having hope can be a significant challenge, especially when we come face-to-face with unprecedented obstacles and fears. Worse still, when hope feels out of our reach, it can seem like yet another failure to be ashamed of.

But bludgeoning ourselves with the idea of hope, resilience, and unwavering optimism does more harm than good. When hope feels heavy, nearly impossible, the way to reach it is through despair: allowing ourselves to express our pain, feel it, and watch it pass through. God will bring us through to the other side.

Just because hope feels unreachable in this present moment doesn't mean our hopelessness will last forever. Jesus, too, experienced a full, complex human life, including moments of sorrow and hopelessness, and he chose to keep his eyes on God. In every trial we endure, we can take comfort in knowing that Jesus understands our pain and bears it alongside us.

Jesus, thank you for coming down to join humanity in our joy and suffering. Thank you for never leaving our side, through good times and hard times. Show us how we, like you, can join alongside others in their sorrow. Amen.

DAY

242 Ephesians 4:31–32

"Get rid of all bitterness, rage, anger, harsh words, and slander, as well as all types of evil behavior. Instead, be kind to each other, tenderhearted, forgiving one another, just as God through Christ has forgiven you." (NLT)

We all know the pain that comes from being wronged by someone we love. We're left questioning how to move forward. How do we address the rift between loved ones? Can we reestablish trust?

For the injured party, it feels tempting to sit in rage. The desire for revenge seems alluring even when we recognize, deep down, that it will not heal our hearts. If we are the wrongdoers, we may feel permanently tarnished, overcome with guilt and shame.

But there is a way forward. Healing comes through forgiveness. To forgive is not to ignore the reality of pain or wrongdoing; forgiveness is wound care. It is the cleaning and bandaging of our emotional injuries. When we forgive, we address the harm done. Much like cleaning a physical wound, this process can be uncomfortable at first. But to refuse to forgive is to allow our wounds to fester and grow infected.

Healing doesn't happen overnight. But we can take comfort that the pain of the present moment will not be everlasting. When we forgive, we work towards restoration. We are reminded of the One who sees our most grievous mistakes and loves us still.

Our errors do not define us. We are defined by Jesus' love. Amen.

Revelation 7:9

DAY
243

"After this I saw a vast crowd, too great to count, from every nation and tribe and people and language, standing in front of the throne and before the Lamb. They were clothed in white robes and held palm branches in their hands." (NLT)

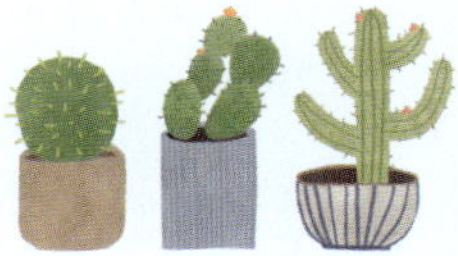

Diversity is baked into creation. Observing nature, we see an abundance of variation. Each aspect of the natural world ebbs and flows in tandem together, serving a unique purpose. Bees pollinate the plants that become our food, and trees clean the air we breathe. But even outside of functionality, diversity is to be celebrated because each variant is an intentionally made aspect of God's grand design. God created the world and said that all of it was good.

Trepidation around those who are different points to our discomfort outside our experience and understanding. The unfamiliar can seem like a cause for fear. But we are all made in God's image. The fact that we are so distinct demonstrates how vast and expansive our Creator is. Rather than denouncing those different from us, we ought to embrace the opportunity to experience a new facet of God. Not only has diversity existed from the beginning, but, as Revelation shows us, it is a part of God's ultimate plan.

Jesus, you assure us that all are welcome in your Kingdom. Our differences make us stronger and remind us of our shared purpose: to love and serve you. Amen.

DAY 244 2 Corinthians 13:11

"Dear brothers and sisters, I close my letter with these last words: Be joyful. Grow to maturity. Encourage each other. Live in harmony and peace. Then the God of love and peace will be with you." (NLT)

Healthy relationships—be they familial, platonic, or romantic—take work. Each of us is a work in progress. We stumble, we grow, we change. Engaging in this process alongside another person means friction is inevitable.

2 Corinthians urges us to lean into these challenges with care and compassion. We should strive to uplift and encourage each other, especially in moments of tension. Conflict will come, but the best way through comes from focusing on harmony and peace, not pride or personal victory.

Yes, growth can be uncomfortable, but it is for our ultimate good. We ought to embrace these stretching seasons, for ourselves and for those we care about. When we live this way, our relationships with one another will be defined by love and peace, even in the rough patches.

God of peace, imbue us with your love and grace. Help us to extend the patience you show us to those we live alongside. Amen.

Psalm 96:11–12

DAY 245

"Let the heavens be glad, and the earth rejoice! Let the sea and everything in it shout his praise! Let the fields and their crops burst out with joy! Let the trees of the forest sing for joy!" (NLT)

Blue ocean waves sparkle with dappled sunlight and crash rhythmically onto the shore. Foam leaps up and dissolves into the sand. The sea resounds, roaring its praise to the One who spoke it into being.

Vast fields of wheat sway like dancers moving to a joyful rhythm only they can hear. Wildflowers bring bright flashes of color along the edges, each petal unfolding quietly, brilliantly, as if to say "thank you" for the gifts of sunlight and rain.

In the forest, humming with life, trees rise like majestic guardians, their branches lifted high, leaves whispering softly in the wind. Birds nest in the shelter of the high branches, their songs weaving melodies of gratitude and delight.

Creation cannot help but praise the One who made and sustains it. Each wave, each flower, each rustling leaf expresses joy simply by existing, fully and vibrantly alive. We, too, are invited to join this chorus, to lift our voices and hearts in thanksgiving to the Creator who breathes life and beauty into all things—including us.

God, help us join creation's song of joyful praise and gratitude for all you have made. Amen.

DAY

246 Isaiah 61:10

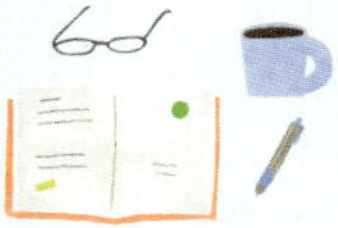

"I delight greatly in the Lord; my soul rejoices in my God. For he has clothed me with garments of salvation and arrayed me in a robe of his righteousness, as a bridegroom adorns his head like a priest, and as a bride adorns herself with her jewels." (NIV)

What does it mean for something to delight us? Delight connotes a high degree of pleasure or extreme satisfaction; when we speak of being delighted, we are conveying more than a vague affection but a deep and abiding joy.

To foster a heart that delights in God means making an intentional declaration of this joy, a soul-deep and expressive state of being. It is not fleeting or dependent on circumstances but rooted in the reality of what God has done for us. Delight is different from happiness in this way; it is not based on what we have but on who God is.

Since God has clothed us in salvation, each day can be the best moment of our lives. Like a bride and groom on their wedding day, we celebrate and enjoy the intimacy and beauty of our relationship with Jesus. We no longer need to strive for worth or approval—we are already covered in divine love. Instead of focusing on what we lack, our hearts remain fixed on the abundance of grace we have received.

Wonderful God, when we ruminate on the care you show us, delight naturally follows. Amen.

2 Corinthians 1:4

DAY
247

"He comforts us in all our troubles so that we can comfort others. When they are troubled, we will be able to give them the same comfort God has given us." (NLT)

There are moments when our lives seem defined by transition, change, and uncertainty. It can be difficult to remain grounded in steadfast faith when we find ourselves continually required to adapt and stretch. Into these spaces, when our foundations feel shaken, God offers resilience—the strength to continue taking on the day's challenges.

Seasons of change are often opportunities for growth. Growth and maturation can be uncomfortable, but when we anticipate the bright and beautiful things God is calling us into, we more easily embrace each new opportunity with a joyful heart. Even so, resilience is not a denial of our worries and pains. God invites us to give voice to our weariness, offering renewal and restoration.

The ultimate Creator governs all things. When the circumstances feel outside of our control, we can lean into that divine power and stability. In relinquishing the burden of control and relying on Jesus, we can find the paths ahead more clearly illuminated.

Almighty God, as we face opposition and upheaval, help us respond with love. Lead us to extend patience to those with whom we are frustrated. Amen.

DAY 248 1 Samuel 1:10-11

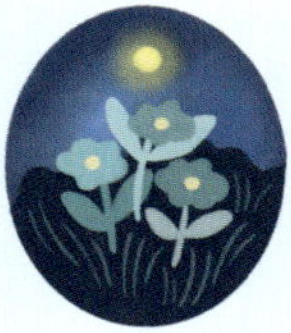

"Hannah was in deep anguish, crying bitterly as she prayed to the Lord. And she made this vow: 'O Lord of Heaven's Armies, if you will look upon my sorrow and answer my prayer and give me a son, then I will give him back to you. ...'" (NLT)

Frustration is often quiet. It builds beneath the surface—grief without language, sorrow without resolution. That frustration can live inside of us, trapped, growing with no outlet in sight. But in scripture, we are reminded that God is not only near to those who exude joy but also close to the breaking point of those who weep.

Hannah wept, neither politely nor privately. She brought her anguish to the altar of the Lord, unedited. And what do we notice? She was not turned away.

We often feel pressure to filter our prayers and approach God with composure. But what if the rawness is the offering? What if our tears, like Hannah's, carry the kind of honesty that makes room for divine response? Frustration is not faithlessness. It is often the beginning of trust.

Let the ache speak. Bring the unspoken disappointments, the unmet hopes, the sharp questions. God is not threatened by our honesty. He meets us in it.

Jesus, may our frustrations be met with your unconditional grace and mercy. Amen.

Hebrews 10:23

DAY 249

“Let us hold tightly without wavering to the hope we affirm, for God can be trusted to keep his promise.” (NLT)

Some days ask everything of us. Each small act of getting up requires every ounce we have to show up. Even when we feel past our limit, there is a quiet refusal to give up.

Hope, on those days, seems less like a soaring feeling and more like a burdened choice. It is a grip that holds when everything else wants to let go. Scripture does not promise ease, but it does offer endurance. A hope rooted not in circumstances, but in the character of Jesus. We believe that this voice can be trusted. We will not forget how Jesus has shown us who he is.

Strength for today is not always found in loud declarations. Sometimes, it’s found in whispers, in breath prayers, in holding on by a thread. And hope for tomorrow? It is not naive. It is anchored in a God who has been faithful before and will be faithful again.

Breathe in: Strength for today
Breathe out: and hope for tomorrow. Amen.

DAY

250 Acts 1:14

"They all met together and were constantly united in prayer, along with Mary the mother of Jesus, several other women, and the brothers of Jesus." (NLT)

Prayer is more than a spiritual discipline—it is the heartbeat of our relationship with God. In Acts 1:14, we see the early believers gathered together "constantly united in prayer." This constancy connotes how important faith was to the disciples; it touched every aspect of their lives.

We pray for many reasons: for guidance when the path ahead is unclear, for gratitude when we recognize God's goodness, in lament when our hearts are heavy, and in praise when we see God's glory. Prayer can also take many forms—specific petitions, quiet moments of stillness, or simple words whispered throughout the day.

But more than a list of requests, prayer is a posture. It is a continual openness to God's presence, a way of tuning our hearts to hear Jesus' voice. It means placing our relationship with Jesus at the very center of our lives, letting everything else flow from that connection. Continual prayer doesn't mean we never stop talking—it means we never stop listening, seeking, and depending on God. In every moment, we are invited to draw near.

May we respond to that invitation daily, living lives grounded in prayer, shaped by your holy presence, and rooted in deep relationship with your Son. Amen.

Matthew 6:24

DAY

251

“No one can serve two masters. For you will hate one and love the other; you will be devoted to one and despise the other. You cannot serve God and be enslaved to money.” (NLT)

There is tension in divided devotion. We feel it when we try to please everyone. When we chase both peace and performance. When we want to be faithful but also in control.

Jesus’ words in Matthew 6 are not merely a rebuke; they are a rescue for all of us who are being torn by our allegiances.

“You cannot serve two masters”—not because it’s morally impossible, but because it’s spiritually exhausting. We were not made to live fragmented. God invites us to return to wholeness, not just with our actions, but with our attention.

We often think we can pretend that this divided worship isn’t fracturing us; Jesus invites us to let that go. He invites us into worship that isn’t based on rigidity but clarity. A clarity centered on focusing our attention solely on him.

So we ask: What has quietly become our master? What voice has grown louder than God’s? And we remember: the divine voice leads us not into performance, but into peace.

Jesus, fix our hearts and minds on you. As we experience communion with you, bring us out of the disunity of the world. Amen.

DAY

252 Psalm 30:4–5

"Sing to the Lord, all you godly ones! Praise his holy name. For his anger lasts only a moment, but his favor lasts a lifetime! Weeping may last through the night, but joy comes with the morning." (NLT)

Suffering is an undeniable part of life. Scripture doesn't ignore this reality—instead, it meets us in it. Psalm 30 gently acknowledges that "weeping may last through the night, but joy comes with the morning."

Pain may linger, and nights may feel long, but they are not forever. God's steadfast love, mercy, and faithfulness outlast every hardship. It is not momentary, but a constant presence that carries us even when we can't feel it.

Holding on to hope means leaning into a deep and abiding confidence in God's goodness, even when our circumstances suggest otherwise. Our suffering does not define us. God's promises do. And God promises the night will not last forever.

The divine timeline often stretches beyond our understanding, but the promise is sure: joy *will* come. Morning *will* break. Amid sorrow, we can hold on—not with shallow optimism, but with rooted hope in the One who brings beauty from brokenness.

Even in our hardest seasons, we can sing praises to you, Jesus. Not because all is well, but because we know that one day it will be. That is the hope we cling to. Amen.

Isaiah 46:4

DAY
253

"I will be your God throughout your lifetime ... I made you, and I will care for you. I will carry you along and save you." (NLT)

We often imagine rescue as dramatic: a miracle in motion, a visible reversal. But more often, it comes quietly. It is carried in small mercies, hidden in ordinary days.

Sometimes, rescue looks like strength to rise again. Sometimes, it sounds like a friend who calls at the right time. It's the breath that comes after a long cry or the stillness that follows unrest. These, too, are moments of rescue.

Heavenly rescue is not always defined by the removal of hardship but by how God sustains us in the midst of it. Jesus' promise that he will hold us and care for us does not come with conditions or expiration.

Isaiah reminds us that God remains with us from beginning to end, not as a distant protector but a personal rescuer. God carries us not once but continually.

There is no place in our story, no matter how dark or distant, beyond His reach. No age limit, depth of sorrow, or failure exempts us from Jesus' love for us. We are released from our need to carry things not meant for us.

God, we recognize that we are not expected to save ourselves; that was never the design. May we be carried by you. Amen.

DAY 254 2 Corinthians 5:17

"This means that anyone who belongs to Christ has become a new person. The old life is gone; a new life has begun!" (NLT)

Scripture promises us that God is making all things new. God is birthing a new kind of world into being, one where people live in healthy, caring relationships with one another, ourselves, God, and our planet. A creation full of harmony, brimming over with life and abundance.

We live in faith that renewal and rebirth is possible—and that it includes us. God is making *us* new.

We get to live in ways of justice and love, shedding our old ways of greed, inauthenticity, timidity, prejudice, exclusivity, the kind of individualism that comes at the expense of community wellbeing, anything else that hinders the thriving of our communities and our world.

God invites us to live in a new and beautiful way today. A way that is being revealed in all the places where God's Spirit is alive and active. New things are coming into being, and Jesus invites us to experience life anew.

God, thank you for making us new, every day and as often as we need it. Help us see your new ways of being all around us, and help us live into these ways. Amen.

Psalm 22:1–2

DAY 255

"My God, my God, why have you abandoned me? Why are you so far away when I groan for help? Every day I call to you, my God, but you do not answer. Every night I lift my voice, but I find no relief." (NLT)

We've all known moments where our prayers seem to hit a wall, where silence is the only response. As he agonizingly hangs from a Roman cross, Jesus, quoting this psalm, relates to this experience, his raw cry affirming how feeling utterly alone resonates with a deep human experience. The psalmist's words remind us that it's okay to express our deepest pain to God. It's okay to question, to doubt, and to feel abandoned.

True faith isn't about pretending everything is perfect; it's about being honest with God, even when God seems far away. The act of crying out to God even amid the silence is itself an expression of faith. The very act of seeking displays a conviction that there is a God who is present, who can hear us, even if we don't perceive or understand God's response.

We voice all our pain and confusion to you, O God, trusting that you are present, you are working in our deepest struggles even though we cannot see or hear you. Amen.

DAY
256 Psalm 119:34

"Give me understanding and I will obey your instructions; I will put them into practice with all my heart." (NLT)

God does not withhold wisdom but is generous with it. When we ask for understanding, we are met with clarity. We wrestle with the delivery and timing of understanding, yet these things are given to us in God's time and in God's way.

Understanding is not about intellectual mastery. It is about alignment—a heart that longs to walk in step with God's will. When we ask Jesus to open our minds, he also shapes our desires. He teaches us not only what to know but also how to trust. Some answers come slowly. Others arrive through lived experience through the practice of surrender, patience, and presence.

This is the posture of faith: to ask, to listen, and then to move, not perfectly but wholeheartedly. Admitting we don't know is an act of humility. But it is also an act of hope to believe that God will provide what we need.

God, you do not expect us to know everything. You draw us close to you for direction and faithfully lead. Even now, we can be still; you are already guiding us. Amen.

Matthew 18:3

DAY
257

"Then he said, 'I tell you the truth, unless you turn from your sins and become like little children, you will never get into the Kingdom of Heaven.'" (NLT)

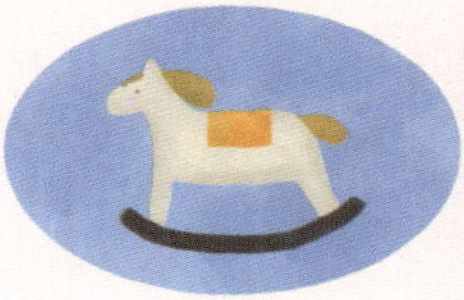

It's easy to overlook the simple gift of childlike wonder. Focused as we are on project timelines and action items, carving out space to marvel and play can seem antithetical. Yet, Jesus tells us to take our cues from children and marvel at the blessings of God.

To become childlike means shedding the layers of cynicism and skepticism that life builds around us and embracing a sense of curiosity. Children have a unique ability to praise without reservation. When we approach God with childlike wonder, we create a stronghold against the doubts and fears that often overwhelm us. Our genuine awe invites us to ponder the great works of our Creator. Each day becomes an opportunity to uncover the beauty that surrounds.

In a world that values grown-up pragmatism, embracing childlike wonder can be a revolutionary act of faith. It means surrendering our need for complete understanding. When we lean into God's guidance with unwavering trust, our paths become clearer, and our lives are filled with purpose.

May we approach you, Jesus, with open hearts, ready to explore the depths of your love. In doing so, we draw nearer to God's heart. Amen.

DAY

258 James 4:8

"Come close to God, and God will come close to you." (NLT)

The invitation of the Gospel is always open: draw near.

We need not search for Jesus in distant places, and we do not have to earn proximity. God's nearness is not conditional; it is constant, waiting to be noticed.

We are the ones who often drift. We fill our days with noise and motion, crowding out the quiet where presence speaks. But God does not retreat in response to our distraction. God waits with patience, not punishment.

To be present with Jesus begins not in effort but in awareness—a slowing, a turning of the heart, a whisper of attention that says, "I'm here." There is no threshold too far, no silence too long. We are welcomed without hesitation, even when we return with heavy hearts or hurried minds.

Jesus is not only someone to follow. He is someone to be with, to linger beside, to be known by, and to rest in. In joy or sorrow, stillness or movement, he remains in every moment.

Remind us, Jesus, that it is not too late to return. We have not missed our chance. You are already near. Amen.

Psalm 103:17

DAY 259

"But the love of the Lord remains forever with those who fear him. His salvation extends to the children's children." (NLT)

"Nothing lasts forever." It's a phrase we say often, usually with a hint of sadness or resignation. Life changes. Seasons shift. Even the most meaningful relationships can fade. In a world marked by impermanence, it's easy to assume that love, too, has an expiration date.

While this may be so for fallible humans, God stands apart. Divine love is not fickle or fleeting. It stands apart from every other kind we know—unaffected by time, failure, or change.

Scripture repeatedly points to the unchanging nature of God. The Creator was here before the world began and will remain forevermore. And because love is at the very heart of who God is, divine love reflects this eternal nature.

This love is not just for today, not just for us—it extends to generation after generation. It is a promise that outlasts our lifetimes, anchoring us in something sure and lasting.

Christ, in a world where so much fades, we can rest in the truth that your love will not. You are steady, faithful, and everlasting—holding us through every change and carrying us into eternity. Amen.

DAY

260 Numbers 6:24-26

"May the Lord bless you and protect you. May the Lord smile on you and be gracious to you. May the Lord show you his favor and give you his peace." (NLT)

Amid division, unrest, and constant noise, the call to live in peace can feel almost impossible. But the peace God offers is not the absence of conflict; it is the presence of wholeness, rooted in unwavering goodness. The words from Numbers 6:24-26 are the Priestly Blessing, a reminder and a promise. They were spoken again and again over the people of Israel, a declaration of God's desire to bless, protect, and bring peace to all. Even today, this blessing serves as a comfort and commission—a call to receive God's peace and become carriers of it.

To live out *shalom* in unpeaceful times is not to ignore the brokenness around us but to be a quiet force for healing within it. It means embodying grace, kindness, and gentleness in our words and actions. It means choosing restoration over retaliation, presence over avoidance.

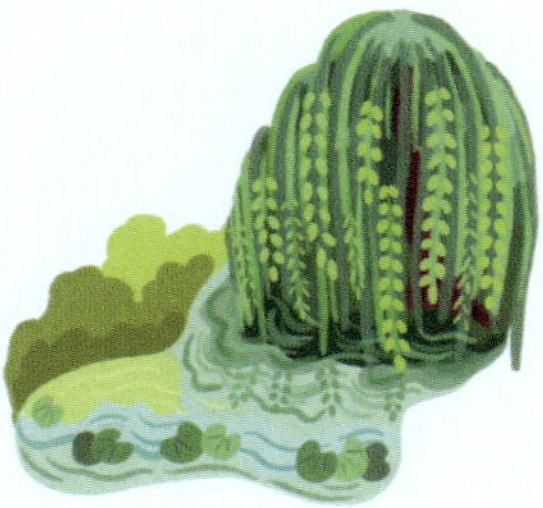

Shalom is not a one-time gift; it's a posture we return to daily. As we receive God's blessing, we are invited to extend it—to be people who, through God's favor, bring peace into every corner of a hurting world.

Jesus, bless and keep us today and everyday. Empower us to be beacons of your light and peace. Amen.

Proverbs 4:25–27 DAY 261

"Look straight ahead, and fix your eyes on what lies before you. Mark out a straight path for your feet; stay on the safe path. Don't get sidetracked; keep your feet from following evil." (NLT)

Distractions will always pull at our focus, tempt us to detour, and ask us to compromise. They rarely appear as threats. Busyness, competition, and comfort slowly seep in as quiet diversions that inevitably nudge our hearts off course.

Proverbs details the beauty of wisdom, which calls us forward and anchors us with purpose. When our eyes are fixed on God, our steps become clearer. This is not about taking perfect steps; it's about direction. We are not called to be flawless but faithful. We will stumble and forget. But even then, the invitation remains: *return your gaze*. Fixing our hearts on God means choosing the steady over the scattered, letting God's love guide everything else.

And it is a choice we make again and again—not once, but daily. To look up. To stay present. To walk with intention.

Set our eyes ahead, Jesus. Let our hearts follow. Even when the path narrows, help us stay the course. You are guiding our every step. Amen.

DAY

262 Mark 14:3

"Meanwhile, Jesus was in Bethany at the home of Simon, a man who had previously had leprosy. While he was eating, a woman came in with a beautiful alabaster jar of expensive perfume made from essence of nard. She broke open the jar and poured the perfume over his head." (NLT)

Beauty, love, generosity. These attributes are at the heart of the Good News of Jesus.

Often, we are ensnared by the ceaseless pursuit of wealth and social status. We become preoccupied with scarcity, always striving for more. Under this mindset, anything not growing our net worth is a waste of time. Mark 14 reminds us to reevaluate our priorities and recognize the beauty in acts of extravagant love.

This woman's story is a poignant reminder that our lives are enriched not by the accumulation of material possessions but by the depth of our relationships and the moments of connection we create. Her actions were not motivated by a desire for recognition or self-gain but by selfless love for Jesus.

Just as the fragrance of the perfume lingered in the air, the impact of the woman's gift resonates across time, inviting us to consider how our actions can leave a lasting legacy. Her devotion is an emblem of the transformative power of love—a love that transcends societal norms and expectations.

May we learn to appreciate the beauty in simple gestures and to pour forth our love without reservation. Amen.

Matthew 4:19

DAY
263

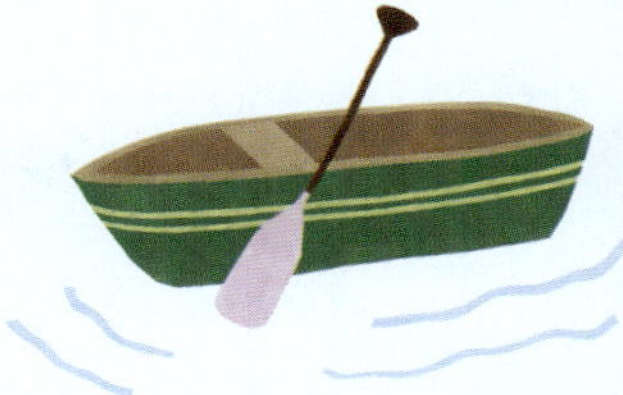

"Jesus called out to them, 'Come, follow me, and I will show you how to fish for people!'" (NLT)

We often imagine that a calling from Jesus must be loud and dramatic—something that radically interrupts our lives with undeniable force. But in Matthew 4:19, the moment is strikingly simple. In the middle of an ordinary workday, Jesus calls out to a group of fishermen: "Come, follow me." There's no spectacle, no thunder from Heaven. Just a quiet invitation that meets them right where they are. This is how Jesus often calls us—not with fanfare but with gentleness. In the middle of errands, meetings, or mundane routines, he offers us the chance to follow, to be part of something eternal.

These soft invitations, though easy to overlook, can lead to seismic shifts within us. For those fishermen, a short conversation changed everything. They left behind what they knew and stepped into a story that would reshape the world.

Jesus is still calling—quietly, persistently—inviting us to participate in the work of his Kingdom. All we need to do is listen and follow. In his gentleness, there is power. And in our ordinary moments, there is the potential for extraordinary transformation.

God, grant us the ears to hear your gentle invitations and the confidence to step out in faith. Amen.

DAY

264 Jeremiah 1:5

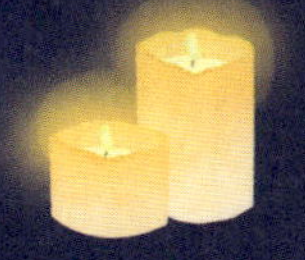

"I knew you before I formed you in your mother's womb. Before you were born I set you apart and appointed you as my prophet to the nations." (NLT)

We all long to be known—to be seen, understood, and accepted in the fullness of who we are. To be cherished—not despite our complexity and imperfection but within it—feels like the deepest kind of love.

This longing finds its fulfillment in God. Before we drew breath, before we even knew ourselves, God knew us. The Almighty saw us fully and called us for a purpose.

We don't need to hide parts of ourselves in God's presence. Our Creator formed every fiber of our being. And even in our failures and doubts, God remains faithful, still offering us a purpose that is uniquely ours.

In a world that constantly urges us to question our identity and value, we can root ourselves in this unshakable truth: we are known and loved by God. Our identity as children of God is the core from which everything else flows.

When we feel lost or unsure, we can return to the One who knows us completely.

In you, Lord Jesus, we are safe to be authentic, and from you, we receive the call to live fully into who we were made to be. Amen.

Psalm 68:19

DAY 265

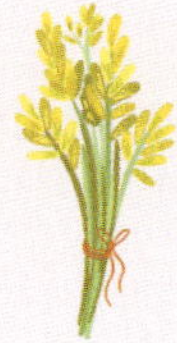

"Praise the Lord; praise God our savior! For each day he carries us in his arms." (NLT)

What do we truly need to get through each day? The world often answers with a loud chorus: more. More stuff, more success, more comfort. We are constantly told that we need something else—one more product, one more achievement—to feel secure or satisfied.

But scripture offers a different vision defined by reliance and trust in our Creator. Living each day not in excess, but in enough. God meets us in our daily needs—giving strength for today, grace for this hour, and peace for this moment.

Simplicity invites us to step back from the noise of consumerism and be present to the quiet abundance already in our lives. When we stop chasing more, we begin to notice the steady rhythm of God's provision.

God is not distant or withholding but near and attentive, carrying us with care. When we trust in Christ's daily provision, we no longer need to hoard or grasp. Instead, we can be content in the knowledge that we are held, fed, and sustained.

Let us praise the One who provides—not always with excess but always with enough.

God, you carry us. Each day, you give us what we truly need. Amen.

DAY

266 2 Thessalonians 3:16

"Now may the Lord of peace himself give you his peace at all times and in every situation." (NLT)

There are seasons when peace feels out of reach.

We may know the words and hold the verses close, but still, we wonder: Can peace find us here, in the middle of uncertainty, heaviness, or silence?

Scripture does not present peace as a prize for the unshaken. Instead, it is a gift from the Lord of Peace Himself. Not someday, but now. Peace doesn't only appear in the absence of struggle but in the heart of it.

This peace does not demand that we be sure of everything. It meets us where we are—tired, questioning, tender. Jesus does not demand that we hold it all together to be held by God in return. He is not impatient with our doubt. He is present within it.

May Jesus' peace settle over us like still waters in every situation. May his peace hold us in everything that feels too heavy to name.

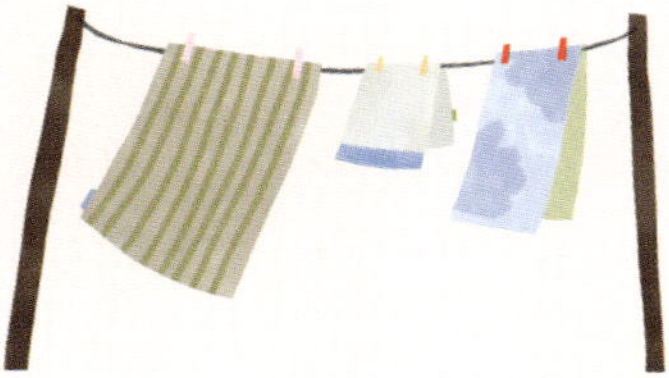

Breathe in: We receive what we cannot create—
Breathe out: perfect peace that holds us here. Amen.

1 Corinthians 12:12–13 DAY 267

"The human body has many parts, but the many parts make up one whole body. So it is with the body of Christ. Some of us are Jews, some are Gentiles, some are slaves, and some are free. But we have all been baptized into one body by one Spirit, and we all share the same Spirit." (NLT)

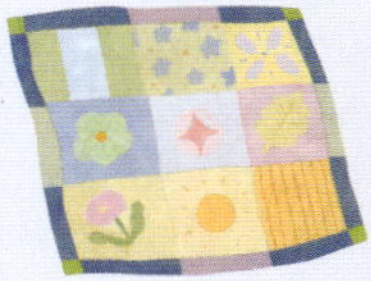

Now more than ever, the call to unity in Christ is radical and necessary. Paul reminds us that though we come from different backgrounds, carry different gifts, and serve in different roles, we are one body, bound together by the same Spirit.

Unity does not erase our uniqueness; rather, it brings harmony through our shared identity in Christ. It is not something we manufacture but something the Holy Spirit births in us. Regardless of ethnicity, status, or story, we are welcomed into the same family of God, baptized into one body. As members of that body, we are called to care for, serve, and honor one another. No one is more important than anyone else. Each person carries value, and each role has purpose.

Living in unity requires humility, patience, and love. It asks us to look beyond ourselves and see Christ in one another. It calls us to resist the spirit of division and embody the peace and belonging found in Jesus.

May we live out this unity, not just in word, but in action, so that the world might see the beauty of a body made whole in you, Jesus. Amen.

DAY
268 Job 11:7–9

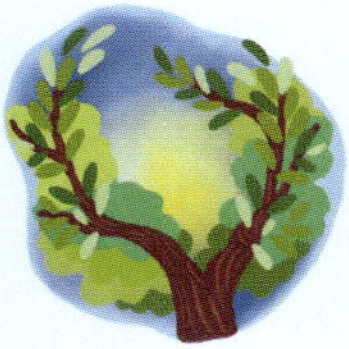

"Can you fathom the mysteries of God? Can you probe the limits of the Almighty? They are higher than the heavens above—what can you do? They are deeper than the depths below—what can you know? Their measure is longer than the earth and wider than the sea." (NIV)

Certainty can be so comforting. Knowing exactly how things are going to play out, exactly what the best choice is, exactly what God has planned for our lives—these are answers we crave, especially when life feels out of our control. But certainty is an illusion, and the relentless pursuit of certainty, the eradication of doubt, can lead us to spiral.

The truth is, we do not and cannot know everything. Our minds and understandings are limited, while God's wisdom is infinite. And it's better that way. The mysteries of God are a key part of why God deserves our worship. When we tune into the feeling of mystery and wonder, we feel the beauty of God's transcendence. And when we leave room for mystery, we open ourselves up to being surprised and amazed by what Jesus has in store.

Almighty God, thank you for your overwhelming glory, the mystery of your power and love. Thank you that we are not in control. We ask that you keep our hearts in a posture of wonder and acceptance in the face of the unknown. Amen.

Isaiah 22:22

DAY
269

"I will give him the key to the house of David—the highest position in the royal court. When he opens doors, no one will be able to close them; when he closes doors, no one will be able to open them." (NLT)

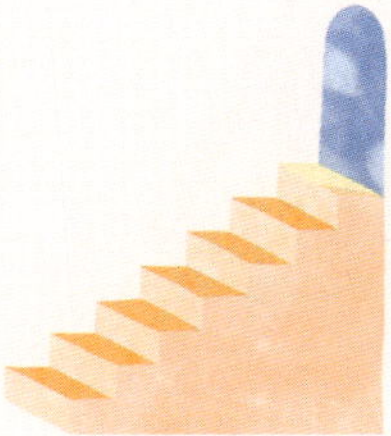

"When God closes a door, He opens a window." It's a clichéd turn of phrase. Said in the face of unexpected disappointment, this aphorism demonstrates our desire to make sense of letdown. When an opportunity we were excited for falls through or when a relationship we counted on breaks, this idea can be a consolation.

But scripture asserts that this is more than just a trite saying. God, as Author and Architect of creation, directs all paths. We will all end up where God is leading us. When forces (be they internal or external) attempt to thwart God, God continues to move mountains, to open doors, to bring us back on course.

Unexpected change and disappointment still hurt. We may struggle to understand the destination God is guiding us to. But amid that frustration, the assurances of scripture can be a balm. There is always a way forward, and God is inviting us through.

Help us to place our confidence in you, Jesus. Let us walk through each new door with anticipation and trust. Amen.

DAY

270 Psalm 103:2–5

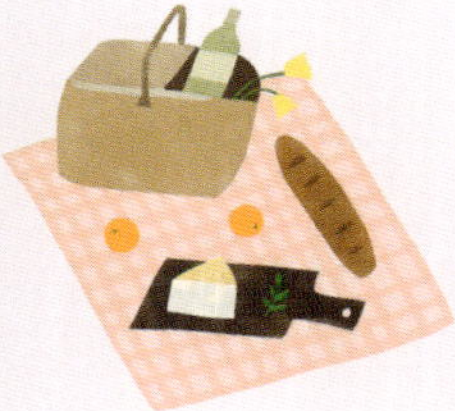

"Let all that I am praise the Lord; may I never forget the good things he does for me. He forgives all my sins and heals all my diseases. He redeems me from death and crowns me with love and tender mercies. He fills my life with good things." (NLT)

It takes intention to recognize and seek out the goodness knitted through our lives' tiny moments and still pauses. Goodness is stitched into our days—not because life is always easy, but because God is always near.

We are quick to forget. Gratitude can slip through our hands as the pace of life pushes forward. But the psalmist calls us to stop and remember: to name the blessings, to notice the grace.

God's goodness is not stored up for someday. It is present in breath, beauty, and unseen kindnesses that sustain us in laughter around a table, in the morning light, and in the strength to begin again.

To enjoy life's blessings is not to take them lightly. It is to hold them with wonder. To receive them as signs of a God who delights in giving.

Generous Jesus, let us not rush past goodness. Let us pause, name it, and give thanks. Amen.

2 Peter 3:18

DAY
271

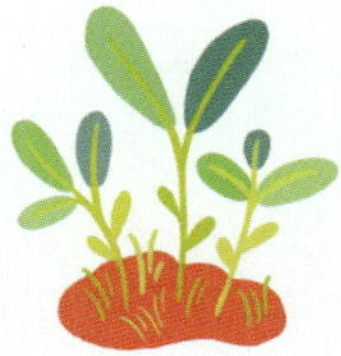

"Rather, you must grow in the grace and knowledge of our Lord and Savior Jesus Christ. All glory to him, both now and forever! Amen." (NLT)

It can be tempting to view faith as a clear dichotomy: we either have it or we don't. From this vantage point, following Jesus is an isolated moment, a single decision. But the truth is, a vibrant faith life means submitting ourselves to constant growth.

None of us is perfect. We make mistakes, we have ever more to experience and learn. The Good News is that perfection is not demanded from us to be in relationship with God. We need not feel burdened or kept back by our shortcomings. However, we also cannot stay locked in them.

To live faithfully means recognizing our growth edges and inviting God into them. Jesus is continually refining our hearts, inviting us to deepen our understanding and step all the more into his example of love, grace, and patience.

We must answer this call. We need not be perfect, but we should not be stagnant. There is room for each of us in the Kingdom of God, and there is also room for us to grow while there.

Jesus, may we bring glory to you as we mature in wisdom and faith. You are the source of all growth; may we embrace your lessons joyfully. Amen.

DAY
272 Luke 6:36–37

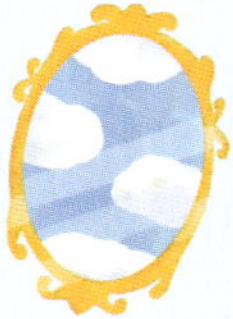

"Be merciful, just as your Father is merciful. Do not judge, and you will not be judged. Do not condemn, and you will not be condemned. Forgive, and you will be forgiven." (NIV)

How we treat others should reflect how God treats us: with compassion. We cannot judge another person's heart because we cannot fully know their heart. We cannot honestly say "that person is irredeemable." Only God knows our intentions, challenges, and context. When we make sweeping judgments about another's character, we make many assumptions. And we have no right to assume!

Instead of judging people, we can offer compassion: "I don't know their situation." "I don't know what led them to make that decision." But how do we balance this perspective with honest acknowledgement of wrongdoing? Rather than making generalizations about someone's character, we can speak to how a specific action made us feel. We can hold compassion and speak up at the same time. Our relationships will often be better for it.

Approaching others with compassion can also teach us to have self-compassion. If we notice ourselves feeling short-tempered or easily offended, it's worth taking a look at how we speak to ourselves. One attitude often informs the other.

Dear Jesus, thank you for showing us compassion with each new sunrise. We ask that you teach us how to show compassion toward others, just as you do toward us. Amen.

Deuteronomy 33:26–27 DAY 273

"There is no one like the God of Israel. He rides across the heavens to help you, across the skies in majestic splendor. The eternal God is your refuge, and his everlasting arms are under you. He drives out the enemy before you; he cries out, 'Destroy them!'" (NLT)

In seasons of uncertainty, we long for something or someone to steady us, for a source of security. Experience has taught us that much of what we hope will be stable turns out to be precarious and fleeting. Help often feels out of reach.

These verses remind us that God is not only a mighty source of help but also constantly near. The everlasting arms of God enfold us—strength and love combined in one embrace.

How radical is our Creator! Clothed in majestic splendor and coming to the aid of humanity nonetheless. God is powerful, but that divine power is not distant. God moves toward us in compassion and care. "The eternal God is your refuge," not just a shelter we run to but a home we live in. God's love isn't a rest stop of momentary comfort but an enduring fortress.

This is the stability we've been searching for. God's arms are strong enough to carry us, gentle enough to comfort. They do not grow weary. While the foundations of the world around shift, God never lets us go.

To be enfolded in your love, God, is to be secure even amid life's storms. Amen.

DAY 274 Ephesians 1:4-5

"Even before he made the world, God loved us and chose us in Christ to be holy and without fault in his eyes. God decided in advance to adopt us into his own family by bringing us to himself through Jesus Christ. This is what he wanted to do, and it gave him great pleasure." (NLT)

We all yearn to understand who we are and why we matter. While the world around us defines identity by achievement, appearance, or approval, scripture offers us a grounding truth: our identity is rooted not in what we do, but in who God is—and in God's eternal love for us.

Ephesians 1:4-5 tells us that even before the world began, God saw us, knew us, and chose us. God lovingly adopts us into the divine family through Christ, not out of obligation, but because it brings God joy. Our identities are not accidental or uncertain. We are chosen. We belong. To be adopted is to be fully integrated into a family, granted full rights, inheritance, and status—and in Christ, we are given the same. We are not distant acquaintances of God but beloved children.

Understanding this identity transforms how we live. We are called to be a set-apart people, not striving for perfection but allowing Christ to shape us in holiness and love.

We are not defined by our past, our failures, or what others say. We are defined by God's choosing, Christ's love, and the Spirit's work in us. Let that shape everything. Amen.

John 20:14–16

DAY
275

“She turned to leave and saw someone standing there. It was Jesus, but she didn’t recognize him. ‘Dear woman, why are you crying?’ Jesus asked her. ‘Who are you looking for?’ She thought he was the gardener ... ‘Mary!’ Jesus said. She turned to him and cried out, ‘Rabboni!’” (NLT)

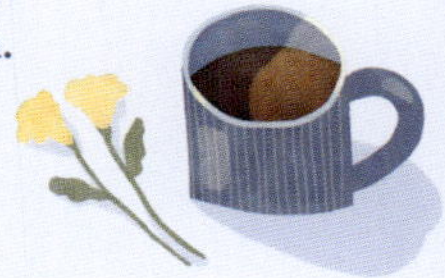

Three days after Jesus’ death, Mary stood outside the empty tomb, overwhelmed by loss. She searched desperately, expecting death but finding only confusion. Then a voice called her name and, in an instant, sorrow gave way to recognition. It was Jesus, alive, surprising her with unexpected joy.

Sometimes we anticipate finding Jesus only in sacred spaces, quiet times of prayer, or familiar rituals. Yet, just as he did with Mary, Jesus meets us where we least expect: in ordinary conversations, in moments of surprising kindness, and even in our grief. We may not recognize him at first, but then he calls our name, and suddenly our eyes open. What once seemed ordinary becomes holy ground. The mundane reveals the sacred; the overlooked moment becomes a place of encounter.

Jesus delights in surprising us. Our invitation is simply to pay attention—to trust that the risen Christ may appear anywhere, speaking our name, revealing that he is alive, near, and profoundly present, even in places where we least expect it.

Jesus, open our eyes and hearts to recognize you wherever you appear today. Amen.

DAY

276 1 Corinthians 16:14

"And do everything with love." (NLT)

Deep down, don't we all crave to be loved without condition, without measure? We yearn for relationships in which grace abounds and forgiveness is readily offered. Yet, in the practicality of our day-to-day lives, we build walls of self-protection, fearing vulnerability. We keep score of offenses, believing justice demands repayment. We set limits based on past hurts or perceived slights. In a world that often seems transactional, the very idea of loving without limits seems idealistic and, therefore, impossible.

Nonetheless, the command of scripture to this kind of love isn't a suggestion. It's an invitation into the possibility of an experience beyond our human limitations—love not from within but from above—love that flows from the heart, the character of the Creator.

God creates us out of love. God continues to love us without condition, sacrificially, even as we don't reciprocate but choose again and again to break the divine heart. It is in both our recognition and reliance upon the divine unconditional love of Jesus that we gain the will and power to fully love others, even our enemies, without limits and in full measure.

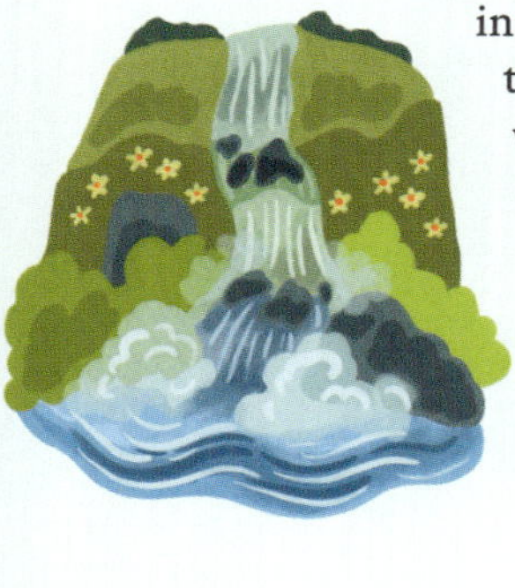

Compassionate God, empower us to love others without reservation, just as you have loved us. Amen.

DAY

2 Thessalonians 2:16–17 277

"Now may our Lord Jesus Christ himself and God our Father, who loved us and by his grace gave us eternal comfort and a wonderful hope, comfort you and strengthen you in every good thing you do and say." (NLT)

We may expect love to thin out over time. We worry that we will do something to lose it. We may even fear we've used up our second chances. But God's grace is not rationed. It arrives endlessly, like waves meeting the shore.

Grace comes again and again: layered, abundant, undeserved.

This is the comfort we are given: that grace is not dependent on our perfection but anchored in God's unchanging nature. It reaches us when we falter, sustains us when we serve, and strengthens us when words feel small and the good we try to do feels unseen.

When we doubt our impact or question our worth, Jesus' grace steadies us—not with grand gestures but with this quiet assurance: *You are not doing this alone.*

This is not the kind of strength we earn; it is the kind that is poured into us. Grace upon grace.

Let us move forward by exuding the grace you give us, Jesus. Amen.

DAY

278 Habakkuk 1:5

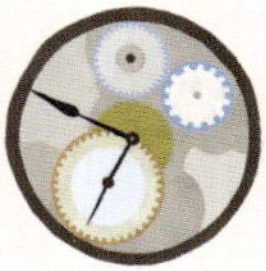

"The Lord replied, 'Look around at the nations; look and be amazed! For I am doing something in your own day, something you wouldn't believe even if someone told you about it.'" (NLT)

Regardless of the tenacity of our faith, we all experience seasons when God seems distant or inactive. Sometimes, our prayers seem to go unanswered, justice feels delayed, and our hope starts to waver. Habakkuk 1:5 reminds us that even when we can't perceive it, God is always moving. The wonder and goodness of God's plans are beyond our comprehension.

God's methods and timing are often unexpected. How we, with our limited and individual perspectives, would anticipate resolution cannot measure up to the plans of the omniscient and eternal Creator. In these seasons, we can rest assured that while God's work may not always look the way we want it to, it is always good, purposeful, and just.

God invites us to look and see, to remain attentive and expectant in periods of doubt. Wonder and awe are spiritual postures that ground us in hope and humility. When the world feels silent, God is working. When outcomes seem delayed, God is still faithful. Our calling is not to fully understand the ineffable but to continually trust.

We wait, expectantly and excitedly, for the great things you are doing, Jesus. Amen.

John 15:15

DAY
279

“I no longer call you slaves, because a master doesn’t confide in his slaves. Now you are my friends, since I have told you everything the Father told me.” (NLT)

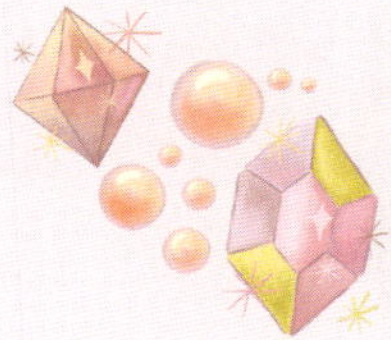

There is something profoundly moving about being chosen not out of obligation but out of love. In John 15:15, Jesus offers us precisely this kind of relationship. Our walk with Jesus isn’t a distant, authoritative relationship—it’s one marked by closeness, trust, and love. The Son of God does not relate to us as mere servants but invites us into friendship. He doesn’t withhold truth or affection but shares the very heart of God with us.

This love isn’t transactional. Our value isn’t derived from our usefulness or success. We are not simply tools in God’s plan—we are companions on the journey. Jesus delights in us. The value Jesus extends to us is definitive; our identity is shaped not by what we do, but by who we are in him. When we begin to grasp this, our striving softens. Our worth is not tied to our status, our resume, or our past. It is grounded in God’s unchanging love and grace.

God, you don’t simply command from afar, but walk with us, speak to us, and welcome us into friendship. Thank you for this gift. Amen.

DAY
280 John 13:14–15

"And since I, your Lord and Teacher, have washed your feet, you ought to wash each other's feet. I have given you an example to follow. Do as I have done to you." (NLT)

We often talk about "random acts of kindness"—small, unexpected gestures that catch others off guard. But underneath that phrase is an assumption: that kindness is surprising, conditional, or something to be earned. At times, we treat it like a favor, a way to feel good about ourselves, or something to be repaid.

But this isn't how scripture defines kindness. In John 13, Jesus kneels to wash the disciples' feet. It's a shocking act of humility, one that unsettles those receiving it. And that's the point. Jesus isn't offering kindness because the disciples earned it. He's showing them—and us—that kindness is love in motion.

God's love is not calculated or transactional. It is complete, unconditional, and freely given. Jesus calls us not just to admire this love but to live it out. "I have given you an example to follow," he says. True kindness flows from a heart shaped by Christ's love. It's not about being polite or "nice." It's about showing up with grace, especially when it's inconvenient or undeserved.

When we extend kindness, we mirror the love you show us, God. Not randomly, but intentionally—every small act is a reflection of you, the One who first loved us. Amen.

DAY

Romans 12:12

281

"Be joyful in hope, patient in affliction, faithful in prayer." (NIV)

Hope can feel naive, like blind optimism out of touch with reality. Who are we to have hope in the midst of our life's hardships and the world's suffering?

But hope is not a silly or trite thing: it is a comfort. It is brave, even strong. Hope keeps us going in our darkest moments. When we face suffering, disappointment, and betrayal, it is hope for the better, for things being set right, for our lives to improve, for God to intercede, that helps us persevere.

Every day holds something new, and positive developments are happening without our knowledge. There is more than meets the eye. While we endure hardships now, we can hope that tomorrow will be different, that soon our circumstances will change. And beyond that, we always have hope in Jesus, because his love is unwavering, his care everlasting.

Jesus, thank you for being the foundation of our hope and preserving us amid challenges and fear. We ask that you show us how to share that hope with others. Amen.

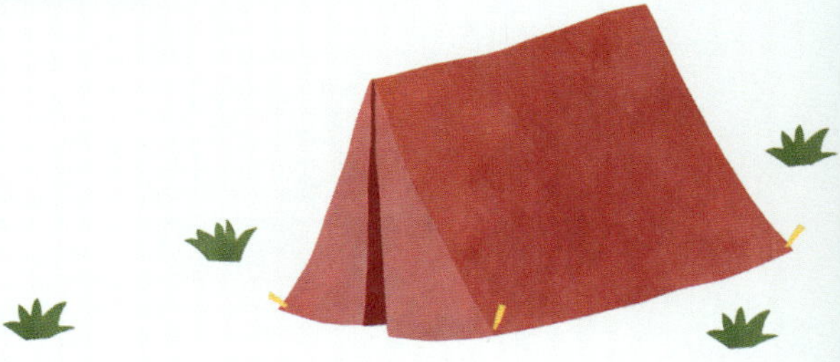

DAY

282 Deuteronomy 8:3

"He humbled you, causing you to hunger and then feeding you with manna, which neither you nor your ancestors had known, to teach you that man does not live on bread alone but on every word that comes from the mouth of the Lord." (NIV)

Our world preaches self-reliance and self-sufficiency. We pedestal so-called "self-made men" and repeat tongue-in-cheek aphorisms like "God helps those who help themselves." In contrast, the actual declaration of scripture may shock us: we are called to walk in daily dependence on God.

Deuteronomy 8 points back to the blessing of manna in the wilderness, when the people of Israel were hungry and God provided food from the heavens. When we feel needy or desperate, we may feel that we need to pull ourselves up by our bootstraps and take care of ourselves. But this story reminds us that seasons of need are not evidence of God's absence but often the very places Jesus uses to point us back to him.

God's provision may not come in the form we expect, but it is always sufficient. Manna was unfamiliar to the Israelites, but it was exactly what they needed. This divine provision extends beyond our physical needs to our spiritual needs as well. God has provided us a feast of spiritual food in the form of the wisdom of scripture. When we feel shaken or uncertain, we can turn to God's Word for guidance and renewal.

Daily dependence isn't weakness—it's where strength is formed. Amen.

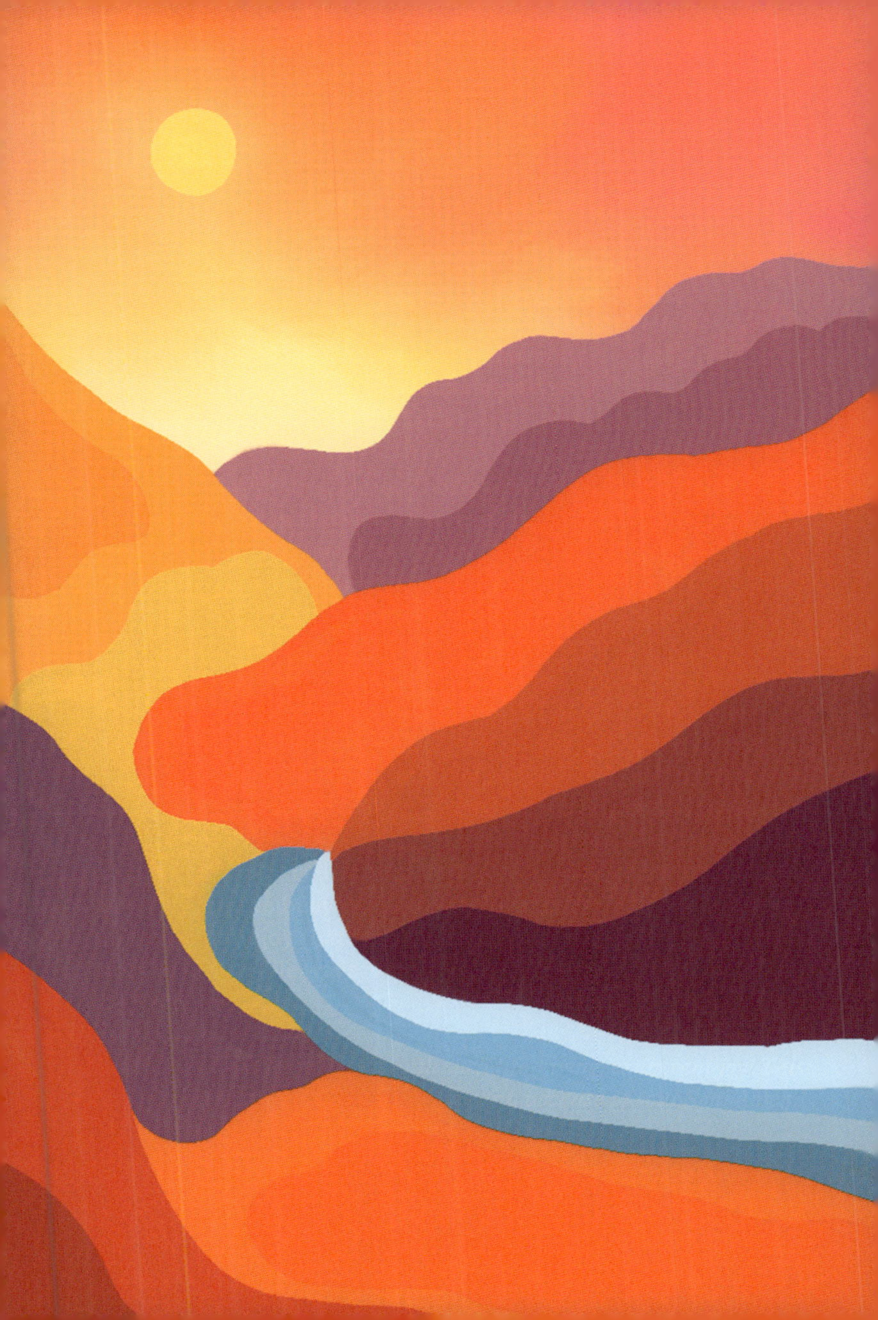

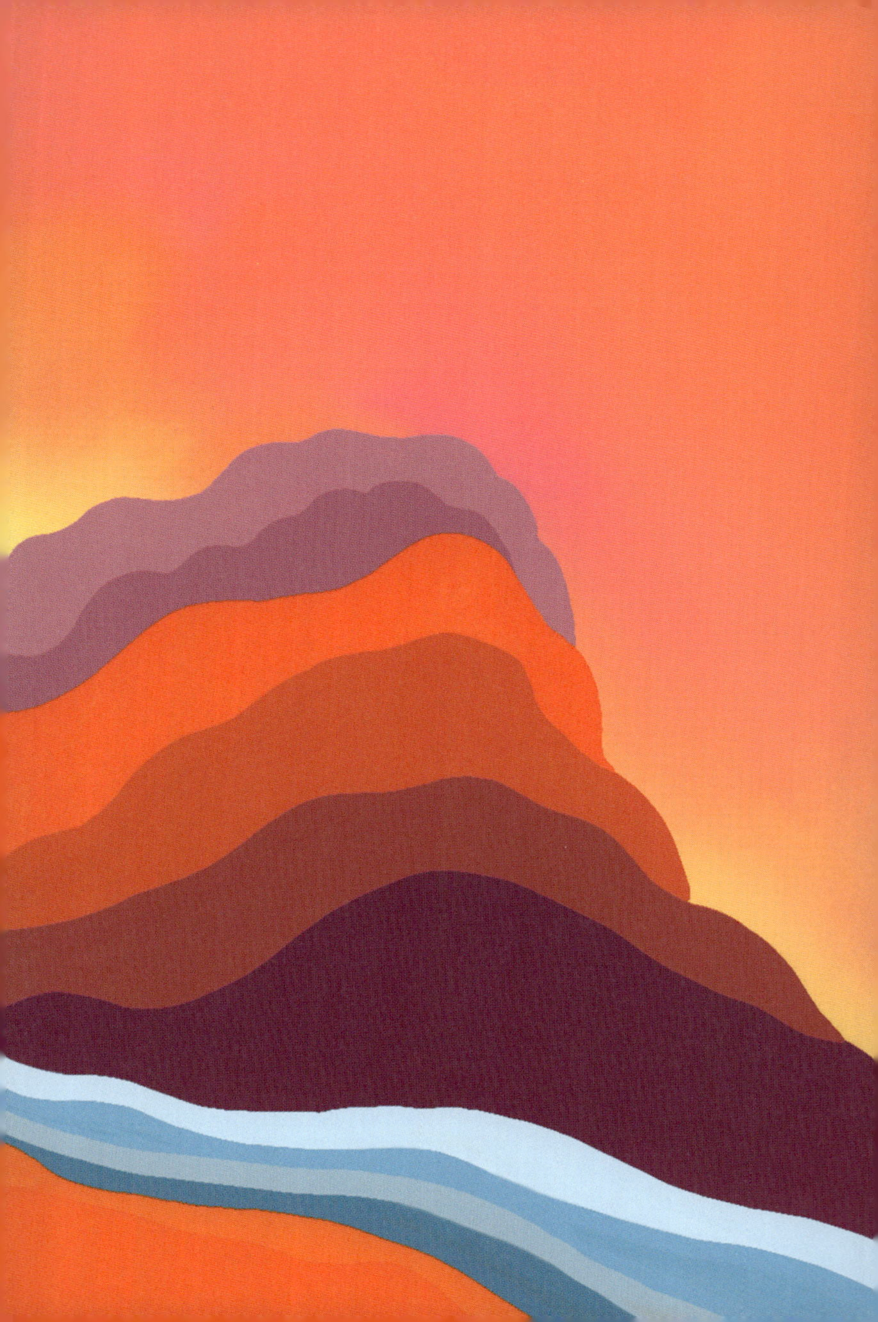

Job 12:7-10

DAY 283

"Just ask the animals, and they will teach you. ... Speak to the earth, and it will instruct you. Let the fish in the sea speak to you. For they all know that my disasters have come from the hand of the Lord. For the life of every living thing is in his hand, and the breath of every human being." (NLT)

From the smallest insect to the mysterious depths of the ocean to the farthest reaches of the cosmos, there is a constant, silent sermon testifying to God's power and wisdom. As we search for evidence of God's existence in grand theological pronouncements, God reveals the divine presence in the intricate patterns of a butterfly's wing and the strength and tenacity of a tree rooted in the earth, far older than we will ever be.

Are we so focused on seeking extraordinary signs that we miss the daily miracles? The intricate dance of nature, the delicate balance of ecosystems, the sheer beauty that surrounds us—these are not accidents. They are tangible expressions of God's love and care, freely given for us to witness and appreciate.

With each breath we draw into our lungs, in the warmth of the sun on our skin, let us not forsake these clear testimonies but worship with all creation as it points to the constant, loving outpouring hand of our Creator.

Open our eyes, Jesus, to see your glory displayed in every corner of your magnificent creation. Amen.

DAY

284 Isaiah 6:3

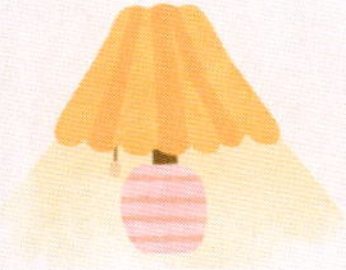

"They were calling out to each other, 'Holy, holy, holy is the Lord of Heaven's Armies! The whole earth is filled with his glory!'" (NLT)

So often, we speak in terms of total dichotomies. We view grief and fear as the opposites of joy and confidence. As we struggle through hard times, we feel as though comfort and peace are impossible or that they will come only if the pain fully dissipates. But Isaiah 6 reminds us that true comfort is not found in the absence of trouble but in the presence of the Holy One who reigns above it all.

Moments of uncertainty and grief can feel earth-shattering, but God is never shaken. The Creator and Ruler is not distant—God's glory fills the earth, including the shadowy places. Jesus is present and active, even in our suffering.

Comfort comes not when our circumstances change, but when we remember God is already here. Holiness means God is completely faithful, just, and loving. Divine glory surrounds us—even when we feel broken. True comfort is found not in understanding everything or banishing uncertainty but in knowing the One who holds all things together.

Holy Spirit, make your comfort known to us here and now. Let us experience your majesty and take heart. Amen.

Psalm 100:2-3

DAY 285

"Worship the Lord with gladness. Come before him, singing with joy. Acknowledge that the Lord is God! He made us, and we are his. We are his people, the sheep of his pasture." (NLT)

As we ruminate on scripture, one refrain repeats again and again: God is always with us. The guiding presence of the Holy Spirit is all around us. This is an important blessing, but the constant assurance can also mean that our awareness of God fades into the background. Caught up as we are in the movement and excitement of life, it is easy for our faith to feel like a footnote or an afterthought.

Psalm 100 urges us to shake off this mindset and instead draw close to God with joy and intention. Jesus desires a deep and personal connection with us, reaching out to us amid our triumphs and our tribulations. God is not merely present but active in our lives, instructing and encouraging us. Are we paying attention?

Our Creator should not be the wallpaper of our lives but the centerpiece. In the face of each challenge we encounter, we should turn to God. Each moment of gladness should move us to give thanks to the source of all blessings.

Jesus, beckon us closer to you. Help us to focus on your voice and not take you for granted. Amen.

DAY 286 Psalm 73:26

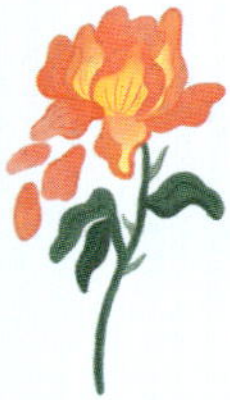

"My health may fail, and my spirit may grow weak, but God remains the strength of my heart; he is mine forever." (NLT)

There are seasons when everything we once held dear and relied upon is stretched to its breaking point. These are moments that reflect a truth we often choose to ignore—the very real fragility of our human experience.

Flesh and heart do fail. Our bodies weaken. Uncertainty and worries weigh us down. Fear and doubt can whisper insidious questions. But, in that very space of vulnerability, there is always a lifeline. It is the outstretched hand of our Creator, of the God who isn't just a distant observer but who comes down into this life in Jesus Christ and takes hold of us.

Following Jesus isn't the promise of an easy journey but the assurance that we are never alone, that we will never be forsaken. Even when we feel like we have nothing left to give, God's love and faithfulness remain inexhaustible. When we believe we can't hold on any longer, God will never let us go. God is and will be the strength that always carries us forward.

God, thank you that even when my faith feels weak, your grip on me remains strong, and your love endures forever. Amen.

Galatians 3:28

DAY 287

"There is no longer Jew or Gentile, slave or free, male and female. For you are all one in Christ Jesus." (NLT)

Every one of us draws lines of separation, delineating between those we deem like "us" and those who are not—"them." But scripture proclaims that, in Christ, there is no separation. No matter our cultural background, place in society, gender, appearance, or age, we are all one before God.

This isn't merely some ideal we aspire towards. It is the very core of the Gospel. Jesus' words and actions reflect that there are no limits to his love. He welcomed everyone, regardless of their past or present. He saw beyond the labels we use to justify distancing ourselves from others. He embraced the marginalized, the outcasts, those deemed "unworthy" and unlovable by society.

The love of Christ levels the playing field, reminding us that we are all equally precious in God's eyes. It challenges us to confront the self-imposed limits we place on our capacity to love and instead allow the boundless grace of God to flow through us to all, without reservation, judgment, or preclusion. To do anything less is to exclude ourselves from the love God offers to us.

Jesus, help us to live out the truth that in you, we are all one, reflecting your boundless love to everyone we encounter. Amen.

DAY 288 Romans 1:7

"I am writing to all of you in Rome who are loved by God and called to be his own holy people. May God our Father and the Lord Jesus Christ give you grace and peace." (NLT)

Before the apostle Paul teaches or corrects—before he writes of belief, sin, or salvation—he begins here: We are loved by God. We are called to be Christ's own.

This is the foundation of faith—not our effort, but our identity.

To walk by faith is to carry this truth through every season: we belong to God. We are not strangers trying to earn attention. We are God's people, already named, already known, even when we feel uncertain, even when the way is unclear.

We do not walk as those guessing at our worth—we walk as those already blessed with grace, already held in peace. Faith does not mean we always feel confident. It means we continue because our steps are anchored in something deeper than feelings.

Grace becomes the path, and peace becomes the rhythm. We are not asked to rush, prove, or perform. We are asked to remember whose we are and walk forward in that truth.

May we walk slowly and deliberately, as those loved and led. Amen.

Psalm 119:105

DAY
289

"Your word is a lamp to guide my feet and a light for my path." (NLT)

The road before us is not always a straight line. It can be easy to get swept away by fleeting currents of opinion or chasing shadows that promise fulfillment but ultimately leave us more lost and less confident of where we are going. This isn't usually a sudden event but more of a gradual drifting, a subtle erosion of direction.

Amidst the dead ends and disorientation, scripture reminds us that God has provided us with a lamp—His very Word. God's Word isn't a fleeting flicker but a constant, reliable source of illumination—our true north in this journey of faith. When we turn to scripture, we aren't just given general directions. Through God's Spirit, we are shown the immediate steps to take to navigate life's twists and turns and stay on the path that God sets before us.

When questions and uncertainty arise, God's Word provides clarity and wisdom. When fear grips us, God's promises offer peace and assurance. Through daily engagement, meditation, and application of God's Word, we are guided every step of the way.

Thank you, God, for the guiding light of your Word; help us to stay rooted in its truth and walk confidently in its illumination. Amen.

DAY

290 Ephesians 3:17–19

"Then Christ will make his home in your hearts as you trust in him. Your roots will grow down into God's love and keep you strong. And may you have the power to understand, as all God's people should, how wide, how long, how high, and how deep his love is. May you experience the love of Christ, though it is too great to understand fully. Then you will be made complete with all the fullness of life and power that comes from God." (NLT)

A faith-driven life is not merely defined by believing in Christ. It is borne out by knowing, trusting, and walking with him in daily relationship. Ephesians 3 speaks to the richness and depth of what it means to truly be connected to Jesus.

Using imagery from nature and architecture, this passage paints a picture of stability, nourishment, and foundation. Love isn't just something we receive from Christ—it becomes the soil in which our whole life grows. Just as a plant cannot be separated from its roots, neither can we flourish apart from Jesus. He is supplying us with boundless love, grace, and wisdom. When we open ourselves up to this relationship, we grow and thrive far beyond what we could ever achieve alone.

As we grow in Christ's love, we are filled with God's very presence. This is the goal of relationship with Jesus: fullness, transformation, and intimacy. It isn't static—it's living, growing, and sustained by love.

Jesus, help us to get to know you as well as you know us. Cultivate in us greater awareness, deeper trust, and fuller joy. Amen.

1 Peter 4:10

DAY
291

"Each of you should use whatever gift you have received to serve others, as faithful stewards of God's grace in its various forms." (NIV)

For some of us, embracing our talents can feel dangerous. What if we're actually seeking attention? What if pride gets the better of us? In truth, we ought to embrace the talents, skills, expertise, and resources we have. God gave them to us for a reason.

To keep ourselves from becoming self-centered, we can also celebrate the talents of others. We have laudable gifts, but so do those around us. When we recognize how essential each person is to the community, we can find it easier to remain humble.

And while we might feel disappointed that we don't have the same talents as another person, this is a beautiful thing. Everyone has something unique to offer. No one is self-sufficient, and it is through our diversity of gifts that we're able to support one another and accomplish even more good.

Almighty Jesus, thank you for blessing us with unique gifts. Please show us ways we can use these gifts to bless our communities and bring joy to people's lives. Amen.

DAY 292 Romans 12:1

"And so, dear brothers and sisters, I plead with you to give your bodies to God because of all he has done for you. Let them be a living and holy sacrifice—the kind he will find acceptable. This is truly the way to worship him." (NLT)

Faith is not confined to our words and thoughts. We live our faith through bodies that ache, move, breathe, and belong. We are invited to bring our whole selves to Jesus: our thoughts, words, bodies, habits, and days. Our physical lives are not secondary to spiritual devotion—they are part of it.

This is what it means to be a living sacrifice—a life laid down once in surrender but offered daily in our routines and rest. We offer what we create, protect, carry, and release. Even the ordinary can become sacred when offered with intention. Preparing a meal, holding silence, and strolling along can all be worship.

Jesus does not desire our performance but rather our presence.

When we treat our bodies as holy ground, we honor the God who formed them. And when we care for our bodies with love, we participate in grace.

Let our worship be not only in song but in how we live. Let our faith be felt in our breath, stillness, work, and care.

Breathe in: This body is yours,
Breathe out: formed and beloved. Amen.

Psalm 46:10

DAY
293

"Be still, and know that I am God! I will be honored by every nation. I will be honored throughout the world." (NLT)

When was the last time we sought out stillness? Not passively, as we try to fall asleep, but actively, finding tranquility in our bodies and the world around us. This is what scripture means when it proclaims, "Be still, and know that I am God!"

Stillness is a radical act of trust in a fast-paced world filled with stress and anxiety. It's a declaration of faith, admitting our lack of control and refocusing us on the presence of God. The world tells us that to pause is to fall behind, but scripture shows us that the quiet and steady moments are gifts. Stillness centers us. It tells the world that who we are and who we're becoming are more important than what we produce.

Embracing a practice of stillness cuts away the flurry of distractions and invites us to experience the blessings and opportunities right in front of us.

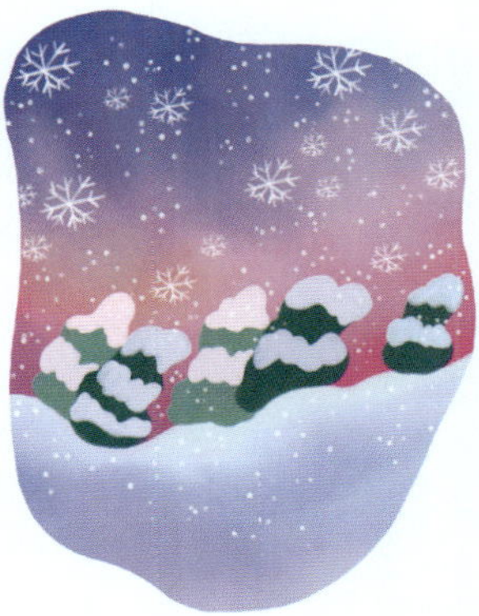

Jesus, teach us to embrace stillness in the face of a world that preaches constant motion. Amen.

DAY

294 Exodus 3:10–11

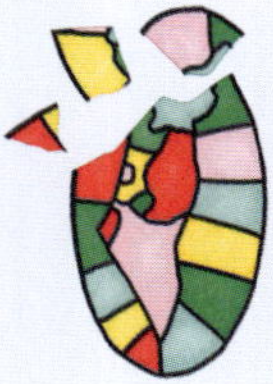

"Now go, for I am sending you to Pharaoh. You must lead my people, Israel, out of Egypt. But Moses protested to God, 'Who am I to appear before Pharaoh? Who am I to lead the people of Israel out of Egypt?'" (NLT)

The call of God often arrives before our confidence. When Moses stood before the burning bush, he didn't feel ready. His past was heavy, and his fears were louder than his faith. God's words were clear: Go. But Moses responded with the question many of us still carry: Who am I?

We assume that becoming who God created us to be will feel empowering. We anticipate that it will be a destination we arrive at rather than a continuously occurring journey. Sometimes, it feels terrifying. We expect clarity, but instead, we receive an invitation.

God never scolds Moses for his fear—doesn't list qualifications or achievements. God simply says, "I will be with you." This is the rhythm of divine calling. God speaks. We doubt it. God stays and step by step, we become what we were intended to be from the beginning. Becoming is not about mastery; it is about movement. God sees beyond what we can and shapes us through the journey we feel unfit to walk.

God, you assure us that we don't need to feel confident or worthy to answer your call. We are sent by you, and that changes everything. Amen.

Acts 17:24–25

DAY 295

“He is the God who made the world and everything in it. Since he is Lord of heaven and earth, he doesn’t live in man-made temples, and human hands can’t serve his needs—for he has no needs. He himself gives life and breath to everything, and he satisfies every need.” (NLT)

Fear loves to interfere with our breathing. Tightness rises in our chests and we struggle to catch our breath, which causes even more anxiety. In Acts 17:24, Paul evangelizes to people in Athens who were accustomed to gods forged by and reliant upon human hands. He reorients their worship towards the God of Heaven and earth, who is unlimited in presence and power.

Philosophers in the crowd must have been impressed to hear of a God whose overarching nature surpasses their spiritual means. Paul highlights the largeness of the Lord, how the author of all is too colossal for their created fixtures.

God does not rely on us; we can rely on God. When we struggle to see anything bigger than our problems, our God is bigger still. The One whose breath lives in every lung. Knowing this, our fear begins to shrink, and breathing becomes easier. We can literally breathe through fear, recognizing that nothing can hold a candle to the majesty and might of the source of our breath.

Lord Jesus, you are bigger than anything we face. Let us inhale this truth as all fear is exhaled out of our systems. Amen.

DAY 296 John 8:34-36

"Jesus replied, 'Very truly I tell you, everyone who sins is a slave to sin. Now, a slave has no permanent place in the family, but a son belongs to it forever. So if the Son sets you free, you will be free indeed.'" (NLT)

It's tempting to build walls around our hearts, each brick forged out of resentments that we hold onto. We cling to past hurts, believing they define us, but in the end, they only confine us in a self-made prison of gnawing bitterness and fear. We trap ourselves in an ever-growing web of contempt toward others that punishes us more than them.

Yet before the door locks from the inside, Jesus comes, knocks, and offers us the key to our freedom. That key is forgiveness, both given and received. It is forgiveness offered to us by God, even as we confront our limitations and failings. Receiving such forgiveness sets us free from fixating on the performance gap we perceive between ourselves and others and allows us to focus on becoming the best version of ourselves.

Forgiveness, once gratefully received, must be extended to others. As we let go of the weight of past wrongs and our need for vengeance, forgiveness sets us free to make peace and be at peace as fellow children of God.

Grant us, God, the courage and grace to forgive so that we may walk in the true freedom you offer. Amen.

2 Timothy 4:16–17 DAY 297

"The first time I was brought before the judge, no one came with me. Everyone abandoned me. May it not be counted against them. But the Lord stood with me and gave me strength so that I might preach the Good News in its entirety for all the Gentiles to hear. And he rescued me from certain death." (NLT)

There is a quiet kind of heartbreak that comes with disappointment. It doesn't always show itself through tears; it lingers in the hollow pause after someone fails to show up and in the silence after a promise is broken.

Paul names it plainly: "Everyone abandoned me." He doesn't pretend it didn't hurt. He doesn't disguise it in spiritual platitudes. He tells the truth. And somehow, in doing so, he makes space for us to tell the truth, too.

We live in a world that tells us to move on quickly. To minimize the pain. But disappointment, when buried, can become bitterness. Instead, Paul teaches us to bring our hurt to God and trust that we are not alone, even in solitude. "The Lord stood with me," he writes. That line is everything.

When people fail us—and they will—God remains. Jesus does not distance himself from our grief. He steps closer. He gives strength not just for survival but also for restoration.

Loving God, guide us through our seasons of disappointment. Wipe our tears and draw us close in your tender embrace. Amen.

DAY

298 Revelation 21:5

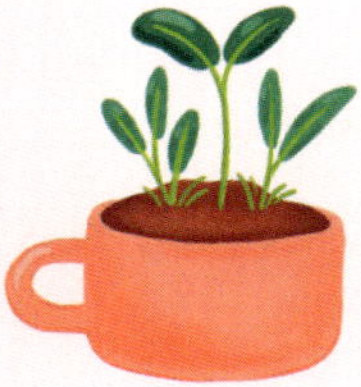

"And the one sitting on the throne said, 'Look, I am making everything new!' And then he said to me, 'Write this down, for what I tell you is trustworthy and true.'" (NLT)

The past can feel inescapable. Mistakes made, systems established, and habits formed can all seem permanent. "People don't change," we say. "This is just the way things are." Yet scripture declares that while what has come before does impact our present and future, we are not trapped in the past.

Ours is the God of creation and restoration. The world was spoken into existence by God out of an expanseless nothing. And, as Revelation assures us, that divine spark will return to make all things new.

To truly embrace the Good News of Jesus is to recognize that God offers second chances. Not only are new beginnings possible, they are promised. Rather than give in to the nihilistic impulses of the culture around us, we ought to be beacons of the forgiveness and grace Jesus offers us all.

The mistakes of the past do not define us; Jesus does. Let us expect the promised new beginnings and partner with God to work towards them.

May we be your instruments of healing and restoration. May all who encounter us experience a hope that points them back to you. Amen.

John 15:11

DAY **299**

"I have told you these things so that you will be filled with my joy. Yes, your joy will overflow!" (NLT)

Sometimes, joy is loud, overflowing with laughter, celebration, and the fullness of goodness made visible. But joy also exists quietly as something that grows over time. It grows in still places. It takes root in the nearness of God.

In John 15, Jesus says, "I have told you these things so that my joy may be in you." His joy—not a fleeting emotion, but a deep, enduring gladness grounded in love and obedience. Not a joy we have to chase, but one we are given.

Contrary to what we may believe, joy is not dependent on ease. It can exist alongside sorrow. Joy is not the absence of pain; it is made available to us because of God's presence in our situations. Bountiful joy overflows, not because life is perfect but because we are connected to the source of life. It is sustainable joy, anchored and full. Do we make room for it? Or have we come to expect just enough to survive?

Joy is not reserved for the untroubled. It belongs to those who remain connected, who trust that even in weariness, God is still pouring out good.

Jesus, let joy overflow within us, knowing it comes from you, the perfect source of all good. Amen.

DAY

300 Psalm 32:5

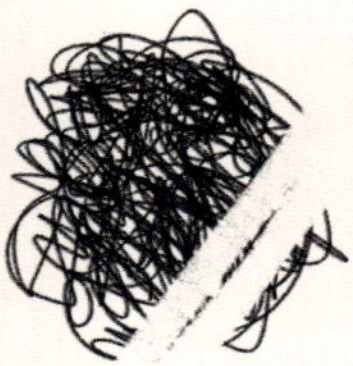

"Finally, I confessed all my sins to you and stopped trying to hide my guilt. I said to myself, 'I will confess my rebellion to the Lord.' And you forgave me! All my guilt is gone." (NLT)

The journey to honest confession can feel like scaling a steep mountain. Our pride whispers that we can manage on our own, that admitting fault is a sign of weakness. We try to rationalize our actions, minimize their impact, or simply bury them deep within, hoping they'll disappear. Still, the weight of hidden mistakes can feel unbearable—a constant, nagging presence in our hearts.

Sweet relief only arrives as we come clean before God. This is the essence of repentance: acknowledging our shortcomings and faults, not to dwell in shame, but to experience liberation. When we truly bring our sins into the light, we allow space for the healing Jesus promises.

It's a courageous act, choosing vulnerability over the illusion of perfection. But freedom is found on the other side, in the humility to admit our need for grace and our embrace of God's willingness to give it, to fill the space where guilt once resided with forgiveness and peace.

God, grant us the courage to approach you with honest hearts, trusting in your boundless forgiveness when we confess our shortcomings. Amen.

Ephesians 4:32

DAY
301

"Be kind and compassionate to one another, forgiving each other, just as in Christ God forgave you." (NIV)

What does it mean to "live well"? In Ephesians, Paul gives a clear and concise answer: "Be kind and compassionate to one another, forgiving each other." In other words, be like Jesus.

While others may offer metrics for success defined by earnings or output, scripture tells us the greatest benchmark for excellence in our lives is how we treat one another. A life well-lived is one dedicated to honoring and glorifying our Creator in response to the blessings we have received—blessings such as unconditional love and boundless mercy. When we truly recognize these divine gifts, we cannot help but extend them to everyone around us.

Kindness, compassion, and forgiveness defined Jesus' earthly ministry. The extent and depths of his care often proved too radical for people. But he insisted that the Kingdom of God—founded on grace and love—was open to everyone. To live according to Christ's example is not only to give thanks for the compassion he has shown us. It is to be vessels for that compassion.

Let us welcome one another into your Kingdom, God. May we follow your lead and live lives defined by love. Amen.

DAY

302 1 Corinthians 13:12–13

"... All that I know now is partial and incomplete, but then I will know everything completely, just as God now knows me completely. Three things will last forever—faith, hope, and love—and the greatest of these is love." (NLT)

How do we understand "love"? Is it a sentimental, warm, fuzzy feeling? A consumerist excuse to sell grocery store cards and heart-shaped candy? Perhaps love, in its larger-than-life orchestral form, is the stuff of movies and fairytales.

Defining love is difficult. It feels ephemeral and tricky to pin down. 1 Corinthians 13 reflects on this multifaceted splendor, asserting that love, more than anything else, is at the heart of all things.

The love of Christ is found even in the disarray of our lives. Available not only to the elite or the exalted but also to the modest and fallible. Love drives God's vision of peace here on earth. It moves us to shout for joy because we know that Jesus cares deeply, intimately, and unequivocally for us.

Giving thanks for the immeasurable love of Jesus, we are moved to extend this love to each other. This means loving people in the face of their brokenness and imperfection, just as Jesus does. It means uplifting one another, supporting our communities, and showing grace and compassion to all.

Jesus, embracing your love is the means for a beautiful, connected life. Help us look for and live out love in unexpected places. Amen.

Luke 6:38

DAY
303

“Give, and you will receive. Your gift will return to you in full—pressed down, shaken together to make room for more, running over, and poured into your lap. The amount you give will determine the amount you get back.” (NLT)

Jesus offers a vision of generosity as an invitation to live with open hands and trusting hearts. To resist the urge to grasp, hoard, or protect what we have out of fear. To hold our time, resources, and gifts loosely, ready to share them freely.

If we keep a handful of seeds in our clenched fist, they remain secure but also lifeless. However, if we open our hands and scatter them, they have the opportunity to sprout, multiply, and grow. Our giving works the same way. Small acts of generosity can take root in ways we may not have anticipated.

Living in a posture of generosity becomes contagious, changing the culture around us. One kind word sparks another. A meal shared inspires further hospitality. God takes what we give, however small, and uses it to stir others, weaving our gifts into a larger movement of provision and grace.

Living with open hands means we give in faith that the God who feeds the sparrows and clothes the lilies with beauty will also fill our lives with what we truly need.

God, help us live with open hands, trusting your abundance and sharing your love freely. Amen.

DAY 304 Isaiah 26:3

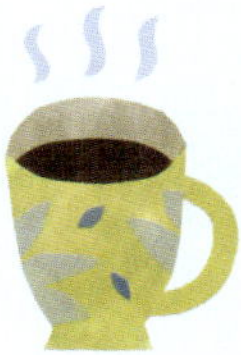

"You will keep in perfect peace all who trust in you, all whose thoughts are fixed on you!" (NLT)

It can feel impossible to preserve peace with so many thoughts pressing heavily on our minds. As the loud world makes serenity seem impossible to reach, we begin to believe that the alarms around and within us are more important to react to than simply pausing to breathe, observing our surroundings, and allowing ourselves to abandon all distractions to trust in the Lord.

This journey of trusting God might very well be compared to a taking a mindfulness walk. As we go about our day, engaging in the five senses to see, feel, taste, smell, and hear nature's activity, we can also hone our discernment, paying close attention to what Jesus is personally telling us.

Mindfulness is challenging work when everyday distractions come to derail us, but it is always worth exercising. When we truly listen, something miraculous unfolds; suddenly, there is no room for worry. We don't have time to entertain false alarms. When we trust God over fear, a supernatural peace washes over us and is promised to remain, as long as we stay focused on Jesus.

Dear Lord, help us to practice mindfulness in your holy presence as we intimately seek you with all of our senses. Amen.

Acts 20:35

DAY
305

"And I have been a constant example of how you can help those in need by working hard. You should remember the words of the Lord Jesus: 'It is more blessed to give than to receive.'" (NLT)

We tend to chase after what we can gain, believing that acquisition equates to happiness. Jesus, however, turns conventional thinking on its head, insisting that true fulfillment lies in the act of giving. The blessing of generosity isn't simply about the recipient's gain; it's about the transformation within the giver.

Consider the joy of seeing a smile on someone's face because we shared our time, offered a listening ear, or extended a helping hand. The satisfaction of giving what we have—our resources and skills—opens our hearts to a deeper joy, a sense of purpose that material gains can never provide.

Recognizing the needs around us and responding out of a spirit of generosity cultivates empathy, strengthens community, and aligns our hearts with the selfless love exemplified by Christ. When we give, not expecting anything in return, but trusting that the act itself is its own reward, we discover a blessing far greater than anything we could ever receive. For in the pouring out of ourselves, we not only meet the needs of another, but we are also filled.

God, cultivate generous hearts within us. Through Jesus' example, may we find true blessing in giving. Amen.

DAY
306 Psalm 46:1

"God is our refuge and strength, always ready to help in times of trouble." (NLT)

Even in seasons of hardship—periods of uncertainty, grief, stress, or fear—it can be challenging to ask for help. Amid shifting sands, we crave stability, but we hate the idea of being a burden.

The wisdom of scripture tells us that no matter what we are facing, we can count on Jesus. Jesus is always with us and always ready to help. Calling out to him is not an imposition; it's the intention. The Bible doesn't promise that God will remove every obstacle from our path, but we are promised that Jesus will tackle every barrier with us.

We often feel pressure to be strong for ourselves or put on a stoic front for others. But in Christ, we're invited to rely on his strength over our own. God is not distant or delayed. The presence of the Holy Spirit is immediate, attentive, and tender. Jesus understands our struggles and meets us right in the middle of them. No matter what comes—be it suffering, stress, or sorrow—we have help.

Jesus, you are our refuge, our strength, and our helper. You are present with us not just someday, but today. Amen.

DAY

307

Psalm 21:6

"You have endowed him with
eternal blessings and given him
the joy of your presence." (NLT)

To abide is to remain. When we abide, we stay even when we are tempted to rush ahead. We root ourselves in being present even when emotions pull us elsewhere. Abiding in Christ is not passive—it is active and intentional. It is the act of repeatedly turning our gaze toward the One who stays until our hearts remember what they knew all along.

Psalm 21 speaks of joy that comes from God's nearness—not the kind we manufacture, but the kind that finds us when we linger. This is a joy made possible by proximity. Abiding joy is not determined by circumstances. It is a product of connection. The more we remain with Jesus, the more we receive.

We live in a culture of restlessness, in which productivity is praised and rest is often mistaken for weakness. But Jesus offers something different: joy rooted not in what we do but where we stay. Are we exhausted by the chase? Distracted by the pull of everything but peace? Let us reorient, not out of guilt but with expectation. God does not shame us for drifting.

Jesus, you always welcome us back, and in that welcome, joy waits. Amen.

DAY 308 Acts 27: 22–24

"But take courage! None of you will lose your lives, even though the ship will go down. For last night an angel of the God to whom I belong and whom I serve stood beside me, and he said, 'Don't be afraid, Paul, for you will surely stand trial before Caesar! What's more, God in his goodness has granted safety to everyone sailing with you.'" (NLT)

In the face of chaos, it is natural to panic. When it feels our lives are hanging on by only a thread, it is easy to bet on the side of death instead of survival. In Acts 27, the men on the ship with Paul were scared by the storm they were facing at sea; it felt fatal, and they were terrified. Sometimes, when we are so consumed by a crisis, we forget that there is a Savior who holds our lives, who has it under control.

In the face of panic today, we are invited to cling to this same comfort. To anchor ourselves to the deep assurance that God shrouds us with a hedge of protection at all times. When we feel the sharp absence of peace in the face of sheer panic, let us return quickly to God's strong and steady presence in our lives; the One who keeps us afloat is weathering every single storm we enter, even before it strikes.

Lord, you are the God who tames the waters. Give us faith that anchors us to the promise that you will always rescue us and bring us out on the other side, alive. Amen.

Luke 6:12

DAY
309

"One of those days Jesus went out to a mountainside to pray, and spent the night praying to God." (NIV)

Meetings, responsibilities, and commitments tend to shape the rhythm of our lives. When the sun sets and the stillness of night unfolds, noise from our day stays with us, with thoughts of unfinished tasks and upcoming challenges replaying in our minds. Intentionally entering into the rest of the evening can be a challenge, encumbered as we are by ongoing demands.

Jesus invites us to consider a new rhythm—a harmonious cadence welcoming the peace of God to dwell within our hearts as our days draw closed. These moments of transition provide an opportunity to find solace, renewal, and connection with God. We set aside our schedules and to-do lists, our commitments and commutes.

This is the space to reflect on the day's blessings. With each breath, we let gratitude fill our hearts like fragrant incense. We recall moments of joy and growth, even amidst challenges. We release our cares, allowing our minds to be still and our souls to be refreshed. We come before God in prayer, knowing that in the hush of the evening, whispers of God's love can be heard most clearly.

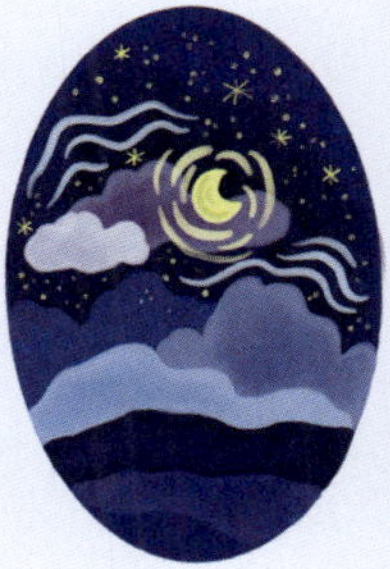

Spirit, hold us this evening in your gentle embrace. As we wind down, may we be attuned to your grace and solace. Amen.

DAY

310 Isaiah 64:8

"And yet, O Lord, you are our Father.
We are the clay, and you are the potter.
We all are formed by your hand." (NLT)

There is something humbling and beautiful about being molded. Clay yields to the hands that form it, soft and responsive, trusting the vision of the one who is shaping. So it is with us. We are held and formed by a patient, purposeful, and artiful God whose hands are strong and tender.

The process of being shaped is not always comfortable. The potter presses, stretches, and rolls the clay. Sometimes we feel weary of the process and uncertain about what we're becoming. But the potter sees the whole design from the beginning. What feels like breaking is often preparation. What feels like a delay is often deep work. Clay is put in a fiery kiln to make it more durable. We may wish to speed the process or to take control of our own shape. But the potter asks for trust. A daily openness to being made new.

And the result? Not something generic or mass-produced but something unique, made with intention and for a purpose. The mark of God, our potter, is found in every curve and dimple. We are the work of divine hands.

God, in the discomfort of our growth help us trust that you are shaping us according to your wisdom and love. Amen.

Hebrews 2:3–4

DAY 311

"So what makes us think we can escape if we ignore this great salvation that was first announced by the Lord Jesus himself and then delivered to us by those who heard him speak? And God confirmed the message by giving signs and wonders and various miracles and gifts of the Holy Spirit whenever he chose." (NLT)

When we think of the word "miracle," what comes to mind? Typically, miracles conjure up images of the supernatural—signs and wonders that we cannot explain. Awe-inspiring, paradigm-shifting, mysterious. We read about miracles in the Bible but in our own lives, do we believe that miracles happen?

Miraculous events throughout scripture allow us to glimpse the world as it was intended, as it could be. A world where death is not inescapable, where restoration and renewal reign—creation in harmony with its Creator. These are not just moments of dramatic emphasis or narrative excitement; they are invitations to step into God's vision for the world.

When the wondrous and astounding break into the ordinary of our lives, we may stumble. Rather than jumping into the invitation we've been offered, we might be tempted to doubt our senses. Even then, Jesus is there to help us understand. God welcomes us into a miraculous world. The wonders our Creator has in store for us are not abstract but real opportunities for transformation and renewal.

Miraculous God, let us trust in your power to provide, heal, bring peace, and renew. May your wonders inspire and comfort us. Amen.

DAY

312 Deuteronomy 32:4

"He is the Rock; his deeds are perfect. Everything he does is just and fair. He is a faithful God who does no wrong; how just and upright he is!" (NLT)

Bombarded with examples of injustice and moral confusion, we long for a standard that is steady and true. Sometimes fairness seems like a fantasy and justice a sliding scale. But when we root ourselves in scripture, we see that righteousness is the very foundation of who God is—unchanging, faithful, and utterly just.

Unlike human leaders or shifting circumstances, God's character is immovable. The actions that God takes always flow out of that character; Christ is never random or unjust. Even when we don't understand, we can trust that God's plans are steeped in perfect wisdom and love.

When everything else feels unsure, we can hold onto one truth absolutely: God does not merely act justly—God *is* just. Jesus never deceives, never compromises, never fails. This divine righteousness is not only judicial but also deeply relational, rooted in God's faithfulness to humanity.

When we are faced with alternative approaches to morality and righteousness, we can judge them against the character of our Creator. Are they defined by love? Guided by wisdom? Characterized by grace? If not, this is not true righteousness.

Let us rely on your perfect example, righteous God. Amen.

1 Peter 1:6, 8

DAY
313

"So be truly glad. There is wonderful joy ahead, even though you must endure many trials for a little while. ... You love him even though you have never seen him. Though you do not see him now, you trust him; and you rejoice with a glorious, inexpressible joy." (NLT)

Joy, unlike happiness, is not contingent upon circumstances. Joy runs deeper in the veins and exclaims an exuberant proclamation of praise upon praise. What inspires such joy? Scripture tells us we rejoice because we know that the best is yet to come in Christ Jesus.

Even though we experience hardship on earth, not even suffering can deter this joy because we know in the depths of ourselves that it was born from an eternal place. When we remember what lies ahead, instead of being stuck in the moment, we get a clear snapshot of our Savior, whom we have not seen yet but look forward to seeing soon.

As we live in the busy demands of our modern day, we can carry this exuberant joy that is too excellent for words! It shines off of us in noticeable ways, with a light that speaks of the brighter days that await us.

Lord! Thank you for filling us with such life-giving, exuberant joy! This is our strength, it is what spurs us onward, because of your Son! Amen.

DAY 314 1 Corinthians 2:9–10

“That is what the Scriptures mean when they say, ‘No eye has seen, no ear has heard, and no mind has imagined what God has prepared for those who love him.’ But it was to us that God revealed these things by his Spirit. For his Spirit searches out everything and shows us God’s deep secrets.” (NLT)

The prophet Isaiah told of God coming down to earth generations before the birth of Jesus. It was a vision of love and redemption that far exceeded any human experience. Isaiah’s promises took on new meaning when Paul quotes them in 1 Corinthians 2. The early believers were able to look back on these words with new wonder in light of Jesus’ ministry, death, and resurrection. They received a glimpse of eternity in the life of Christ and an outpouring of the Holy Spirit. What once seemed fantastical took on new reality.

The same gift of holy imagination is available to us, too, through the work of the Spirit. Just like Isaiah, we can continue to dream of the Kingdom of God. Like Paul, we can also look to scripture and see evidence of God revealing secrets to us. Jesus, as he ascended, promised the gift of the Spirit and more. So, in anticipation, we imagine all the goodness yet to come.

Holy Spirit, stir your imagination in us as we hope for your glory. Amen.

Hebrews 4:16

DAY 315

"So let us come boldly to the throne of our gracious God. There we will receive his mercy, and we will find grace to help us when we need it most." (NLT)

How do we imagine approaching the throne of God? Many of us come before God timidly, ashamed, or uncertain of our welcome. Who are *we*, we wonder, to ask something of the Creator and Sustainer of the universe? Hebrews 4:16 offers a powerful invitation: because of Jesus, we can approach God boldly, expecting mercy and grace in our times of need.

God's throne is a place of authority but not condemnation. It is a place of generosity and welcome, where we are met with compassion. Before we even ask, God knows the exact help we need, be it strength, forgiveness, patience, or peace.

We don't need to be uncertain; Jesus has declared that we are forgiven. God's grace is not rationed or earned but generously bestowed. The way to God's throne has been cleared by Christ. We don't need to linger in the back or make ourselves presentable; we can approach God with confidence.

Lord, your heart is open. Grace is waiting. Let us come. Amen.

DAY

316 Genesis 28:15

"What's more, I am with you, and I will protect you wherever you go. One day I will bring you back to this land. I will not leave you until I have finished giving you everything I have promised you." (NLT)

We're in the midst of a loneliness epidemic. Despite the prevalence of social media, many of us feel disconnected and isolated. We struggle to make connections. We feel that we need to rely on ourselves. But the truth is, no matter how alone we may feel, God is always by our side.

God walks with us through difficult seasons and circumstances. Our Creator protects and provides for us. When we recognize this—breaking free from the myth that we must be self-reliant—our eyes open to opportunities to embrace connection with others.

Knowing that God is on our side, we can feel empowered to reach out to our communities. We are all united by our common identity as children of God. When we embrace this truth, healing begins. We find the courage to be vulnerable, to let others in, and to extend grace. In God's presence, loneliness loses its power. We are seen, known, and deeply loved. And from that love, we are invited to love others with openness and compassion.

Jesus, we delight in your presence. Remind us we are never alone and encourage us to join together with those you have placed before us. Amen.

Zechariah 13:9

DAY 317

“I will bring that group through the fire and make them pure. I will refine them like silver and purify them like gold. They will call on my name, and I will answer them. I will say, ‘These are my people,’ and they will say, ‘The Lord is our God.’” (NLT)

The process of being refined by fire in the spiritual sense is as intense as it sounds. As blacksmiths use extreme heat to shape their fine metals, Zechariah 13 shows us the necessity of spiritual fire as a tool to transform us into people of God, free from our sins. This divine flame may be painful, but it is also healing.

The Lord is devoted to cleansing us from all iniquity that prohibits us from being in fellowship with Jesus. This holy fire leaves us renewed, better equipped for the life God calls us to.

Oftentimes, walking through the fire doesn’t make sense to us, but it is essential to form us into who we are meant to become. In metalworking, fire allows for reshaping but also reinforces the metal. Likewise, as God guides us through the process of refinement, burning away the impurities that hold us back, we emerge on the other side stronger and more stable. We can embrace refinement by faith, knowing that the One shaping us sees us as more precious than silver or gold.

Christ Jesus, you never waste our pain. Give us faith to endure the fire we face. Thank you for refining us and burning us pure. Amen.

DAY 318 Colossians 3:23–24

"Work willingly at whatever you do, as though you were working for the Lord rather than for people. Remember that the Lord will give you an inheritance as your reward, and that the Master you are serving is Christ." (NLT)

We often approach work as a necessary burden rather than an opportunity. Scripture challenges our tendency to separate the sacred from the secular, transforming our perspective on the daily tasks that fill our lives, including the jobs that we do. Even the most mundane tasks can be infused with divine purpose. Every project, interaction, and chore can be a way to honor God—to reflect the goodness of our Creator.

Reframing our work as service to God transforms our motivation. We focus less on working for outward approval and more on sharing the blessings that God showers upon us for the benefit of others. Whether in a boardroom or a classroom, sweeping floors or writing code, raising a child or caring for an aging parent, our labor holds divine significance. No longer are we just working for a paycheck. As we embrace each task, big or small, with enthusiasm, diligence, and integrity, we are taking greater hold of the inheritance of love that is ours, thanks to Jesus.

Jesus, help us to embrace our work today not as a burden but as a sacred service—a sincere offering of praise and testament to your glory. Amen.

Mark 16:15

DAY
319

"And then he told them, 'Go into all the world and preach the Good News to everyone.'" (NLT)

The Great Commission is often misunderstood. In the call to share the Gospel, we may feel pressure to say the right words, to "win souls," or to measure our faithfulness by visible results. At times, it can even feel like a task list—one that risks reducing people to projects and faith to performance.

But when we return to Jesus' words with fresh eyes, we discover something far more beautiful. This final instruction isn't a burden to carry but an invitation to participate in the love we've received. It's a call to embody and extend the Good News, not as a formula but as a way of life. Living out the Great Commission begins not with urgency or pressure but with deep compassion.

Rightly oriented, we proclaim Christ's love wherever we are. It's declared in how we live: by listening well, loving patiently, serving humbly, and acting justly. The Great Commission isn't a sales pitch—it's participation in the restoration of all creation.

Jesus' love is wide enough to embrace all people and deep enough to renew all things. Living the Great Commission means living in response to love, not in fear or obligation.

As you have loved us, Jesus, let us go and love others. Amen.

DAY
320 Luke 1:38

"Mary responded, 'I am the Lord's servant. May everything you have said about me come true.' And then the angel left her." (NLT)

Mary's words in response to the news that she would be the mother of Jesus echo through time: "I am the Lord's servant. May everything you have said about me come true." These words are simple but not small. Trust and obedience often appear that way on the surface—quiet decisions and subtle responses. But underneath, they are movements of courage.

Mary had questions, and she was likely afraid. But her posture was one of surrender, not the surrender that gives up, but the kind that opens up to mystery, purpose—a story far greater than her own.

Trust is not the absence of uncertainty. It is the choice to say yes, even when the outcome is unclear. Obedience is not rigid compliance; it is love in motion. We are invited into the same posture Mary adopted: one of willingness, one that makes room for God to do more than we can understand.

What if trust doesn't always resemble certainty? What if it is simply saying, "Let it be so?"

Lord, we come to you with the same trust as Mary. May it cultivate an obedience full of love and courage. Amen.

Isaiah 30:20–21

DAY
321

"Though the Lord gave you adversity for food and suffering for drink, he will still be with you to teach you. You will see your teacher with your own eyes. Your own ears will hear him. Right behind you, a voice will say, 'This is the way you should go, whether to the right or to the left.'" (NLT)

At times, the way forward feels obscured. Clarity seems beyond reach, and God's silence feels louder than divine guidance. Isaiah 30:20-21 reminds us that even in seasons of scarcity, even in sorrow or correction, the voice of God still speaks: "This is the way you should go."

God does not abandon us to confusion. The paths God prepares are not always visible in advance but are revealed in real time, step by step. Sometimes, the path unfolds through detours, recontextualizing what we thought were failures, and opening doors we never would have chosen. Still, the Holy Spirit leads. What feels like wandering is actually formation.

God's guidance does not always announce itself with certainty. But it is present, persistent, and near. The path may not be illuminated in advance, but it is never without a guide.

Jesus, grant us the acceptance that you guide our every step and the confidence to trust your leading. Amen.

DAY

322 Deuteronomy 1:31

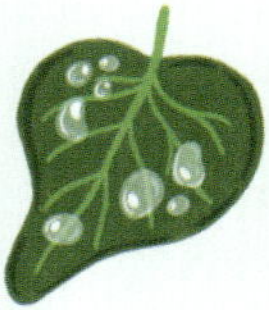

"And you saw how the Lord your God cared for you all along the way as you traveled through the wilderness, just as a father cares for his child. Now he has brought you to this place." (NLT)

Most parents carry a bag of necessities full of diapers and wipes, snacks, water, sunscreen, and maybe even a change of clothes. The child rarely has to worry about their needs when all they have to do is ask the loving parent who totes around the heavy load for what they require.

The Bible is full of stories of God providing for the Israelites out of a heavenly supply in their long journeys through the wilderness. There was manna, quails, and fresh water along the way, with dry ground for steady feet. Every step of the way, God provided.

Thankfully, we serve the same God who will continue to hold what feels too heavy for us as we journey through our lives. God still journeys with us in our own wilderness seasons. And when we are like children asking for a snack while exploring, God will be the good parent, faithful to open the heavy bag and provide.

God, thank you for carrying our heavy loads and faithfully providing our every need. Amen.

1 Peter 2:23

DAY
323

"He did not retaliate when he was insulted, nor threaten revenge when he suffered. He left his case in the hands of God, who always judges fairly." (NLT)

Holding tight to our anger and resentment can feel like a position of strength. Desiring suffering for those who hurt us can give us a sense of power. But as the familiar saying goes, clinging to anger and resentment is "like drinking poison and waiting for the other person to die." In the end, it hurts *us*.

Jesus models for us another way through: the profound strength found in choosing forgiveness.

Forgiveness takes wrongs and pains seriously, but instead of keeping them clenched tightly in our fists, it places judgment in God's hands. Even in his moments of greatest suffering, Jesus trusted God. He released bitterness and resentment and showed us that true strength lies not in revenge but in bringing our wounds to the care of our God, who is full of wisdom, justice, and love.

The path of forgiveness allows us to exchange our bitterness for healing. It frees us from cycles of hurt, making room in our hearts for peace and new life. This does not erase the past, but it can begin to transform it, turning scars into testimonies of grace.

God, give us the strength to forgive as you forgive, trusting fully in your justice and grace. Amen.

DAY

324 Joel 2:28

"Then, after doing all those things, I will pour out my Spirit upon all people. Your sons and daughters will prophesy. Your old men will dream dreams, and your young men will see visions." (NLT)

Imagination is not childish; it is sacred. In the face of a rigid and rationalistic world, it is the ability to conceive of more, of better.

God does not dismiss dreamers or visionaries. When children of God dare to hope for more than what is seen, we are given inspiration through imagination.

The Spirit of God is not only found in tradition and memory but also in creativity, vision, and the ability to imagine a future that aligns with God's Kingdom.

This is not empty dreaming. It is Spirit-filled seeing. What possibilities have we silenced in ourselves? What callings have we dismissed as unrealistic? God speaks through dreams. Jesus inspires ordinary people to live with extraordinary courage.

Let our imaginations be sanctified, not tamed, but trusted. The same Spirit who hovered over the waters now stirs within us.

Breathe in: Come, Holy Spirit
Breathe out: and stir what
is sleeping in us. Amen.

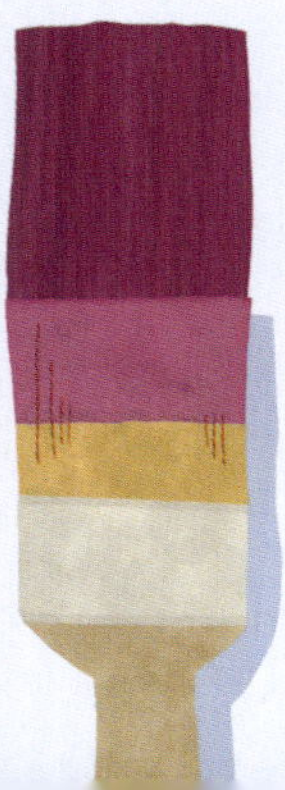

Isaiah 12:5–6

DAY
325

"Sing to the Lord, for he has done wonderful things. Make known his praise around the world. Let all the people of Jerusalem shout his praise with joy! For great is the Holy One of Israel who lives among you." (NLT)

In the hushed moments of morning, when the air crackles with anticipation and the sky is veiled in a soft, ethereal glow, the world begins to sing with a profound sense of joy. Joy is a transcendent feeling, beyond mere pleasure or fleeting satisfaction. It is the serenity found in a quiet moment of reflection, the bliss that arises from genuine connections, and the contentment derived from embracing life's simplest blessings.

Joy reveals itself in the unspoken language of heartfelt gestures. It's the contagious laughter of a child, echoing through the halls and reminding us of the innocence and wonder that resides within us all. It's the comforting warmth of a loved one's embrace, a tangible reminder of the enduring bonds that tie us together.

It is also intrinsically linked to hope and faith. Joyful spirits fill us with hope to face adversity. Faith leads us through the darkest nights and allows the radiance of joy to pierce the shadows. Joy is the beacon that reminds us of the eternal promise of love, echoing through the ages and finding its culmination in Christ.

Almighty God, fill our souls to the brim with joy. Let us abound in delight for your good works. Amen.

DAY 326 Jeremiah 31:3

"Long ago the Lord said to Israel: 'I have loved you, my people, with an everlasting love. With unfailing love I have drawn you to myself.'" (NLT)

What does everlasting love really entail? We hear it sung about in songs, questioned by philosophers, and doubted during seasons of heartbreak. What the world does not know is that the love of God is distinct from any version of earthly love.

God has lavished creation with a love that is infinite and indestructible in every way. Amidst our stubborn wanderings and rejections, God continues to extend this love, drawing all of humanity in and going to any lengths to get us back.

When other relationships falter, Jesus shows us a love story that never wavers but rather restores us from the inside out. This love is real, reliable, and unbreakable, even when the world is crumbling around us. What's more, this love keeps us close and stable when all else is uncertain. If there is one thing we can be sure will never let us down, it is the power of God's love, the very agent for a perfect relationship, with the One who is head-over-heels devoted to us.

God, who embodies all love! Thank you for stabilizing us with your unending, perfect embrace. It forever completes us. Amen.

Isaiah 6:8

DAY 327

“Then I heard the voice of the Lord saying, ‘Whom shall I send? And who will go for us?’ And I said, ‘Here am I. Send me!’” (NIV)

Stepping into our callings can be scary. It’s intimidating to tackle a new challenge, venture into uncharted territory, or do something unprecedented. What if we have to risk something important? What if we fail?

But to answer God’s call for our lives, we can’t just believe. We need to act. Our callings come directly from God, so we can trust that anything God is leading us into, He is preparing us for.

In times of uncertainty, when our confidence falters and we second-guess our path, we can take comfort in this: we are never alone. Jesus is always by our side as we answer his call for our lives. We can also find strength and encouragement in our loved ones. When we have moments of fear and doubt, they will be there to revive us, pray for us, and remind us why we’re on the path.

God, thank you for giving our lives a calling. We ask for the bravery to boldly pursue that calling, to your glory. Amen.

DAY

328 Psalm 27:4

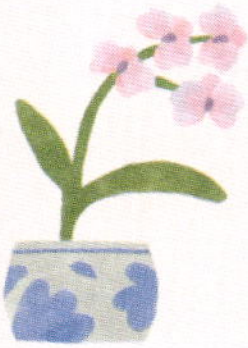

"One thing I ask from the Lord, this only do I seek: that I may dwell in the house of the Lord all the days of my life, to gaze on the beauty of the Lord and to seek him in his temple." (NIV)

Amid our responsibilities, we can easily slip into utilitarian thinking. "What purpose does this serve?" we ask. "How does this get me closer to my goals?" From this perspective, it can be hard to appreciate beauty.

But there is more to life than mere utilitarianism, only seeking out and valuing what tangibly serves us. Our Creator didn't have to make the world beautiful, but still chose to. When we take time to appreciate beauty, we feel refreshed, inspired, and more connected to the rest of God's creation.

Beauty itself does have value. The beauty of service, community, generosity, and love helps inspire us to give more of ourselves. The natural beauty of creation reminds us of God's glory, the vastness of the universe, and our small place in it. It's a source of wonder and comfort, pointing us to something beyond ourselves. When we pursue a beautiful life, we're striving to answer God's unique calling.

Holy Creator, thank you for filling our lives with beauty, from the wonders of creation to the tenderness of friendship. Open our eyes to appreciating the everyday beauty in front of us, and help us make the world a more beautiful, good place. Amen.

Matthew 6:9–10

DAY 329

"Pray like this: Our Father in heaven, may your name be kept holy. May your Kingdom come soon. May your will be done on earth, as it is in heaven." (NLT)

Prayer. It's one of the most foundational aspects of our faith lives, and yet, it can feel intimidating. What do we say? How do we carry ourselves? Should we speak aloud, or stay quiet? Jesus offers a model for prayer, a framework for communicating with God that is rooted in love, reverence, and trust.

In other words, prayer is not about performance—it's about relationship. Jesus invites us to approach God not as a distant deity but as a loving Father. We "hallow" God's name in recognition of the uniqueness of this relationship compared to every other we have. Prayer begins with honor and worship, not requests.

The outline Jesus offers is a prayer of longing for the world to reflect the beauty, justice, and righteousness of God's Kingdom. It also encourages a posture of surrender, trusting that God's will is also best, even when it isn't what we would choose. The Lord's Prayer is not merely something we recite by rote; it is a rhythm for living in daily communion with God.

Jesus, lead us in prayer that is grounded in love, marked by awe, and shaped by surrender. Amen.

DAY

330 Isaiah 25:6

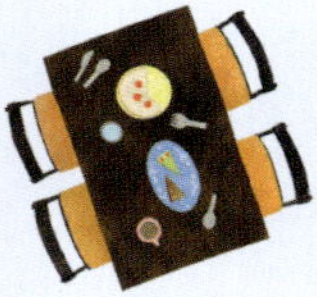

"In Jerusalem, the Lord of Heaven's Armies will spread a wonderful feast for all the people of the world. It will be a delicious banquet with clear, well-aged wine and choice meat." (NLT)

Imagine that the greatest chefs came together to prepare a meal with no ingredients off limits. Our souls and stomachs would leave filled from the rich conversations, hearty laughter, and culinary mastery. A celebratory feast for the ages! Isaiah 25:6 celebrates the future of Heaven as a delicious banquet open to all. How wonderful it will be to dine at the table described!

Many of the conversations in Jesus' ministry happened around meals that left a lasting impression. He transformed water into wine, multiplied fish and bread, and shared tables with people from all walks of life. During the Last Supper, Jesus declared that his body is the bread broken and his blood is the wine spilled. And after the resurrection, the meal Isaiah describes took on a new reality.

In remembrance and anticipation, we embody the celebration with new hope. As the Spirit makes ordinary tables holy, we begin to model Heaven's banquet here and now, and we glimpse our common call to celebrate.

Holy Spirit, we thank you for the times when you have joined us at our table, and we ask that you grant us greater glimpses of the banquet to come. Amen.

Ephesians 1:9–10

DAY 331

"God has now revealed to us his mysterious will regarding Christ—which is to fulfill his own good plan. And this is the plan: At the right time he will bring everything together under the authority of Christ—everything in heaven and on earth." (NLT)

A life lived in pursuit of Jesus is often marked by tension between what we know and what we don't. We speak of the ways of God being outside our comprehension, of wisdom beyond our understanding, but mysteries and uncertainties tend to irritate us. We dislike the not-knowing.

Ephesians 1:9-10 urges us to set aside our search for digestible meaning and marvel at the mystery that is the unfolding of God's eternal purpose in Christ. God's plan is not a riddle to solve but a Person to follow. We are invited to live not with perfect clarity but with deep trust.

Even when we can't see the whole picture, we can trust the character of the One writing the story. God's mysteries are not random; they unfold from love and grace. They point us towards a greater hope: Jesus will make all things whole.

Embracing mystery means walking by faith, holding wonder, and trusting the goodness and trustworthiness of Christ.

Help us release our need for certainty in all things and step out in confidence with you, the One who holds all things. Amen.

DAY

332 Matthew 18:12–14

"If a man has a hundred sheep and one of them wanders away, what will he do? Won't he leave the ninety-nine others on the hills and go out to search for the one that is lost? And if he finds it, I tell you the truth, he will rejoice over it more than over the ninety-nine that didn't wander away! In the same way, it is not my heavenly Father's will that even one of these little ones should perish." (NLT)

We all have seasons when we drift away from the centering of our faith, whether by distraction, pain, doubt, or weariness. Jesus' parable of the lost sheep paints a picture of a shepherd who notices, seeks, and rejoices over the one who strays. This is more than a story of rescue—it's a revelation of God's character.

In the parable, the shepherd doesn't wait for the sheep to return on its own; he goes out to search. Jesus seeks us. His pursuit is not reluctant but eager and intentional. And once we are brought back into the fold, God does not greet us with scolding but with joy. This is the tone of God's grace: celebration over shame, delight over reproach.

God's desire is always restoration, always reunion. The seeking love of Jesus flows from his very nature. No one is too far gone, no one beyond his reach. We don't have to prove anything to be loved.

Let today be a moment of returning and resting in your arms, the arms of the God who seeks. Amen.

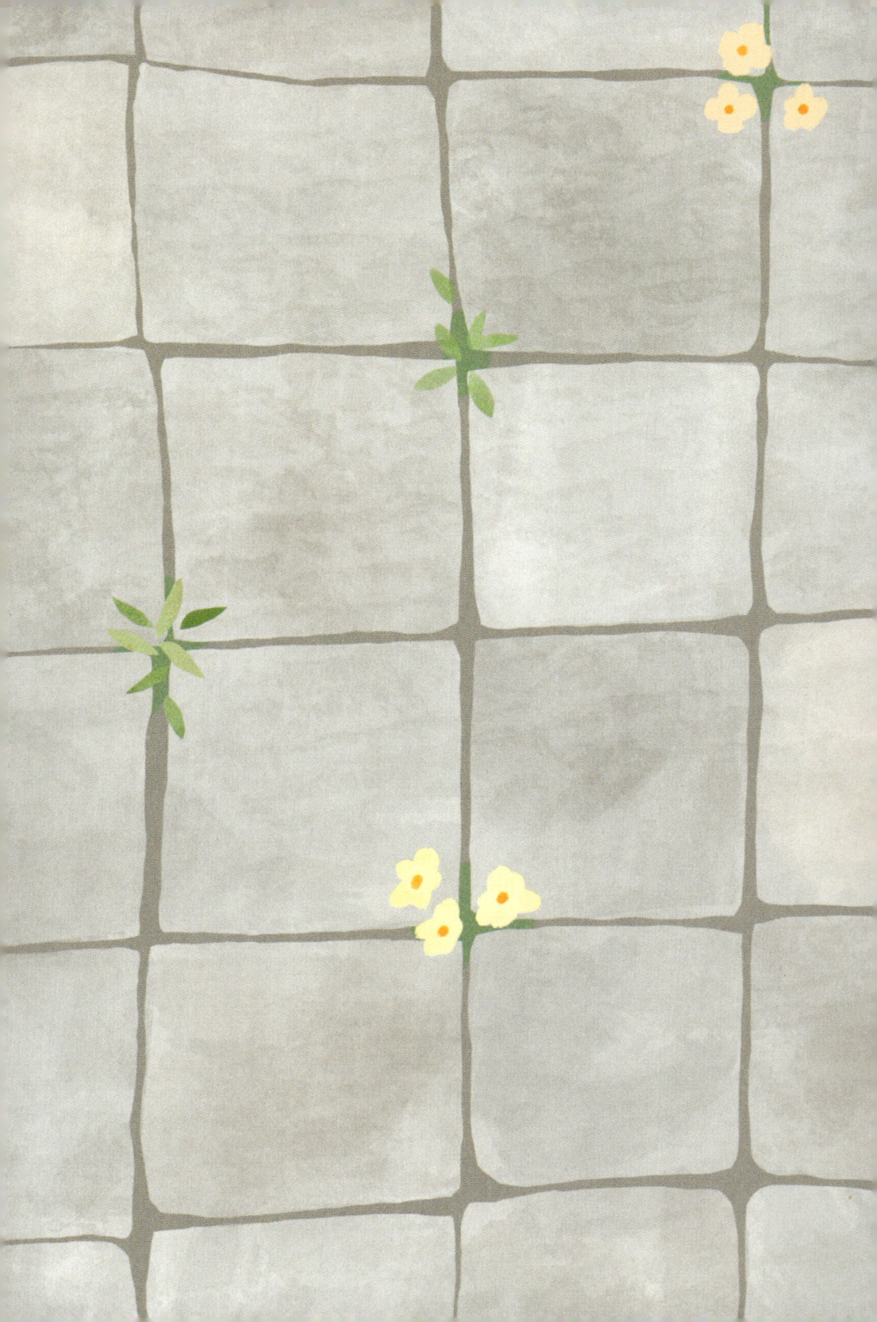

Psalm 111:2–3

DAY 333

"Great are the works of the Lord; they are pondered by all who delight in them. Glorious and majestic are his deeds, and his righteousness endures forever." (NIV)

When we seek out the beauty of creation, we safeguard ourselves from being bogged down by hardship, sorrow, and boredom. Observing the delicate, precise wings of a bumblebee, the mathematical force of a wave, the funny appearance of a platypus, or our beloved pet—these are opportunities to be revived, encouraged, and amused.

Knowing that we aren't in control of everything, even our own circumstances, can be frightening. But reminding ourselves that we have a God who is both almighty and unwaveringly good is a comfort. When we seek out moments of wonder and delight in our daily lives, we point ourselves back to God's power and benevolence. We find ourselves even more confident in God's ultimate, restorative plans.

Jesus, forgive us for the times we've felt too busy to stop and marvel at the beauty of creation. Show us opportunities to savor the small wonders around us as they point us to your eternal wisdom and love. Amen.

DAY 334 Galatians 5:25

"Since we are living by the Spirit, let us follow the Spirit's leading in every part of our lives." (NLT)

There is a cadence to life. Our pace may be chaotic and rushed, but the Spirit's is steady, attuned, and alive.

To walk in step with the Spirit is to release the constant pressure to lead. It is to listen, not just for direction, but for rhythm. We trust that the Spirit's pace is not just right—it is right for us.

Spirit-led living can feel countercultural in a world that idolizes productivity and speed. But it is also freeing. It frees us from the need to perform and from the fear of falling behind.

The Spirit does not drive us forward in urgency. It draws us forward in obedience and trust. Walking in step requires presence. It asks us to slow down, notice, and discern. Sometimes, this looks like bold movement, and other times, it looks like sacred stillness.

What would shift if we stopped trying to run ahead of Jesus? What might we hear if we slowed down enough to match the Holy Spirit's pace?

May we have the grace to accept your pace for our lives, Spirit. Amen.

Galatians 5:22–23

DAY 335

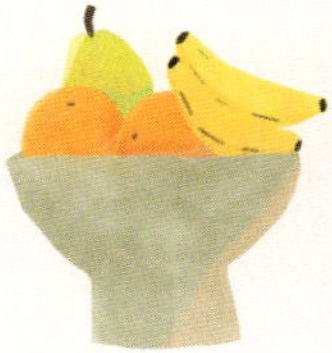

"But the Holy Spirit produces this kind of fruit in our lives: love, joy, peace, patience, kindness, goodness, faithfulness, gentleness, and self-control. There is no law against these things!" (NLT)

When trees bear ripe fruit, they beam with vibrant color and bless those who pick from their full branches. Likewise, when the Holy Spirit is planted in us through faith, we become most fruitful, transforming our inner worlds and blessing those who encounter us. Unlike the seasonal offerings of the trees, the fruit of the Spirit is nonperishable and continues to yield in willing hearts each new day.

Love compels us to show the compassion of Jesus to others. Joy inspires us to give thanks. Peace calms and comforts us. Patience equips us to endure lengthy journeys. Kindness makes the stranger or the sick feel seen and cared for. Goodness treats others with integrity. Faithfulness enables us to stand the test of time. Gentleness extends a soft and tender touch to the vulnerable. And self-control instills a temperance in us to resist sin and pursue what is right.

These nine virtues are the essence of God's character, visible in us when we live well. Each virtue is distinct from the other, yet they work in harmony to make us whole.

Holy Spirit, you make us most beautiful. We invite you to bear your fruit within us, for our good and God's glory. Amen.

DAY

336 Leviticus 25:4

"But during the seventh year the land must have a Sabbath year of complete rest. It is the Lord's Sabbath. Do not plant your fields or prune your vineyards during that year." (NLT)

A garden left unpilfered bursts through artificial boundaries and becomes wild, growing freely towards the sun. Untamed growth like that takes more than a few days; it takes seasons. What if we embraced this example in our spiritual lives?

For soil to stay fertile, it has to be allowed to rest every few years so that nutrients are replenished. Spiritually, an unproductive harvest can seem like death, and it can be easy to feel like we are far from God. We struggle to see how a lack of planting and pruning helps. Yet, it is in rest that we can grow more freely towards God's light.

Relying on continuous busyness that inhibits our growth, we struggle to see God's care for us. God urges us to prioritize rest, so much so that even the very soil used for growing is given respite. As we trust in God's provision, our spiritual lives are replenished with all we need. Who are we to think we can produce more than our Creator will allow?

Creator God, you created rest and called us to spend it in relationship with you. Grow in us a desire for rest so that the soil of our lives may be refreshed in you. Amen.

Isaiah 42:16

DAY 337

"I will lead blind Israel down a new path, guiding them along an unfamiliar way. I will brighten the darkness before them and smooth out the road ahead of them. Yes, I will indeed do these things; I will not forsake them." (NLT)

Change can be scary. When we look down the untread paths of our lives and see only darkness, it's easy to instead search for a more familiar way forward. But darkness doesn't always represent something bad; sometimes, darkness is just waiting for the light we carry to come.

The people of Israel frequently found themselves in uncharted territory and on unfamiliar paths. Abraham was called to a country he didn't know. The Israelites were led to an unknown Promised Land, and later to a foreign country in exile. Though darkness was in front of them, God's light would eventually reveal a path that was good and helped Israel grow into who God called them to be.

God's care and promises to us are good. When we're called down an unfamiliar path, we can trust God to guide us through the darkness. Jesus' light will come.

Christ, grant us the courage to keep walking forward, even when the path feels unfamiliar. Amen.

DAY
338 Lamentations 2:19

"Arise, cry out in the night, as the watches of the night begin; pour out your heart like water in the presence of the Lord. Lift up your hands to him for the lives of your children, who faint from hunger at every street corner." (NIV)

We tend to rush through uncomfortable feelings. We try to speedrun the stages of grief. We acknowledge pain only to, in the same breath, declare that it will pass. This is understandable; hope is valuable. Reminders that better things are ahead can be helpful. But sometimes, we need a moment to sit in our sadness and frustration. We need to lament.

The spiritual posture of lament invites us to openly express our griefs and sorrows to God. It is the divinely sanctioned space for venting anger, voicing doubts, and asking tough questions. Lament is not a signifier of feeble faith but a demonstration of a relationship with God that is active and vibrant. To acknowledge that things are not how they should be isn't weakness. It is born out of confidence in the vision of creation that Jesus promises.

Lament calls out to God amidst our pain and asks God to work for healing and restoration. The injustice and inequity that break our hearts also enrage God. There is space for our lament. Reckoning with the wrongness of the world allows us to work towards righteousness all the more intently.

Spirit, hear our cries. Pour out your presence upon us. Amen.

Ephesians 5:8–9

DAY 339

"For once you were full of darkness, but now you have light from the Lord. So live as people of light! For this light within you produces only what is good and right and true." (NLT)

Before we embrace faith in Jesus, our lives are completely consumed by a spiritual darkness. We may not have been fully aware of it at the time—sin is an expert blinder. And if light comes from Christ, we know that without him, we wander aimlessly without the light.

What comes after our old life of darkness is so much better. With Jesus shining in our hearts, we live in this light every day and resist reverting to the shadows of sin. The light becomes intimately one with us so that in return, we would become walking lights that embody Christ's radiant character.

Darkness may still exist outside of us. But Christ's light is inextinguishable. Its burn length is eternal, and we can choose to keep burning brightly for him, no matter the shade or shadows that are viciously shot our way. In Jesus, we are now walking lights, so let's be vessels that shine.

Jesus, you are the light of the world who has made us who believe in you little lights in return! Help us to shine brightly in this dark world, and keep our flame burning within. Amen.

DAY 340 1 John 4:8–10

"But anyone who does not love does not know God, for God is love. God showed how much he loved us by sending his one and only Son into the world so that we might have eternal life through him. This is real love—not that we loved God, but that he loved us and sent his Son as a sacrifice to take away our sins." (NLT)

Love is not simply something God does—it is the very substance of who God is. And because the divine does not change, divine love does not flicker even in the face of our failings.

This truth steadies: we are loved completely and continuously.

This love comes not because we deserve it nor because we earned it, but because love, real love, originates with God. It was love that moved Jesus toward us, love that took on flesh, that bore the weight of distance and closed the gap forever.

Sometimes, we forget. We measure divine love by our moods or our mistakes. But the Cross has already answered the question. Let there be no mistake: we are not merely tolerated, and we are not on trial. We are loved, chosen, and delighted in.

Let this truth fall fresh, like rain on hardened soil, and let it soak deep into the places that resist affection.

God is love. God loves us and calls us by name. Amen.

DAY

Ecclesiastes 3:12–13 341

“I know that there is nothing better for people than to be happy and to do good while they live. That each of them may eat and drink, and find satisfaction in all their toil—this is the gift of God.” (NIV)

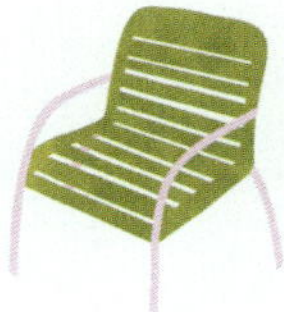

Life’s never-ending responsibilities and challenges can be overwhelming. As we strive for big wins, little pleasures can seem insignificant, even trivial. But small joys matter. Satisfaction in a job well done, celebrating with loved ones, sharing good food: these everyday sources of comfort and connection can provide us with the strength to continue in hard times.

After all, Jesus did not limit his ministry to grand miracles and wonders; he also provided wine at weddings and enjoyed sharing meals with his friends. Every small joy is a divine gift and therefore deserves to be savored. Paying attention to “the little things” is in Jesus’ nature: he praises the widow’s small offering, seeks the one lost sheep, and welcomes the smallest of children. He reminds us to appreciate what’s easily forgotten.

It can be difficult to feel encouraged by ordinary comforts when life’s challenges loom large. But as we tune into the present moment, celebrating little blessings, it becomes easier to find more and more indications of God’s love, care, and beauty.

Heavenly Father, thank you for the small joys in our lives, the everyday wellsprings of comfort in the midst of hardship. May we continue to seek out and appreciate every blessing you bestow. Amen.

DAY
342 Isaiah 50:4

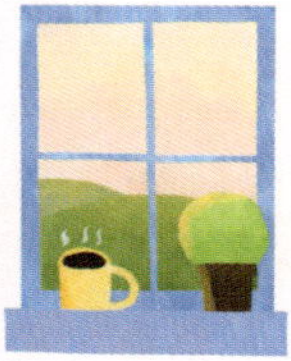

"The Sovereign Lord has given me his words of wisdom, so that I know how to comfort the weary. Morning by morning he wakens me and opens my understanding to his will." (NLT)

When the world is hushed and the first light of a new day begins to touch the edges of the horizon, there lies a sacred opportunity to approach the morning with intention. Morning time brings the gift of a fresh start, a chance to release the burdens of yesterday and embrace the possibilities of today.

Before the hustle and haste of the day have taken over our focus, we can carve out a moment of stillness. This period of pause allows us to be fully present, acknowledging our connection to our Creator and inviting God's guidance to lead us. We can use this morning's stillness to converse with Jesus through prayerful reflection.

Each day we awaken is a step forward, a gift from God to deepen in wisdom. Likewise, the rest of the previous night is a blessing in itself. Renewed and refreshed, we wake up ready to care for others, honor creation, and pursue God's Kingdom.

Holy Spirit, open our understanding to your will. Help us to embrace the stillness and mindfully embrace the gift of today. Amen.

Proverbs 27:23–24 DAY 343

"Be sure you know the condition of your flocks, give careful attention to your herds; for riches do not endure forever, and a crown is not secure for all generations." (NIV)

Everything we have—our time, money, skills—is something God has chosen to bless us with. How can we be faithful, intentional stewards of these blessings?

First, we need to understand what we have. A good salary, lots of free time or flexible commitments, extra room, plenty of food? When we know the state of our affairs, we can better plan, prepare, and provide, not just for ourselves, but for our wider community.

Jesus continually fed the hungry, comforted the grieving, and spent time with social outcasts. While he was a man of few financial means, Jesus of Nazareth still saw opportunities to give what he did have. Our resources are not for ourselves alone. May our thankfulness spur us to be generous with others, just as God has been generous with us.

Generous God, we desire to be wise and compassionate stewards of your blessings. We know we can't hold onto our material comforts forever, nor should we want to. Show us ways to improve the lives of people around us in the here and now. Amen.

DAY

344 Nehemiah 5:6, 8

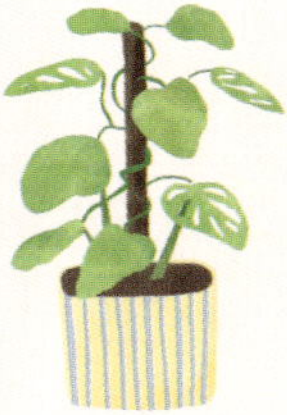

"When I heard their outcry and these charges, I was very angry. ... and said: 'As far as possible, we have bought back our fellow Jews who were sold to the Gentiles. Now you are selling your own people, only for them to be sold back to us!' They kept quiet, because they could find nothing to say." (NIV)

Anger can seem like a harmful emotion, something that makes us more prone to sin. We might envision yelling, even getting aggressive with loved ones or strangers. What good can possibly come of anger? Is it a danger to be avoided, a temper to be subdued? Emotions are sources of information: they tell us something about a situation and how we relate to it. Anger can be an indicator that something is fundamentally wrong, unjust.

There are many injustices worth our anger: needless hunger and illness in poorer communities, rampant abuses of power, the withholding of much-needed resources by the greedy. Righteous, justified anger can spur us to address these things. The feeling itself is not the conundrum; it's the action we take in light of that anger. Jesus felt righteous anger when cleansing the Temple and confronting the Pharisees. Likewise, we need to steward our anger wisely, moving forward with care and intention.

God, help us sit with our anger and reflect on the causes of it, that we may act with intention and care. Move us to just, righteous anger, and show us how to amend wrongs. Amen.

DAY

Genesis 17:7

345

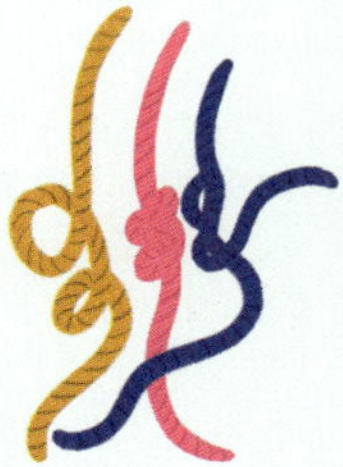

"I will confirm my covenant with you and your descendants after you, from generation to generation. This is the everlasting covenant: I will always be your God and the God of your descendants after you." (NLT)

Despite our best intentions, human promises often falter. Broken by forgetfulness, failure, or unexpected circumstances, we don't always live up to our commitments. But the promises God makes are different.

In Genesis, God bestows an enduring covenant upon Abraham—one that echoes through generations. Covenants are more akin to legal contracts than our more informal promises. Traditionally, both parties agree to certain terms, and if one or both of them don't make good on the agreement, the terms are void. And yet, God follows through even if we do not. Divine promises are not rooted in our worthiness but in God's mercy and choosing.

The covenant God establishes with Abraham reveals the character of God's heart: faithful, enduring, and deeply personal. The promises of God are not temporary or shifting; they endure forever. They are not transactional but relational, meant to draw us into deeper trust and communion.

Jesus, what you speak, you sustain. In every season, we can hold fast to your word. Amen.

DAY 346 Romans 8:9

"But you are not controlled by your sinful nature. You are controlled by the Spirit if you have the Spirit of God living in you. (And remember that those who do not have the Spirit of Christ living in them do not belong to him at all.)" (NLT)

The war between the flesh and spirit is depicted as an intense struggle in scripture, even after becoming a person of faith. However, when we embrace Jesus as our personal Lord and Savior, the Holy Spirit moves in and makes a home within us.

Romans 8:9 boldly declares that once we invite God in, we are no longer in bondage to the sinful tendencies that once enslaved us. Rather, those who have the indwelling Spirit of God are powerfully directed in how they should think, act, and live a fruitful life.

We might compare this experience to a candle being lit within a hollow cave, wherein, before the flame of the Spirit illuminated inside our hearts, we were stumbling in sheer darkness. But when the wick is lit, our inner worlds are filled with living light, never to burn out. The Spirit is our sacred seal that shows evidence that we belong to God.

Spirit of God, thank you for living in us and making us beautiful from within. Lead us and keep us, please. We surrender to you. Amen.

Isaiah 1:17

DAY
347

"Learn to do good. Seek justice. Help the oppressed. Defend the cause of orphans. Fight for the rights of widows." (NLT)

We often equate righteous living with avoiding wrongdoing. In God's eyes, however, acting justly goes beyond following the rules and not breaking the law. It means actively working to foster a world where the vulnerable are cared for and protected, where the needy are offered a helping hand, and where everyone is treated with dignity and has enough to thrive.

Our thoughts and prayers may be a place to start, but it is far from where we are called to finish in doing good. Our actions matter. Living justly means embodying the proactive love of God in everything we say and do, including what and who we support. It is challenging systems that perpetuate oppression and inequality. It is remaining committed to setting things right even where there is opposition.

If we perceive ourselves as having no real power or resources, we might wonder how we can make any difference in a broken world. But even the smallest gestures of kindness, compassion, and advocacy can be manifestations of Jesus' restorative touch to those who believe they have been forsaken and left behind. Other can experience God through our witness.

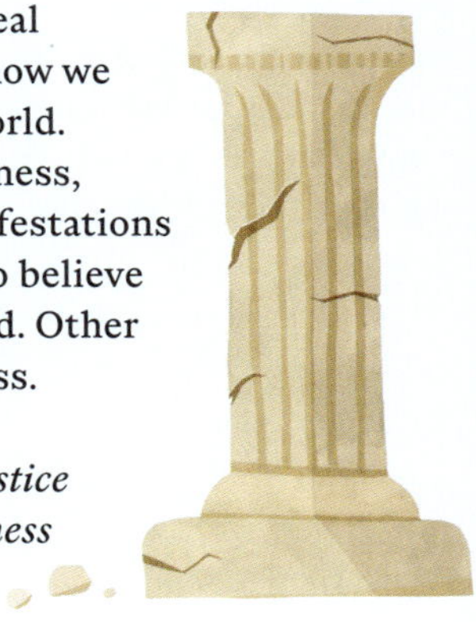

God, ignite within us a passion for your justice and empower us to be agents of righteousness in our broken world. Amen.

DAY
348 1 Corinthians 1:10

"I appeal to you, dear brothers and sisters, by the authority of our Lord Jesus Christ, to live in harmony with each other. Let there be no divisions in the church. Rather, be of one mind, united in thought and purpose." (NLT)

More and more, division is the name of the game. We speak of in-groups and out-groups. We set ourselves apart from anyone whose approach to life differs from our own. But, as people of faith, we are called to something different: a fellowship rooted not in sameness but in a shared life in Christ.

In 1 Corinthians 1:10, Paul asks us to embrace a unity shaped by love, humility, and mutual belonging. This isn't a call to uniformity but to a love that transcends our differences. True fellowship isn't built on preference, personality, or shared interests; it's built on Jesus. If the love of Christ can reach us all, surely we can find space for everyone within our communities.

Where division often begins in pride, fellowship thrives in humility and grace. It doesn't require us to agree on everything—just to navigate the conflicts that arise in love. This type of community is not passive; it requires a commitment to one another and a shared pursuit of Jesus.

As we choose you, Jesus, over ourselves, help us to embody the heart of your Gospel in all aspects of life. Amen.

James 1:22

DAY 349

“Do not merely listen to the word, and so deceive yourselves. Do what it says.” (NIV)

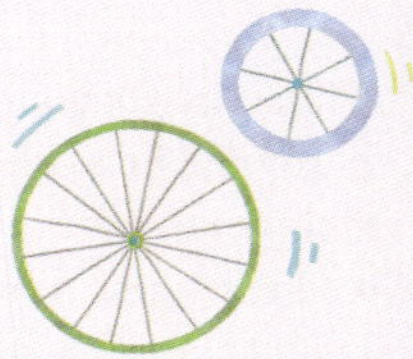

Jesus says all we need is the faith of a mustard seed. Our salvation rests on our conviction that Jesus is truly God and is the way toward a more beautiful, fulfilling life and a healed world.

But conviction is more than mere belief: it is choices made and actions taken. In the words of James, we cannot “merely listen,” we must “do.” Our faith informs our lives on a practical level. Inspired by the Holy Spirit, we change in obvious, visible ways.

Listening, feeling, and processing are essential to growth, but they are incomplete without action. When we don’t enact what we have learned, it calls our beliefs into question. When we take the Gospel to heart, when we love Jesus and earnestly desire to continue his ministry, our lives will bear fruit.

How we live should be an effective witness of Christ himself. When people interact with us, do they experience Christ’s love? Can they feel our values—witness them—from our actions?

Jesus, thank you for setting an example of action rather than mere words. Embolden us to live out our convictions in tangible ways, as representatives of your love, justice, and mercy. Amen.

DAY 350 Luke 14:12–14

"Then he turned to his host. 'When you put on a luncheon or a banquet,' he said, 'don't invite your friends, brothers, relatives, and rich neighbors. ... Instead, invite the poor, the crippled, the lame, and the blind. Then at the resurrection of the righteous, God will reward you for inviting those who could not repay you.'" (NLT)

In a transactional society, our hospitality is often based on reciprocity. But Jesus flips this understanding. While we tend to seek comfort among equals, expecting a favor to be returned in kind, Jesus calls us to embody a deeper, sacrificial love, having a heart that mirrors God's.

Biblical hospitality isn't about what we get back but about how much we are willing. It is less about reinforcing existing social bonds than it is about disrupting the status quo by breaking down social barriers and creating a new community of equals. Such radical hospitality, which recognizes and protects the inherent worth and dignity of every person, is but a reflection of God's extravagant grace, freely given to us all.

It's not about grand gestures. It's about simple acts of kindness. A listening ear, a shared meal, a helping hand extended toward those in need, regardless of their social standing or ability to repay. In these moments of welcome, we embody and experience the blessing of Christ's love, not just in theory but in practice.

Help us embrace radical hospitality, opening our lives and reflecting boundless compassion to those most in need. Amen.

Lamentations 3:25–26

DAY 351

"The Lord is good to those who depend on him, to those who search for him. So it is good to wait quietly for salvation from the Lord." (NLT)

Cultivating dependency on God can be very difficult when we are so independently driven. Our culture leads us to believe that we can be self-sufficient when, in reality, we are always in desperate need of the Lord's care. Only when we truly lean on God can our burdens be lifted and our souls be gently hushed.

Lamentations reveals God's goodness to those who realize they need Him and wholeheartedly seek God in return. When we take matters into our own hands without relying on the Lord, we enter into a place of pure chaos. Our inner worlds become loud with expectations that we are simply not fit to fulfill. When we forsake this tendency to take control and trust in God's ability to carry us, our souls lighten up as a bird that finally rests its full weight in a sturdy nest. Let us wait with quiet expectation for salvation that comes only from Jesus, and be still.

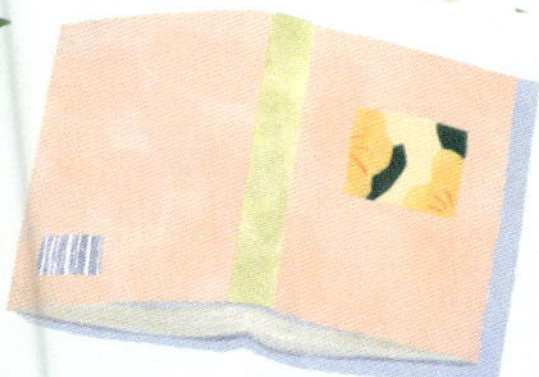

Lord, when the world is loud around us, help us to depend on you, and quiet our souls in the process. Thank you for caring for us so well. Amen.

DAY

352 Luke 10:38–39

"As Jesus and the disciples continued on their way to Jerusalem, they came to a certain village where a woman named Martha welcomed him into her home. Her sister, Mary, sat at the Lord's feet, listening to what he taught." (NLT)

We are constantly looking for the next thing to do. Rest is an unpopular rhythm. For Martha, preparing the perfect dinner for her special guest took precedence over giving him her undivided attention. But what if we saw stillness as equally essential and even more honoring to God?

How many times have we gotten so distracted by the demands of hosting that we forget to visit with our guests, spend quality time with them, and listen? When we worry about our performance, is there room to really hear them?

Mary, on the other hand, chose to lower herself and sit at Jesus' feet as an obedient child, the place she could best commune with the Lord. When we hold this posture of submission, we can ponder and cherish each lesson and insight Jesus offers us.

God is waiting for us to spend time in His company. Let's still ourselves and make room to visit with Jesus.

Lord Jesus, teach us how to be still and sit at your beautiful feet; help us to lay it all down so we can find true rest in you. Amen.

DAY

James 1:19 353

“Understand this, my dear brothers and sisters: You must all be quick to listen, slow to speak, and slow to get angry.” (NLT)

If we let it, anger will find its way into the deepest corners of our hearts. Its presence becomes overwhelming, clouding our judgment, straining relationships, and hindering our spiritual growth. Anger can seem like a means of feeling powerful amid pain or fear. Yet, scripture tells us this is an illusion. Left unchecked, anger is a distraction that keeps us locked in our hurt.

When fury rears its head, we need not feel ashamed. Emotions are a natural part of being human. What matters most is how we allow our feelings to direct our actions. We can acknowledge our anger and open ourselves to self-reflection and divine guidance.

While righteous anger may spring from our desire for justice, God advises us to approach conflict with humility and wisdom. Instead of responding out of rage, we can pursue peaceful resolutions, guided by the love and grace of Christ. We can strive to extend forgiveness to one another as Jesus forgave us. Faced with roadblocks of wickedness and corruption, we can look to the One who promises goodness and justice.

God, help us build bridges of understanding and foster reconciliation. Through your grace, we can release anger and embrace a spirit of forgiveness and love. Amen.

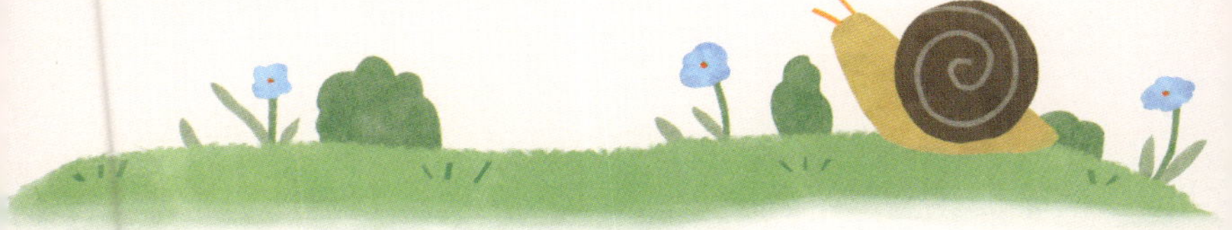

DAY

354 Isaiah 28:16

"Therefore, this is what the Sovereign Lord says: 'Look! I am placing a foundation stone in Jerusalem, a firm and tested stone. It is a precious cornerstone that is safe to build on. Whoever believes need never be shaken.'" (NLT)

It can sometimes feel like the only places left to build on are sandy shores. We need a firm foundation, but we fear a single wave could demolish everything we have carefully crafted.

Jesus, the Master Carpenter, spent his earthly ministry clearing the soil for the foundation of the Church. With the sacrifice of his death and resurrection, Jesus became the tested, precious cornerstone used by God to build a permanent relationship with humanity. Over generations, believers have placed the stones of their faith upon the solid foundation of God. Earthquakes have struck and the ground has shaken, but like a strong fortress, the foundation of the Church hasn't faltered. We have the security Isaiah prophesied and hoped for but never saw come to fruition.

Now, when things around us seem unsteady, we know that we are not balancing our lives on shifting sands but have placed our stones on the firm foundation of Jesus.

Jesus, we thank you for the steady place you provide for us. Amen.

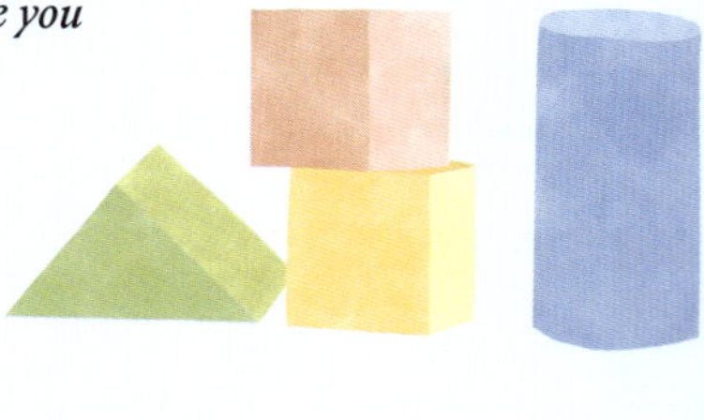

Romans 13:8

DAY
355

"Owe nothing to anyone—except for your obligation to love one another. If you love your neighbor, you will fulfill the requirements of God's law." (NLT)

We often get caught up in questions of right and wrong, wondering if we've done enough, obeyed correctly, followed the rules as we should. There is wisdom in seeking to live rightly, but occasionally we can become so focused on the laws themselves that we lose sight of the heart beneath them.

Paul reminds us that all commandments, all guidance, all ethical striving find their fulfillment in one thing: genuine love for God and for our neighbor. If we get everything else right but fail to love, we've missed the point. But if we love well, truly and deeply, we are living in step with the heartbeat of God.

And what does this call to biblical love look like? It's patient, self-giving, and enduring. It means showing up with compassion, extending grace, and making room for others to be fully human. When we cultivate this kind of love in the practices of our lives, we step into the fullness of what God desires for us.

We love because we have been loved first, and that love points our way forward.

Dear Jesus, teach us to love others sincerely and deeply, just as you have loved us. Amen.

DAY

356 Philippians 3:13–14

"No, dear brothers and sisters, I have not achieved it, but I focus on this one thing: Forgetting the past and looking forward to what lies ahead, I press on to reach the end of the race and receive the heavenly prize for which God, through Christ Jesus, is calling us." (NLT)

Some say life is a marathon. Others suggest it's a sprint. Either way, scripture agrees that this life is a race—one defined not by earthly achievements but by pursuing a deeper relationship with our Savior. Following Christ, however, is a journey that is not without its moments of doubt, temptations to quit, and times when we question whether we can make it to the end.

To press on, we first have to let go of the past—the regrets, disappointments, perhaps even prior triumphs that might hold us back. Not remaining stuck in the past pushes us to look ahead, focusing on what God sets before us each day while also keeping our eye on the horizon of eternity—on the full, abundant, and everlasting life that awaits us beyond this one.

On this journey of faith, we never walk or run alone. Jesus goes before us as our guide, even as he also comes alongside us as our encourager. Fueled by his grace, we find the strength to reflect the light of his love and finish the race well.

God grant us strength and focus to run our race with endurance, pressing toward the glorious prize you have set before us. Amen.

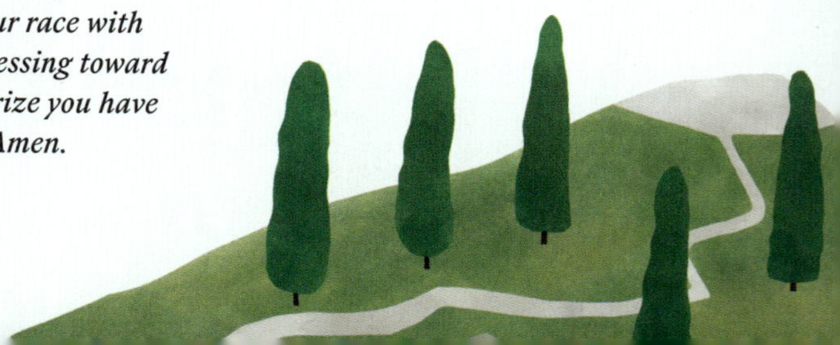

Exodus 13:21–22

DAY
357

"The Lord went ahead of them. He guided them during the day with a pillar of cloud, and he provided light at night with a pillar of fire. This allowed them to travel by day or by night. And the Lord did not remove the pillar of cloud or pillar of fire from its place in front of the people." (NLT)

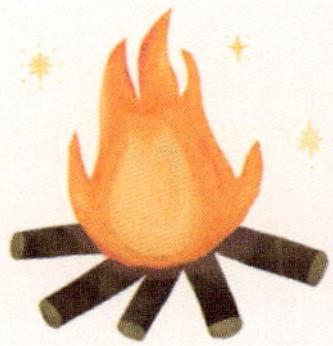

God speaks in beauty. This is how the Israelites experienced God's presence in the wilderness—through a pillar of cloud and a column of fire. Day and night, the miraculous wonders of God were on display, traveling as a guide, always leading the way.

Our Creator is just as present in our hearts and through leaders like Moses today. God doesn't have to be magnificent and beautiful. But in the dry deserts of life, sometimes we need reminders of God's faithfulness on display. When we feel as though we are the only living things in sight, God delights in providing encouragement as well as guidance.

God's faithfulness to believers in the wilderness remains as consistent for us as it was for the Israelites. We can see it in sunsets and when the beauty of nature radiates. God will be a guide ahead of us, directing us out of captivity and into where the milk and honey flow.

Lord Jesus, we thank you for being an ever-present guide for us and uncertain seasons. Remind us of your presence through ways only you can as we wait for your magnificent evidence in sunsets. Amen.

DAY 358 Psalm 78:15–16

"He split open the rocks in the wilderness to give them water, as from a gushing spring. He made streams pour from the rock, making the waters flow down like a river." (NLT)

Psalm 78 recounts the history of faithfulness that the people of God experienced. Generation after generation, God was there to intercede and aid them in wondrous and miraculous ways. When they were thirsty, God split the rocks open. Not gently, but with force, because sometimes the places of our provision must be broken open. When there was no water, God poured it from stone, the least likely source of water. He created it out of impossibility.

This is the pattern of supernatural provision. It is rarely predictable, but it is always enough. We are provided for even in the wilderness and when our hearts are hardened. God gives—not because we are faithful, but because God is.

We often pray for immediate comfort, but God offers living water. We ask for the familiar, and Jesus responds with the miraculous. Perhaps what feels like scarcity is actually fertile soil nurturing something sacred.

God is not limited by the landscape—not discouraged by the dryness. Our Creator and Sustainer sees the thirst before we speak of it, and His kindness does not delay.

Direct our focus, God. Where is the rock already splitting open? Where are you pouring out your living water? Amen.

1 Corinthians 10:13

DAY 359

"The temptations in your life are no different from what others experience. And God is faithful. He will not allow the temptation to be more than you can stand. When you are tempted, he will show you a way out so that you can endure." (NLT)

Temptation is a universal experience. We're all faced with situations in which we think to ourselves, "Just this once." As we struggle to resist forbidden fruits, we often feel overcome by guilt or shame. 1 Corinthians 10:13 offers not condemnation, but comfort. We are not alone, and we are not without help.

One of the biggest lies temptation tells is that of isolation—that no one else struggles or wrestles as we do. But scripture counters this lie, reminding us that others face these same battles. And others have overcome them by God's grace.

Amid overwhelming temptation, God promises a way through—an opportunity to choose obedience. We can slow down, offer a prayer, reach out to a friend, anything that reminds us of who we are in Christ. Facing temptation is an exercise of partnership: God provides strength, and we respond with faith and trust. We aren't defined by our struggles, but by the One who gives us strength to stand. Temptation is real, but so too is God's faithfulness.

In our darkest moments, God, make your light all the brighter. Lead us away from damaging paths and toward your goodness. Amen.

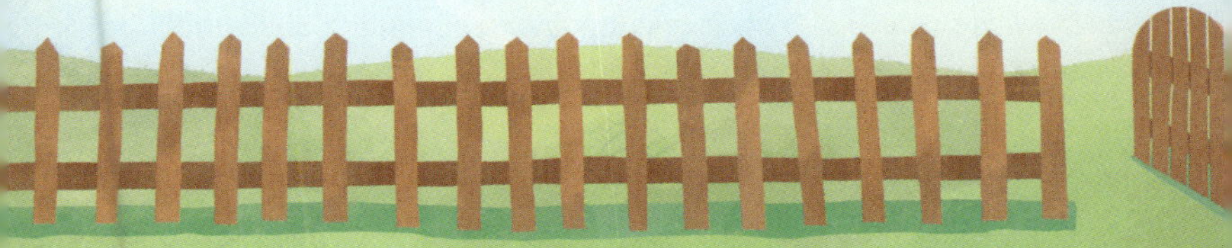

DAY 360 Psalm 146:7–9

"He gives justice to the oppressed and food to the hungry. The Lord frees the prisoners. The Lord opens the eyes of the blind. The Lord lifts up those who are weighed down ... The Lord protects the foreigners among us. He cares for the orphans and widows, but he frustrates the plans of the wicked." (NLT)

God's justice is not a concept; it's a current. A movement that flows toward the ones forgotten, lifting the low, setting the bound free. The psalmist speaks plainly: God gives food to the hungry, frees prisoners, watches over the vulnerable, and brings the wicked's ways to ruin. This is not a poetic exaggeration—it is the heartbeat of the Kingdom.

To know God is to feel this beat in our own chests, not as momentary outrage but as a holy ache. We are not called to be reactive but to respond with a steady resolve to stand with God on the side of justice.

It begins when we open our eyes, listen more closely, and allow our compassion to interrupt our comfort. And when the pain feels too great or the work too slow, we remember: we are not the source of justice but its stewards.

We may not be able to do everything. But we are all called to do something, operating as conduits for the current of divine justice.

Righteous Jesus, help us to partner with you in your vision of restoration and renewal. May we, like you, seek justice in all things. Amen.

Psalm 143:8

DAY
361

"Let me hear of your unfailing love each morning, for I am trusting you. Show me where to walk, for I give myself to you." (NLT)

At the break of each new day, a miracle unfolds—God renews mercy toward us. Each morning offers us a fresh beginning, even if the night before may have felt impossibly dark. Just as the sun rises faithfully, so does the Lord display mercy that never runs out.

Psalm 143 invites us to recall the presence of God's unfailing love every day when we wake up. When we rise, do we immediately rush to get ready without meditating on this miracle?

Remembering God's mercy also instills great gratitude in us as we reflect on the undeserving nature of it. Mercy, by its definition, echoes this, revealing pardon rather than punishment. We can actively trust in God's restorative love for us, assured that Christ will show us where we should sojourn next.

When we give ourselves wholly over to Jesus, we invite him to occupy every area of our lives, completely surrendering to mercies that sustain us from day's beginning to night's end, and in the morning, once again.

Merciful Lord, thank you for lavishing your mercies on us each new day; help us to embrace them every day we wake up. Amen.

DAY

362 Matthew 7:7–8

"Keep on asking, and you will receive what you ask for. Keep on seeking, and you will find. Keep on knocking, and the door will be opened to you. For everyone who asks, receives. Everyone who seeks, finds. And to everyone who knocks, the door will be opened." (NLT)

It has been said, "A little curiosity is a dangerous thing," but this is never the case in our relationship with God. Jesus encourages us not to remain at a distance but to come close enough to explore the contours of God's love and generosity. Like the inquisitive child constantly asking, "Why?" we are called to keep asking questions, to grow bolder in our exploration and experience of the wisdom, character, and will of our Creator.

Holy curiosity pushes us beyond surface-level understanding toward greater intimacy with God. It prompts us to explore, study, and find deeper meaning in scripture. It involves actively engaging with our faith by asking the tough questions and embracing even more challenging answers. It beckons us to pray with intention, seeking guidance in all things by knocking on the door of spiritual revelation.

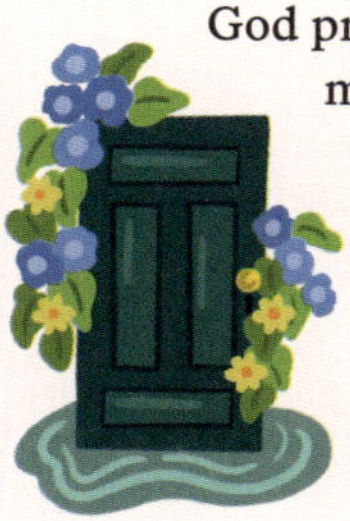

God promises to respond. What we discover and receive may not always look as we expect, but it will always be what is truly good and beneficial for our spiritual growth in the richness of Jesus' grace and wonder in our lives.

Ignite within us, God, a holy curiosity that compels us to seek you more deeply and discover the wonders of your love. Amen.

DAY

Psalm 131:2-3

363

"Instead, I have calmed and quieted myself, like a weaned child who no longer cries for its mother's milk. Yes, like a weaned child is my soul within me. O Israel, put your hope in the Lord—now and always." (NLT)

Ours is a world that screams for speed. As we rush, scroll, and consume, we demand instant gratification. But for all the content we ingest, we remain restless. Amid the frantic pursuit of more, yet never having enough, scripture offers a different path: resting in the quiet presence of God.

Such peace does not come easily or instantaneously. Like a babe who has grown attached to his mother's milk, we must be weaned from our dependency on the next big thing. Bombarded by enticements for our attention that pull in countless directions, we must let go of constant cravings. We learn to find contentment not in the rush but in the steady, loving, nurturing presence of God. The key to shedding the discontent of insatiable want is abiding in the truth that God always gives us what we need.

In a world obsessed with doing, God invites us to simply be. To slow down, to breathe, to trust. To find our hope and peace every day in God's promises and provision.

Jesus, quiet our restless hearts and help us find peace in your loving presence amidst the clamor of the world. Amen.

DAY

364 Mark 6:31

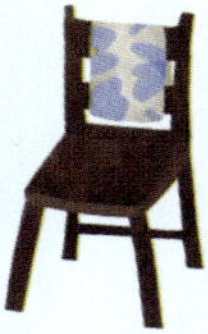

"Then Jesus said, 'Let's go off by ourselves to a quiet place and rest awhile.'" (NLT)

"Come away with me," Jesus said, "and rest." The invitation is so gentle that we almost miss its urgency.

Rest is not a luxury. It is how the soul returns to itself, how we remember we are more than what we produce, more than what we carry. Jesus offered rest in the middle of need, not after all demands were met. He knew what our bodies forget: even sacred work requires sacred pause. Even as we live out our purpose, we need rest.

Rest is a form of trust. It says: the world will keep spinning, even if we do not. It believes that God sustains more than we ever could. Rest is not just about stopping. It is about being met. In stillness, we make space for God to remind us who we are: beloved, held, and wholly seen.

So we stop, not because we're finished but because we're human. We breathe, we sleep, we step away. The quiet becomes holy ground. And in it, we meet not absence but presence.

Rest is not an interruption to the work but part of it.

Breathe in: We choose to slow down.
Breathe out: You are already here. Amen.

Psalm 91:1–2

DAY 365

"Those who live in the shelter of the Most High will find rest in the shadow of the Almighty. This I declare about the Lord: He alone is my refuge, my place of safety; he is my God, and I trust him." (NLT)

Sometimes, stress and anxiety invade every facet of our lives, disrupting our days and interrupting our sleep. In times of stress, our brains send a signal to our bodies that we aren't safe, and we produce hormones that keep us awake, allowing us to be ready for danger. Even when our stresses are more abstract, like worries over finances or relationships, they still trigger the same biological response. Our bodies don't feel safe.

We can calm our nervous systems by listening to soothing music, stretching, or regulating our breathing, but the message of Psalm 91 offers us an important reminder: God offers us safety. When we live and move in the ways of God, we can always find rest in God's shadow; we always have a safe refuge there. In times of stress or anxiety, this passage can be our guide back to rest and trusting in God.

Jesus, thank you for offering us a space to rest. You are our refuge, our place of safety, and we trust you. Amen.

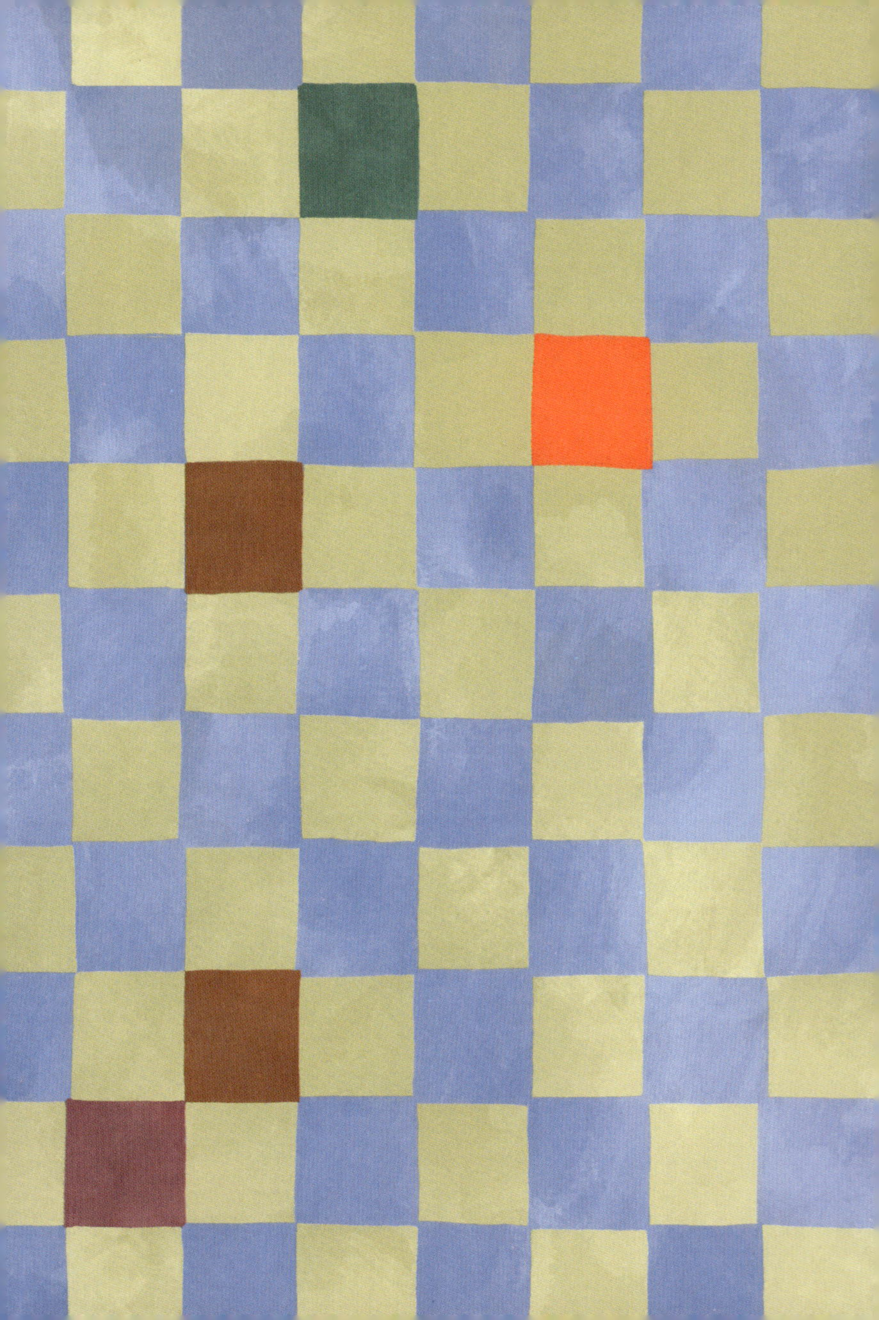

ALABASTER

Team

Brian Chung

Christina Woo

Collin Eldridge

Daniel Han

Ellen Wei

Emaly Tweitmann

Emma Tweitmann

Gabriel Quintanar

John Han

Josh Jang

Joyce Tan

Minzi Bae

Samuel Han

Tyler Zak

Valerie Hui

Willa Jin

Artwork

Rachel Yumi Chung

Katie Chan

Layout Design

Janice Park

ALABASTER

Writing

Bethany Fox

3, 6, 9, 28, 38, 40, 44, 48, 57, 58, 64, 69, 80, 82, 90, 114, 126, 129, 138, 165, 192, 210, 218, 227, 245, 275, 303, 310, 323, 355

Liz Jenkins

5, 23, 25, 45, 47, 55, 61, 75, 79, 88, 91, 94, 113, 117, 118, 124, 139, 172, 181, 190, 191, 194, 196, 203, 207, 213, 232, 240, 254

Jackie Aviles

2, 17, 20, 34, 54, 67, 78, 81, 89, 96, 97, 99, 100, 102, 104, 110, 111, 132, 133, 134, 137, 142, 147, 149, 151, 156, 159, 164, 169, 171

Betsy Sunny

176, 177, 183, 216, 234, 236, 248, 249, 251, 253, 256, 258, 261, 266, 270, 277, 288, 292, 294, 297, 299, 307, 320, 321, 324, 334, 340, 358, 360, 364

Emma Tweitmann

26, 29, 32, 35, 41, 43, 52, 56, 60, 66, 71, 72, 74, 76, 84, 86, 93, 98, 101, 103, 107, 108, 120, 125, 135, 141, 143, 148, 182, 199, 204, 219, 223, 225, 230, 237, 238, 239, 242, 243, 244, 246, 247, 250, 252, 257, 259, 260, 262, 263, 264, 265, 267, 269, 271, 273, 274, 278, 279, 280, 282, 284, 285, 290, 298, 301, 302, 306, 309, 311, 312, 315, 316, 319, 325, 329, 331, 332, 338, 342, 345, 348, 353, 359

Published in Los Angeles by Alabaster Creative Inc.

FSC
www.fsc.org
MIX
Paper | Supporting responsible forestry
FSC™ C136333

Printed in China through
Asia Pacific Offset

Contact
hello@alabasterco.com
www.alabasterco.com

Alabaster Co explores the intersection of creativity, beauty, and faith. Founded in 2016. Based in Los Angeles.